THE VICTOR HEROES

BY
ROBERT PIKE

D1354544

FIRST PUBLISHED IN MM BY
ANCRE PUBLISHERS

COPYRIGHT © ROBERT PIKE

ISBN 0-9539507-0-0

PRINTED BY HART TALBOT PRINTERS LTD
SHIREHILL INDUSTRIAL ESTATE
SAFFRON WALDEN, ESSEX CB11 3BE

ANCRE PUBLISHERS
66 VICTORIA AVENUE, SAFFRON WALDEN, ESSEX CB11 3AE

FOREWORD.

THE RT HON SIR ALAN HASELHURST, M.P.

WAR AT ANY TIME is a dreadful experience. For all we have increasingly learnt about the First World War - the Great War - it must throughout its length have been absolute, merciless hell. It produced casualties on a huge scale. A whole generation was virtually wiped out. Hardly anywhere in this country remained untouched by tragedy. What Robert Pike has done in this book is to remind us in chilling detail the impact on Saffron Walden and its neighbouring villages.

This is not a history of the Great War, but its course is followed as the author tells his tale of death, heroism and despair. Of course the men of Saffron Walden went to war along with others from all over Britain and the Empire, but this is the first complete record of those who failed to return or did not survive. It has to be a satisfaction for the town that the full list of heroes should be known. It must also be a comfort to their descendants that their sacrifice is properly acknowledged.

What emerges is a tapestry depicting human waste and personal sacrifice. The reality of death is made graphic as the story is told. The loss for families and the local community is profound as each victim's fate becomes known and as the total steadily accumulates. Eighty years on a sense of melancholy prevails.

It was a futile war, not in its cause or its outcome, but in its conduct. Human beings were devalued in the slaughter, which was allowed to endure. Families and society were robbed. In these pages brave men are re-humanised and their memory honoured. We shall grateful to them – and never forget. Robert Pike has performed a service to Saffron Walden and to future historians in producing this comprehensive record. I compliment him on his dedication and perseverance and above all the respect he demonstrates for these Victor Heroes.

ACKNOWLEDGEMENTS .

This book was born out of two of my great interests, the conflict once known as the Great War and the lovely town in which I am fortunate to have lived for the last seventeen years. As I have almost qualified as a local, I felt able to tackle this tale of our local heroes, men who deserve never to be forgotten and after six or more years research, the result is here with.

Many people and organisations have helped me and I am most grateful for their assistance and support. It is almost invidious to single out individuals, but I feel I must, at the same time offering my humble apologies for those I have overlooked.

I am indebted to The Right Honourable Sir Alan Haselhurst, M.P. for kindly agreeing to write the foreword to this book.

Many relatives of the men concerned have supplied stories, memories, anecdotes and photographs and I would particularly like to thank Mr. Marks of Elsenham (William Marks), Mr. Smith of Newcroft (Frederick H Smith), Brian and Janice Sharpe (Arthur Brand), Fiona Wright, Fred Rushmer, Keith Braybrook (Joseph A Braybrook), Gary Sell (Ernest Mansfield), John Maddams (Albert and Harry Kidman), Mr. Wells (Charles, George and Joseph Pearson), Mrs. Barker of Thaxted (William Adams), Mr. Hill (Walter Hill), Lewis Wiseman (C Lewis Gardiner), Eileen Clarke (Harry and Sidney Clarke), Mrs. Margaret Warner (C Tom Smith), Mrs. A Rogers of Duxford (Arthur and Ben Halls), Mr. P Housden, Mr. Downham (George and Stanley Downham).

In addition my sincere thanks go to Sir Henry Marking for permission to publish Frank Marking's letters, Martin Everett and the staff at Saffron Walden Library, The Commonwealth War Graves Commission, The Western Front Association, Essex branch, Jim Horne, Kyle Tallett, Ken Wood of Hart-Talbot Printers Ltd, John Brooker and the Walden Local, the late Ron Powell, Ian Miller, Ian Hook and the Essex Regimental Museum, Pauline Allwright at the Imperial War Museum.

I must mention dear friends whose encouragement, help and goading have led to the completion of this tribute, David Green of Ashdon for his humour, his friendship and ventures to Gallipoli, Alan and Alma Walker, John and Carol King and my brother-in-law, Ken Sinyard, without whose artistic expertise this book would never have seen the light of day.

Finally, it would not have been possible, or nearly as enjoyable without my wife, Carrie, my sons, Ben and Sam and my daughter, Kate, who have traipsed in all weathers round cemeteries, memorials, museums and battlefields in France, Belgium, Italy, Germany and Turkey and who never moaned (well, not much !).

THE VICTOR
HEROES

ON SATURDAY MAY 7TH. 1921 at 2.30 p.m. Saffron Walden came to a standstill and men, women and children gathered silently at the top of the High Street to see the unveiling of the town's war memorial. On it were inscribed the names of 158 (later 159 see Appendix 3) men who fought in the so-called Great War and who died in all the different theatres of that terrible struggle, and some of wounds, in England itself. In 1919 when the concept of a memorial first became a fact, relatives and friends were encouraged to examine a list on three framed parchments in the parish church to see if their loved ones' names were included. The roll of honour was to embrace Saffron Walden and the hamlets of Sewards End, Little Walden and Audley End and to comprise of men whose home was in Saffron Walden when they joined His Majesty's Forces and men whose parents resided here and who had gone away to work, but had not established a home for themselves elsewhere. In August 1919 the names numbered 134.

The war memorial was the last and most splendid of a number of memorials created to remember these men in Saffron Walden. There had been the painted board which once stood in the market square on the Victorian fountain, the names being added as news of a death arrived (to be seen in the parish church until November 1996 and now in the museum) with the names of 132 officers and men in seemingly random order ; there was and is the illuminated roll of honour in the Town-Hall council chamber and there was an Odd fellows roll of honour in their Lodge Room. The Boys' British School roll was unveiled on November 11th. 1919 with 75 names on it (this disappeared mysteriously on the school's closure) and the Comrades Club opened. There is also a memorial in the Friends School (see Appendix 2), but this contains the name of only one man from the town, but it was the white war-memorial that focussed people's grief and their need for praise and remembrance.

On that bright May afternoon the address spoke of, *" The victor heroes (who) rest in many lands, but here the symbol of their glory stands, "* but who were those victor heroes and where do they rest?

This is not a military history, no more is it an history of a conflict that changed the world for ever, it is simply a record of those men who marched away and never returned. It is a small tribute to them, their courage, steadfastness, patriotism and stoicism, but it is also a tribute to the men who returned scarred physically and mentally to try and rebuild their lives and most poignantly to the relatives - wives, children and parents whose existence lost its purpose when that fateful telegram dropped through their letter-box.

If ye break faith with us who die
We shall not sleep, though poppies grow
In Flanders fields.

War was declared on August 4th. 1914 and two weeks later the paper reported that 123 Army and Navy men had left the town and district and there had been forty-three applications to enlist, five of which were rejected. Recruitment took place at the Armoury at the top of the High Street. On Tuesday 1st. September a meeting in the Market Square was held to gain recruits and a further thirty gave their names. The realisation that the *" War could be over by Christmas ! "* gave impetus to recruitment and by September 11th. the paper reported that, " *now the position was realised there was "no hanging back."* On Monday 7th. September the first batch of fifty recruits had left followed by another thirty the following day.

In Belgium the British Expeditionary Force, comprised of the Regular Army hurriedly shipped over to combat the Schlieffen Plan, had already entered into battle with the German troops and was now being inexorably pushed in retreat south, in the famous forced march of the self-styled *" Old Contemptibles."* At sea, however, Britain was regarded as the great maritime superpower with the Royal Navy expected to play a decisive role in the war. But as on land where the use of artillery revolutionised, at such terrible cost, the soldier's war, in the same way at sea it was not the great sea-battles between huge battleships, with the exception of Jutland in 1916, but the threat of the U-boat that changed the face of the war.

There are seven names on the memorial who perished in the Royal Navy and all but one of them has no known grave, except the immensity of the ocean. One of them carries the tragic honour of being Saffron Walden's first casualty.

ABLE-SEAMAN WILLIAM EDWARD **GILBEY** (221975) ROYAL NAVY, H.M.S PATHFINDER, DROWNED 5TH. SEPTEMBER 1914, AGED 27. COMMEMORATED ON CHATHAM NAVAL MEMORIAL, KENT, PANEL 2.

William Gilbey was born in Braintree on 18th. March 1887, the son of Mr. and Mrs. Walter Gilbey who later moved to 11 Mill Field, Ashdon Road. In March 1902, aged 15 he joined the Royal Navy as a Junior Seaman attached to H.M.S Warspite. On attaining the age of eighteen William signed on for twelve years and was attached to H.M.S Impregnable. Over the next eleven years he saw service in a range of ships, including a Dreadnought, Cruisers and Light Cruisers. Oddly, in October 1907, his record states that he was, " *...recovered from desertion and sent to H.M.S Pembroke and sentenced to forty-two days. "* This aberration does not seem to have affected his record as in 1908 his character is desribed as, *" Very Good. "*

During this period of service he married Florence, who later went to live in Bermondsey. On October 1st. 1913 he joined H.M.S Pathfinder classed as a light cruiser/destroyer in the " Scout " class launched in July 1904 and completed in 1905 at 2940 tons armed with nine four-inch guns. On 5th. September 1914, the cruiser was off St. Abb's Head a promontory off the east coast of Scotland, near the Firth of Forth. The captain was Francis Martin-Leake, a brother of the first man ever to win two Victoria Crosses - Arthur Martin-Leake (buried in High Cross Churchyard, Hertfordshire), - and H.M.S Pathfinder had a complement of 264 men. Three days previously a German submarine the U21 had, undetected, entered the Firth of Forth and penetrated the sea defences. It cruised around until at 4.30 p.m. on September 5th. it fired a single torpedo at H.M.S Pathfinder striking it square on, causing the forward magazine to explode. The ship went down in four minutes. At the time the men were relaxing on the mess decks and were caught by the full explosion. Only fifty-six survived and William Gilbey was not one of them. Thus the first British naval ship to fall victim to an enemy submarine contained Saffron Walden's first fatal casualty of the war. The submarine U.21 survived the perils of sea warfare, but was sunk in the North Sea on February 22nd. 1919, on its way to England to surrender !

It was not long before two more families were in mourning for the loss of their beloved sons killed in similar circumstances and their stories are tragically intertwined.

ABLE-SEAMAN ERRINGTON HOUNSOME **NORMAN** (SS 2428) ROYAL NAVY, H.M.S HOGUE, DROWNED 22ND. SEPTEMBER 1914, AGED 27. COMMEMORATED ON CHATHAM NAVAL MEMORIAL, KENT, PANEL 1.

Errington was born on June 5th. 1887 the son of William John and Susan Norman of 34 Victoria Avenue, a railway guard on the Saffron Walden branch line. On leaving the Boys' British school, where he knew Alexander Perkin, he obtained work as a foot-man, before joining the Royal Navy in May 1908 signing on for five years. During this first year of service aboard H.M.S. Achilles, a cruiser, he was awarded the Messina Medal. This had been given to the men from eight Royal Naval ships involved in the relief of the Sicilian town when 80% of it was destroyed in an earthquake. Only some 3,500 were issued.

In 1913, when Errington's period of service was up he left the Navy in the Royal Fleet Reserve and obtained a job working at Mr. Joseph Wright's Motor Works, 26 High Street. On the imminent outbreak of war he was called up on August 2nd. and joined H.M.S Hogue. From this point, Errington's tragic story and that of his old school-fellow, Alexander Perkin are linked.

On September 22nd. 1914, The Hogue, the Cressy and another armoured cruiser of the same class, H.M.S Aboukir were on patrol in the Broad Fourteens off the Dutch coast, when they were sighted by the German submarine U 9.

The three ships were steaming ahead with a distance of three miles between them, when the Aboukir was torpedoed and sunk. The survivors were picked up by Errington's H.M.S Hogue, but no sooner had they started to clamber aboard than another torpedo struck the Hogue and she went down in three minutes.

Again the accumulated survivors of both cruisers, possibly including Errington, swam to Alexander Perkin's H.M.S Cressy and were hauled on board. Minutes later she was torpedoed and sank firing all her guns at the U 9 which was some 200 yards off.

LEADING-SEAMEN ALEXANDER **PERKIN** (227224) ROYAL NAVY, H.M.S CRESSY, DROWNED 22ND. SEPTEMBER 1915, AGED 26. COMMEMORATED ON CHATHAM NAVAL MEMORIAL, KENT, PANEL 1.

Alexander Perkin was born on February 28th. 1888, the son of Charles and Mary Perkin, who lived at 24 East Street. Like Errington Norman he attended the Boys' British School leaving to become a gardener before joining the Royal Navy in 1906 as a Boy Seaman on H.M.S. Ganges. Alexander progressed rapidly in the Navy becoming an Able-Seaman on H.M.S. Illustrious in 1907, a Leading-Seaman on H.M.S. Tyne in 1910 and passing his exams to be a Petty Officer on H.M.S. St.George in December 1911. He was also attached to Torpedo Boat No. 24, until after the Spithead Review he was transferred to the armoured cruiser of 12,000 tons, the H.M.S. Cressy in July 1914.

Three months later his path once more crossed that of his school friend. On September 22nd. 1914, the Cressy witnessed the sinking of, first the Aboukir, whose survivors swam to the Hogue, and then the Hogue itself. The accumulated survivors of both cruisers, possibly including Errington Norman, swam to H.M.S Cressy and were willingly helped on board. Minutes later a torpedo hit H.M.S Cressy and she sank taking Alexander Perkin, and conceivably Errington Norman with her.

Three hundred survivors of the three ships were saved by a Dutch trawler but 1460 men were lost including Norman and Perkin whose friendship not even death could part.

History will now forever link these two friends together, when the Roll of Honour at the Boys' British School was dedicated after the war, the first two names on it are those of Errington and Alexander and ironically, on October 19th. 1914 the two friends' names appeared side-by-side in the local paper's roll-of-service of those joining up (when they were already both dead).

As a chilling postscript it was later written by a naval officer that, " *Those three old cruisers* (they were only twelve years old)*...had been expected to be sunk every day for weeks... (it) had been repeatedly warned that it is madness to allow ships to patrol up and down at the same speed...I only hope the person responsible for putting them there gets hung.* " Sadly no notice was taken - twenty-three days later the cruiser H.M.S Hawke was sunk in the North Sea by the submarine captained by the same officer who had sunk the Cressy, the Hogue and the Aboukir with the loss of another 500 souls, including Stoker Petty-Officer James Lofts of Saffron Walden.

The news of the sinking of four ships of the seemingly invincible Royal Navy shocked the British public as yet unaware of the casualties in Belgium, but this was soon brought home to one family in Saffron Walden when news came of the death of the first soldier from the town.

SHOEING-SMITH WILLIAM HENRY **SAWARD** (415) 9TH. (QUEEN'S ROYAL) LANCERS, KILLED IN ACTION 24TH. SEPTEMBER 1914, AGED 20. COMMEMORATED ON THE LA FERTE-SOUS-JOUARRE MEMORIAL TO THE MISSING, FRANCE.

William Saward was the son of William Henry and Alice Lewis Saward of 5 Ingleside Place, the High Street. Very little else is known of William Saward, except that he was born in Plumstead and lived in Hoddesdon, Hertfordshire ; he was a farrier who was mobilised in Hertford immediately war was declared and rushed to Belgium as part of General Allenby's 2nd. Cavalry Brigade, 1st. Cavalry Division. It is possible that William was involved in the saving of the guns of the 119th. Battery Royal Field Artillery, for which a Victoria Cross was awarded to Captain Francis Grenfell and the cavalry charge by the 9th. Lancers at Quievrain (not for nothing were they nicknamed "The Delhi Spear men") described as " *a modern version of Balaclava,* " with the same results, which he fortunately survived. In September the 9th. Lancers were positioned on the River Aisne and took part in the Battle of the Aisne in the area of Soupir and

Chavonne and it is likely that he met his death here probably in the heavy artillery bombardment suffered by the British. His body was never found.

The lessons to be learnt from the sinking of the Pathfinder, the Cressy, the Aboukir and the Hogue were studiously avoided by the Admiralty with inevitable consequences.

PETTY-OFFICER STOKER JAMES **LOFTS** (306070) ROYAL NAVY, H.M.S HAWKE, DROWNED 15TH. OCTOBER 1914, AGED 33. COMMEMORATED ON CHATHAM NAVAL MEMORIAL, KENT, PANEL 4.

James Lofts was born in Linton on November 12th. 1881, the son of Mrs. Marie Rushforth, and the late George Lofts, who later lived at 2 Hodson's Yard, Castle Street. He was married to Annie, with two children, and living at Prospect House, Castle Street.

He was first employed as a fireman before enlisting in the Royal Navy in 1904 joining H.M.S Acheron as a Stoker 2nd. Class in 1905. By 1911 he had been promoted to a Stoker Petty-Officer. When war erupted James had been a member of the crew of H.M.S Hawke, a cruiser of some 7350 tons, since April 1914, though he had served on her previously in 1912.

On 7th. October Mrs. Lofts received a postcard from her husband saying he was in the best of health and spirits, but giving no intimation of where he was. In fact, H.M.S Hawke was patrolling the east coast between Peterhead and the Naze as part of the 10th. Cruiser Squadron. On 15th. October 1914 the flagship H.M.S Crescent went to restock coal leaving definite instructions for the method of cruising to avoid U-boats, to the rest of the squadron. At 1.20 p.m. H.M.S Theseus reported being attacked, but not hit, by a submarine. All ships were ordered north-west at full speed and all acknowledged the order except H.M.S Hawke. A destroyer was sent to look for her at her last known position where she sighted a submarine, but no Hawke.

The events had been all too-familiar. The ships had been spread in ten mile intervals when suddenly H.M.S Hawke had been hit by a torpedo abreast of the forward funnel and there had been an explosion. She immediately listed and there was only time to lower two boats. James had been in the engine-room below deck and was not one of the seventy survivors. 500 sailors were lost.

Thus twenty-three days after the loss of Cressy, Hogue and Aboukir another ship was lost, this time to the submarine U-29. The commander of this submarine was Lieutenant-Commander Weddigen who had also sunk the other three ships in the U-9 (which survived the war surrendering in 1919). Thus with the war only some ten weeks old four sailors from Saffron Walden had shared a similar, and arguably avoidable, fate.

In Flanders after the mobile warfare of the retreat from Mons and the battles of the Marne and Aisne, the conflict had settled down into the static trench-warfare that symbolises the Great War with two lines of trenches varying distances apart, facing each other from the North Sea to the Swiss frontier - the incorrectly named Western Front. Also at this time a small town in Flanders became synonymous with the suffering of the First World War and to this day conjures up the destruction and muddy horror of those years - Ypres and the Salient round it.

On 12th. October 1914 began the First Battle of Ypres and this claimed three victims from Saffron Walden, two on the same day and with the same regiment, the Pompadours or the Essex Regiment.

PRIVATE GEORGE ALFRED **DOWNHAM** (10003) 2ND. ESSEX REGIMENT, KILLED IN ACTION 21ST. OCTOBER 1914, AGED 20. COMMEMORATED ON THE PLOEGSTEERT MEMORIAL TO THE MISSING, BELGIUM, PANEL 7.

George Downham was the son of William George and Louisa Downham of 15 Mount Pleasant, Debden Road. He was single and was a reservist at the outbreak of war and was thus mobilised immediately at Warley. His elder brother Stanley also joined up . George landed at Le Havre on 24th. August as part of 12th. Brigade 4th. Division and was soon involved in the heavy fighting on the Aisne as part of III Corps, but it was in fighting during the battle of Armentieres that George met his death.

The 2nd. Essex Regiment were in the area of Hill 63 with the line extending to Le Gheer. Initially in reserve, the 2nd. Essex were called forward at 5.15 a.m. on Wednesday, 21st. October 1914 to combat a heavy enemy attack by the German XIX Corps. However, they were forced back towards Le Gheer, until a counter-attack by two platoons of D company drove the Germans back north of Le Touquet. Heavy casualties were involved, amongst them George Downham.

It was not until August 1915 that his parents heard the details of his death from a comrade, Private G Bacon. He described how they were near Armentieres when George was wounded in the arm, with his friend Andy Porter who had received a similar wound. They were both eager to get to the dressing-station and got out of the trench. As they were running back over exposed ground a machine-gun was turned on them and they both fell. George's body was never found. He is also remembered on the Baptist Church memorial.

PRIVATE ANDY **PORTER** (8802) 2ND. ESSEX REGIMENT, KILLED IN ACTION 21ST. OCTOBER 1914. COMMEMORATED ON THE PLOEGSTEERT MEMORIAL TO THE MISSING, BELGIUM, PANEL 11.

Andy Porter was also mobilised at the outbreak of the war as a reservist, enlisting in Saffron Walden the town of his birth. He was the son of Mr. George Porter of 15 Debden Road and had three brothers all of whom were to be killed in the war, Bertram, Henry and Joseph. He landed at Le Havre on 24th. August as part of 12th. Brigade 4th. Division. He lived in Liskeard, Cornwall with his wife and two children.

To this happy family came his last letter dated 17th. October, written in the trenches, saying how he always thought of home and that things were, *" looking black."* The details of Andy's death are those of George Downham, his friend, but a real insight into the comradeship of the trenches is given in a postcard dated the day George and Andy died, sent by one of their friends and received on November 14th. Private F Braybrooke wrote how, *" he had lost both his mates killed on the same day."* Like George, Andy Porter has no known grave.

Andy Porter was one of four brothers to die in the war. Possibly on the same day, the first of three other Saffron Walden brothers to die, was mortally wounded.

SHOEING-SMITH CHARLES STEPHEN **PEARSON** (5533) 47TH. BATTERY, ROYAL FIELD

ARTILLERY, DIED OF WOUNDS 25TH. OCTOBER 1915, AGED 38. BURIED AT BOULOGNE EASTERN CEMETERY, FRANCE, PLOT 13 ROW A GRAVE 8.

Charles Pearson was the second son of Stephen and Sarah Pearson of 38 Fairycroft Rd. His brothers George and Joseph were also to die although a fourth, Herbert who served in the Wiltshire Regiment survived. He had been in the Army for twenty-one years and 1914 was to have been his last year of his service. He lived in Aberdeen Road, Brighton with his wife Elizabeth and two children. After enlisting at Stratford, East London, he had been in France and Flanders since the early days of the war with the British Expeditionary Force at Mons in the 2nd. Division Artillery 44th. Howitzer Brigade RFA.

By October the war had become more static, but there was an acute ammunition shortage - at one time there were only 150 rounds per gun in the whole of France ! Charles was probably wounded on October 21st. in support of the 5th. Infantry Brigade who were hotly engaged at St. Julien meeting the attacking Germans on an eleven mile front from Menen to Steenstraat. Three days later the whole Division was hastily transferred to Polygon Wood in a desperate holding operation.

On being wounded he was taken to the Base hospital at Boulogne where on the Sunday he died. Unusually the headstones in Boulogne East Cemetery are flat because of the sandy soil, and on Charles' is the touching inscription from his family, *"Oh for the touch of a vanished hand and the sound of a voice that is still."*

Charles Pearson is the first casualty from Saffron Walden to have a known grave because he died in hospital and was not buried on a repeatedly fought-over battlefield or literally blown to pieces by a shell.

The onset of winter quietened down military operations apart from the desultory shelling and sniping that was always a constant threat. Indeed, at Christmas 1914 a truce existed in many parts of the line where Tommy and Fritz exchanged whisky, schnapps and songs, not unlike the portrayal in *" Oh, What a Lovely War. "* We know that some of the soldiers from Saffron Walden were involved in this so-called time of *' goodwill to all men '*.

1915 opened quietly and it was not until the end of February that any major engagements were fought. Just before that the first soldier to die in 1915, from Saffron Walden, was killed.

PRIVATE GEORGE HENRY **CORNELL** (3/2370) 2ND. ESSEX REGIMENT, KILLED IN ACTION 14TH. FEBRUARY 1915, AGED 39. BURIED IN CALVAIRE (ESSEX) MILITARY CEMETERY, PLOEGSTEERT, BELGIUM, PLOT 1 ROW G GRAVE 3.

George Henry Cornell was the son of Thomas and Emma Cornell and was a pre-war reservist. He was thus called upon immediately, enlisting at Warley, when war was declared, departing from Saffron Walden on the 7th. or 8th. November 1914. The roll of honour describes him as a union porter and he was also a member of the Oddfellows Lodge, where his name appeared on their memorial roll.

The exact circumstances of his death are unknown, but he was on the fateful Sunday in the area of Le Bizet with the 2nd. Essex Regiment and involved in sharp fighting along parts of the line where the Germans were searching for weak spots. It is likely that he was killed by an enemy sniper or a rifle grenade. Interestingly, Aubrey Smith, whose classic book, *" Four Years on the Western Front, "* by ' a Rifleman ' was in the same area and there is an entry for the day Henry died. *" We are in a big field and our trenches are on one side, to the right they are manned by our company (the London Rifle Brigade) for some few hundred yards and the the Essex right continues the line onwards in the direction of Armentieres....300 yards away is the German trench which we observe through a periscope.... the Germans appear to have superiority of fire, as regards musketry in this part of the line. They have snipers posted and plenty of loopholes and keep up a constant fire all day. "*

Henry is buried in a typical regimental cemetery next to the building known as Essex Farm, so named from its occupation by the 2nd. Essex from November 1914. Henry thus lies amongst friends and comrades.

Sadly, many men have no known graves, usually because their hurriedly dug resting-place had disappeared as future battles were fought over old ground, but many soldiers were literally blown to shreds, no trace of their mangled remains ever found. These are commemorated on the huge memorials created after the war to remember these countless missing. The Menin Gate in Ypres is one such in a place where many of the men whose names are upon it would have passed through on their way to the trenches. It bears nearly 55,000 names - three from Saffron Walden, two of whom were the next fatalities.

Sergeant Herbert **WREN** (7235) 2nd. Duke of Cornwall's Light Infantry, killed in action 14th. March 1915, aged 31. Commemorated on the Menin Gate Memorial to the Missing, Belgium, Panel 20.

Herbert Wren (the Town Hall roll of honour describes him erroneously as Hubert) was a pre -war regular soldier with the Duke of Cornwall's Light Infantry serving in many different parts of the world - Gibraltar 1905 ; Bermuda 1907; South Africa 1910 ; Hong Kong 1913 and home to Crownhill Barracks, Plymouth in the same year. It is likely, however, that at least part of Herbert's service would have been spent as an instructor at the Depot or Territorial battalion, or with the 1st. Battalion or at extra regimental duty elsewhere. We do know that he spent some time in South Africa and had a son H G L Wren who lived in Durban.

In 1914 the regiment were rushed home refitted, and equipped at Winchester, before crossing to France on 20th./21st. December 1914, and arriving in the Ypres Salient 12th. January 1915.

At 5 p.m. on Sunday 14th. March 1915 the Germans opened a very heavy bombardment of the British trenches in front of St.Eloi. Herbert's battalion were in the frontline from the night before. The day had been very quiet, but in addition to the bombardment, two mines were exploded under the Mound - a thirty foot artificial heap covering half-an-acre, and trenches 17 and 18. The whole area was plastered with shells and the German infantry swarmed out of their trenches, bombing the British trenches and forcing them back. By 6 p.m. many trenches were in the hands of the enemy with a machine-gun set up on the Mound. At mid-night the battered battalion were withdrawn with forty-two dead and thirty-five missing. Sergeant Herbert Wren was one of the missing and his body was never found.

The Second Battle of Ypres started on 22nd. April 1915 and lasted until 14th. May 1915. It was in the latter stages, in conditions archetypal of every photograph and image seen of Flanders mud that an artilleryman from Saffron Walden died and became another name on Portland stone.

CORPORAL WALTER **PARSLEY** (22131) 22ND. TRENCH MORTAR BATTERY, ROYAL FIELD ARTILLERY, KILLED IN ACTION 13TH. MAY 1915, AGED 32. COMMEMORATED ON THE MENIN GATE MEMORIAL TO THE MISSING, BELGIUM, PANELS 5 AND 9.

Walter Parsley was the youngest son of the late Robert Parsley who lived in Thaxted Road and had been for many years a foreman plate-layer on the Saffron Walden branch line of the Great Eastern Railway. Walter had attended the Boys' British School and had been with the Royal Field Artillery from the beginning, when he enlisted at Stratford, East London, as part of the 14th. Brigade 1st. Corps under Haig at Mons.

In May 1915, Walter found himself with the Artillery on a line from Sanctuary Wood through Hooge and Frezenberg to Mouse Trap and Turco Farms. The British were both outgunned and seriously short of ammunition. The German attacks were supported by a tremendous concentration of fire. On Frezenberg Ridge alone the shell craters touched each other !

On May 7th. the 22nd. Battery lost two guns by direct hits and the following day many batteries withdrew through Ypres. The situation was critical until reinforcements and supplies came on May 16th. In the words of Aubrey Smith, " ....*the Germans made a colossal attempt to break our line, an attempt that was nearly successful. The weather was cold, wet and squally and the bombardment lasted over four hours targeting, amongst other objects, every field-gun position, and as it continued to rain, turning the ground to mud. The plain was wreathed in fire and smoke so that it seemed impossible for anyone to exist on it.* " During this period Walter was killed. We shall never know whether he was directly hit by a shell or drowned, wounded in the sea of mud but his body was never found.

The scene shifts from the Western Front to a different killing-ground - the shores of the Bosphorous and the Gallipoli peninsula about forty miles long and twelve miles across at its widest point. This harsh finger of land was the scene of a campaign to capture the prize of Constantinople (now Istanbul), yet it ended in defeat, with 250,000 casualties in only eight and a half months. Gallipoli is a tragic, yet heroic name particularly for Australians and New Zealanders (ANZACS), and it was a son of Saffron Walden in a Digger's hat who next laid down his life in ' *those tortured ridges and heat-filled ravines.* '

TROOPER ARTHUR JOHN **HAILSTONE** (641) 1ST. AUSTRALIAN LIGHT HORSE, AUSTRALIAN IMPERIAL FORCES, KILLED IN ACTION 7TH. JUNE 1915, AGED 22. BURIED IN SHRAPNEL VALLEY CEMETERY, ANZAC, GALLIPOLI, TURKEY, PLOT 4 ROW D GRAVE 17.

Arthur Hailstone was born in London in July 1882 and was the second son of Mr. A J Hailstone of Ivy Cottage, South Road. On leaving school he had emigrated to Australia where he worked as a station-hand until war broke out when he immediately answered his Mother country's call and enlisted on September 8th. 1914. His records describe him as being 5 feet 9 inches tall, weighing 10 stone 7 pounds with yellowish-brown hair, blue eyes and of a florid complexion. He became a private in the 1st. Australian Light Horse (the regiment immortalised in Peter Weir's epic film, "Gallipoli.") and on December 20th. 1914 embarked from Sydney on H.M.A.T A 42 for the Dardanelles, joining his regiment on 15th. February 1915.

On 20th. May 1915 Arthur was wounded in the left arm, and was in convalescence for a while until he returned to his battalion judged fit for light duties. On Monday 7th. June 1915 he was shot and died immediately.

The time schedule of his father receiving the news highlights the tragedy. He did not hear of his son's initial wound until a fortnight after he was already dead, and the news of his death not until the end of July ! This news followed a letter from Arthur written three days before his death when he confided, *" A dummy attack was made by the Turks and directly we put our heads above the parapet to fire, they turned a machine-gun on us. "* These words were tragically prophetic for in another letter from one of Arthur's chums to his father he says, *" He was the whitest man I ever met... hit in the temple by a shot from a machine-gun... he was always more daring than the rest, he stayed above a trench too long...his grave has a small cross."*

Today Arthur lies in one of the most beautiful of the peninsula' s cemeteries with 526 of his adopted countrymen. The gully obtained its name from the heavy shelling of it by the Turks in April 1915, because it was an essential road from the beach up to Lone Pine. Wells were sunk and water obtained from it in small quantities, and in its lower reaches were camps, depots and gun positions. It is no wonder the Turks called Shrapnel Valley, Korku Dere - the Valley of Fear.

A sad, but typical postscript to this story is that Arthur's father received his son's worldly effects - a purse, coins, two knives and a silver watch and chain, all in one brown paper parcel and in 1920 was forced to write a letter *"..and since I sacrificed a good deal for his education, I would be glad, if there is any gratuity in his case, to have it. I would not have mentioned the latter were it not for the hard times we are enduring here and the difficulties of making ends meet. "* A land fit for heroes and the loved-ones left behind ?

This post-war feeling of disillusion spawned a wealth of creative enterprise but, ironically, the horror and sacrifice during the Great War also engendered a remarkable amount of memorable literature - poetry, novels, autobiographical accounts, posthumous memoirs, letters and personal diaries. The poetry of Wilfred Owen and Siegfried Sassoon particularly, created a vivid catalogue of suffering, comradeship, heroism and fear which still has a stark relevance today. The next name to appear on the roll represents more modestly the literary flowering of those years, a soldier whose letters were privately published by his grieving mother in 1915. (see Appendix 5)

PRIVATE FRANK **MARKING** (2168) 1ST. CAMBRIDGESHIRE REGIMENT, KILLED IN ACTION 26TH. JUNE 1915, AGED 25. BURIED IN HOUPLINES COMMUNAL CEMETERY EXTENSION, FRANCE, PLOT 3 ROW A GRAVE 13.

Frank Marking was the son of Isaac and Annie Marking of 24 Church Street. His father was a well-known local butcher and Frank had been able to attend Saffron

Walden Grammar School. In 1914 he enlisted in Cambridge for General Service and after training in England set sail for France from Southampton on 15th. February 1915 and it is here that his letters begin.

These letters cover a period of only four months till just before his death in June. It is by no means a unique document, but it is well-written, articulate and vividly portrays the life of the Poor Bloody Infantry or P.B.I, alternating between periods of discomfort or stultifying boredom and sheer exhilaration and terror.

Frank's letters, mainly to his father and mother begin with mundane details of route marches, inspections, requests for money, cigarettes and food. Details of where exactly he was, were censored, so there are references to, *"..a village the size of Littlebury"*. But in early March came news of the first casualties and soon Frank had his first experiences of the trenches, *" the mud is really rather terrible, but the worst thing is the fearful stenches everywhere...it isn't really so terrible...I shouldn't want it as a hobby though ! "*

The next letter is written on his birthday while at rest behind the lines at a chateau down the road, his battalion having been relieved. But he finishes, *" I didn't funk, and it is certainly no good to do so."* As his periods in the trenches continue more disturbing details emerge, *" Our first experience of the actual fire-trench, the Germans, in some part being only about ten yards away..About five of A Company fellows went off their heads, owing to the strain, and they were only in four days ! "*

On April 18th. he writes, *" We had our first casualties in the gun-section ...one our fellows was shot through the head and killed. "* But amidst the horror never far away is a sense of humour, *" You ought to see us frying steak and onions in our mess-tins. That always seems to annoy Fritz* (the sniper over the way), *as about dinner time he always potted our sandbags...he must have a rare nose for onions ! "*

Another aspect of Frank's letters is his compassion, *" Two big shells put 127 men out of action. It is fearful to see the women and kiddies and the dead civilians,"* and never far-away the sense of his own mortality, *" They shelled us pretty considerably and also sent some 'lobdobs' from trench-mortars...one fellow near us had his head blown off and every stitch of clothing."*

In late May the battalion moved to the area of Ploegsteert Wood (Plugstreet Wood to the Tommy, ever adaptable in his coming to terms with strange French and Flemish words) where Frank casually recounts how he and another volunteered to go out into no-man's land to try and rescue a badly wounded officer (Lt. Eric N Hopkinson who died June 2nd. 1915 and is commemorated on the Ploegsteert Memorial) , reluctantly being driven back by intense fire from the enemy some fifteen yards away. It is here on Thursday, June 24th. that Frank writes his last letter requesting, *" some cigarettes and some stuff for making lemonade to be mixed with cold water. We go back to the trenches tomorrow for twelve days."* He finishes, *" Love to all."*

Two days later he was dead, an hour after he had been recommended for promotion. He had been an acting corporal for some time. *" The Germans started shelling about eight o'clock* (wrote a friend, Gunner J Brand) *and we had just been debating whether we should move. Frank said -' Well, boys we have been lucky up to the present, no rea-*

11

son why we shouldn't be now. ' *Myself and two others just moved away - what made us do it, I couldn't say..when we heard another shell coming....saw (it) explode in the trench...saw Frank's hand sticking out of the top of some rubbish, as the shell had struck a dug-out...a piece of shell must have struck him on the side of the head. Death must have been instantaneous.*"

2Lt. F A Mann, the Cambridgeshire's Machine Gun officer wrote to Frank's mother a week later, "*..I feel I have lost the best of a good section, and shall miss him greatly....He was buried some distance behind the firing line...and his grave will be honoured by us as long as our Regiment is in the district.*"

Frank's own words are a fitting epitaph, " *We are having lovely weather here now; if it were not for this war and other small enemies, things would be very enjoyable. As it is, we make the best of things and have many a good laugh in spite of everything.*" His parents chose this inscription for his headstone, " Adjuvante deo floremus. " (We flourish and are encouraged with God's help).

The ability of the ordinary soldier to make the best of trying circumstances is legendary, but it is amazing to modern sensitivities the conditions the men in the trenches endured and joked about, particularly in the morass of mud, shell-hole and nightmare that was the Ypres Salient.

CORPORAL WALTER GEORGE **THORPE** (6312) 1ST. NORFOLK REGIMENT, KILLED IN ACTION 5TH. JULY 1915. BURIED IN PERTH CEMETERY (CHINA WALL) ZILLEBEKE, BELGIUM, TRENCH RAILWAY CEMETERY SPECIAL MEMORIAL 88.

Walter Thorpe was a rural postman between Radwinter and Hempstead and lived in East Street with his wife and child. Born in Catton, Norfolk, he had, through his wife's family, still maintained connections with the county of his birth and at the outbreak of war was a reservist, so was immediately mobilised in Norwich and went to France in August 1914, landing at Le Havre with the British Expeditionary Force as part of II Corps under Smith-Dorrien in the 5th. Division 15th. Brigade. His early days saw him take part of the battle of Mons and the retreat, the battles of the Marne and the Aisne and finally First Ypres. Deservedly after these campaigns he was sent back to base for a rest and innoculation, where he contracted fever and was allowed home on leave for convalescence.

On Walter's return to Belgium he was in the vicinity of the notorious Hill 60, which had been created in the last century when the nearby railway had been built, and in the flatness of Flanders was of great strategic importance. After bitter and prolonged fighting and mining, it had been in German hands since May and remained so until June 1917, heavily fortified.

Although there were periods of time between the heavy fighting described as, ' lulls' in regimental histories, it was still a dangerous place with constant infantry probing, sniping and artillery bombardment. On July 5th...., a cool day, heavy shelling started at 2 p.m, a shrapnel shell exploded in the back of the Norfolk's trench and a bullet from it hit Walter in the head killing him instantaneously (letters home invariably used this word to spare the relatives the pain of their loved ones' actual dying circumstances). A few days later his widow received a postcard written on the day he died saying he was fine.

He was buried in the nearby Trench Railway Cemetery, which after the war was closed and Walter and twenty other bodies were reburied in Perth Cemetery (China Wall), so called after the communication trench, the Great Wall of China, that was to the north up to the front-line.

Meanwhile in Gallipoli - the campaign which began as, *"one of the great strategical conceptions of the World War."* before it plunged into suffering for all and defeat for the Allies continued, and it is apposite to remember that we *" commemorate in stone those who never questioned the worth or wisdom of the idea. The sacrifice and valour were things far greater than the unacquired victory."* One such name, commemorated in stone died in the searing heat of a summer's day, came from Saffron Walden.

CORPORAL JULIUS **JACKSON** (8743) 1ST. ESSEX REGIMENT, KILLED IN ACTION 6TH. AUGUST 1915. COMMEMORATED ON THE HELLES MEMORIAL TO THE MISSING, SEDDULBAHIR, GALLIPOLI, TURKEY, PANELS 133 TO 140.

Julius Jackson was the son of George and Elizabeth Jackson of 5 Copt Hall Buildings Ashdon Road. We know little of his early life but he seems to have been a pre-war regular serving with the Essex Regiment in Mauritius when war was declared. They arrived in England in December and went to Harwich, joining the 88th. Brigade 29th. Division at Banbury. On March 21st. 1915 the regiment embarked on the *" Caledonia "*, landing on 3rd. April 1915 at Alexandria on their way to the Dardanelles. After a short stop at the Mudros on the Greek island of Limnos, the harbour being the original assembly point for the fleet that landed the first troops at Gallipoli, they landed on " W " Beach during the morning of April 24th., taking part in the attack on Hill 138 the same day.

In August Julius found himself in the line having been warned that he would be engaged a big attack on the Turks, this a diversionary attack at Cape Helles, the villages of Krithia and the heights of Achi Baba being the objectives, to enable the landing at Suvla Bay to succeed. The Essex Regiment, some 700 strong were detailed to take the trenches H 12a, H 12 and some trenches under construction to the north-east of H 12, near Krithia. At about 2.30 p.m. the artillery opened up, but the Turks replied with shrapnel and high explosives which rained down on the Essex trench system. At 3.50 p.m. the attack was launched in two lines on the Turkish trenches. H 12a was seized and secured, but there were heavy casualties (3,480 British and 7,510 Turks) and they were forced back. One of the fifty killed and 180 missing Essex men was Julius Jackson. His body was never found.

By the middle of 1915 the Great War had spread to many parts of the globe and troops were being transported to varying theatres of war. The huge convoys carrying this manpower were an attractive target for German U-boats, which had proved their deadly efficiency earlier in the conflict with the Royal Navy, as four grieving Saffron Walden families were all too well aware, and it was a man who wanted to save lives rather than to take them that was their next victim

PRIVATE CHARLES LEWIS **GARDINER** (99) 54TH. (1ST/1ST.) EAST ANGLIAN CASUALTY CLEARING STATION, ROYAL ARMY MEDICAL CORPS (TF), DROWNED 13TH. AUGUST 1915, AGED 29. COMMEMORATED ON THE HELLES MEMORIAL TO THE MISSING,

Lewis Gardiner was a man of devout faith. He was the son of the late Charles Walter and Mary Ann Gardiner of 23 South Road, and he had three sisters and a brother. He worked for Webb and Brand, Seed and Nurserymen of 10 East Street, at their greenhouses opposite the police-station. He was also the Superintendent of the Sunday School at Saffron Walden Baptist Church at the top of the High Street.

On the outbreak of hostilities in 1914 Lewis joined the Saffron Walden Voluntary Aid Detachment of the Red Cross before volunteering for foreign service and being attached to the Royal Army Medical Corps (R.A.M.C). At this time the campaign in the Dardanelles at Gallipoli was resulting in a huge loss of life, not only from enemy action, but from disease, which also debilitated the ones who recovered and replacements were urgently required.

Lewis found himself bound for Gallipoli on a transport troopship, the *Royal Edward*, formerly a Canadian Northern Steamships liner, from Alexandria to the Greek island of Limnos (Lemnos). On Friday August 13th. 1915, off Andileousa Island, about eighteen kilometres south of Kos and near the entrance to the Gulf of Kos (Kerme Korfezi) in the Aegean, where a landfall on the island had become part of the regular route, the troopship was torpedoed by the German submarine UB 14 under the command of Korvettenkapitan Heino von Heimburg.

The 11,000 ton vessel sank in minutes, taking with it Lewis and 867 other men, mostly drafts of the 29th. Division. There were only 500 survivors. Lewis' body was never found, and his name along with all who lost their lives is on the Helles Memorial, where on a clear day most of the Gallipoli peninsula can be seen, as well as to the south the blue Aegean Sea where Lewis met his God.

Lewis attended the Boys' British School and is also remembered in the Baptist Church where he worshipped. An enlarged portrait was hung in the Sunday School, an inscribed desk and a pine communion rail were commissioned in his memory. Sadly, the communion rail was destroyed in the Second World War, when soldiers were billeted in the church. A brass plate remains in the archives and the desk is at the back of the lower hall.

Five days after Lewis Gardiner drowned, another " promising young townsman, " was mortally wounded in France, and died two days later; another fellow-citizen with so much to offer his community, snuffed-out too soon.

Corporal Arthur William **PENNING** (29471) 31st. Heavy Battery, Royal Garrison Artillery, died of wounds 20th. August 1915, aged 24. Buried in Etaples Military Cemetery, France, Plot 4 Row C Grave 2A.

Arthur Penning had attended the Boys' British School and was the only son of William and Alice Jane Penning of 44 Gold Street. His father owned the grocer's shop in the Market Square, a magnificent feature of Saffron Walden until only a few years ago. After leaving school he joined the army, and had been in it some six years when war broke out. Immediately mobilised at Warley, he was soon in France and took part in the retreat from Mons with the 31st. Heavy Battery and their 60-pounder guns. Arthur was also present at the beginning of First Ypres, receiving as a council member, a Christmas parcel from the town's gift-fund in 1914.

On 18th. August 1915 he was severely wounded in both legs and taken to the base hospital at Etaples (Eat-apples) where he died on the Friday - the cause, possibly, being shock with exhaustion.

It was not until September when a friend visited his parents that the exact circumstances of his death were known. Arthur and a group of friends were having dinner at a rough wooden table when four or five shells exploded near them shattering one of his legs and causing a severe flesh wound in the other. He never recovered.

In addition to the town memorial his name appeared on the Oddfellows' roll of honour in their lodge room and he is commemorated on his parents' gravestone in the town cemetery in Radwinter Road. On his headstone in France, they chose these lines, *" Faithful unto death. Sadly missed. "*

One of the most sobering facts of the Great War is the human cost, an estimated nine million men, most under the age of thirty. One in eight who served was killed and the effect of their death on a small community is incalculable, but until now the casualties in the war for Saffron Walden had been relatively light, but it was deaths like Arthur Penning and two friends killed on the same day a month later that brought the true facts of the war home to the community and illustrate the aptly named Lost Generation.

PRIVATE OSBORNE **WHITEHEAD** (G/4615) 13TH. MIDDLESEX REGIMENT, KILLED IN ACTION 28TH. SEPTEMBER 1915, AGED 29. COMMEMORATED ON THE LOOS MEMORIAL TO THE MISSING, FRANCE, PANELS 99 TO 101.

Osborne Whitehead was one of five sons born to Osborne (Senior) and Maria who lived at 4 Common Hill. He attended the Boys' British School and was well-known locally as a footballer with the town's first eleven. When war was declared Osborne enlisted immediately with ten other men from Saffron Walden, including his best friend George Wren in the 13th. Middlesex Regiment., "The Diehards."
The Middlesex Regiment were part of the 73rd. Brigade, 24th. Division, a New Army division which, after training at Hove, Shoreham and Pirbright, arrived in France on 2nd. September just before the biggest battle the British army had yet been engaged in - the battle of Loos.

Osborne wrote to friends on September 24th., *" We are not in the firing-line yet, but every march brings us nearer; in fact we are getting quite used to the thunder of the guns."* Writing again the next day, *" We were awakened by gunfire at six o'clock and thought it was the Germans, but found it was our guns. They made a great noise and shook the windows where we were billeted. The Colonel told us this morning the action we are going into will be the biggest in history, so expect to see something in the papers soon. All the men seem to be in good spirits, especially after the good news we heard this morning. I am in good health and feel fit for anything."*

Thus on a wet, cold day began the battle, a huge attack with Osborne's battalion in the front-line by· Fosse 8 on their left (a twenty-foot high slag-heap behind the Hohenzollern Redoubt which commanded the whole area). For the New Army battalions it was an awful baptism of fire, inexperienced, exhausted by the long marches to get to the area and inadequately fed they suffered terribly. One survivor described it as

" an absolute shambles." After three days in the trenches, two without water, Osborne volunteered to fetch some and was never seen again. It was not until three weeks later that his parents were told he was missing. His body was never found. His name also appeared on the roll of honour in the Lodge Room of the Oddfellows Society.

PRIVATE GEORGE **WREN** (G4620) 13TH. MIDDLESEX REGIMENT, KILLED IN ACTION 28TH. SEPTEMBER 1915, AGED 24. COMMEMORATED ON THE LOOS MEMORIAL TO THE MISSING, FRANCE, PANELS 99 TO 101.

George Wren was the younger of two sons of Mrs. Eliza Gray Frances Penning of 1 Little Walden Road and his story is the shared tragedy of his great pal, Osborne Whitehead. They were friends at the Boys British School and played soccer for the town together. George also worshipped at the Baptist Church - his name appears on their memorial, but in 1914 they joined up together and were both posted to the same battalion of the same regiment.

Whether the circumstances of their death were the same is not known. George disappeared on the same Tuesday taking part in an infantry charge and like his friend his body was never found. It was not until 16th. September a year later that their deaths were confirmed, an agonising period of forlorn hope for all who knew them.

George is remembered on his parents' grave in the town cemetery (his father died soon after, perhaps of grief), *" For him the path of duty was the way to glory and we bow our heads in reverence to his memory."*

The deaths of these two young men, both under thirty and heavily involved in the community must have had far-reaching effects on parents, friends, children, perhaps still with us today. The Wrens and the Whiteheads seem innocents of that remote conflict, *" those sweet, generous people who pressed forward and all but solicited their own destruction."* As Philip Larkin observed, *" Never such innocence again."*

Every day on the battlefield and in the trenches countless acts of bravery took place; deeds warranting the Victoria Cross were commonplace, but often passed unnoticed and unreported, but in July 1915 a soldier from Saffron Walden performed an heroic task which was to lead to the award of the Distinguished Conduct Medal (the D.C.M.), sadly posthumously. This was one of two bravery awards given to men of our small town who became fatalities.

PRIVATE FREDERICK **DAVIES** D.C.M (12407) 7TH. SUFFOLK REGIMENT, KILLED IN ACTION 17TH. OCTOBER 1915, AGED 24. COMMEMORATED ON THE LOOS MEMORIAL TO THE MISSING, FRANCE, PANELS 37 AND 38

Fred Davies was born in Great Chesterford, probably the youngest son of a baker, John Davies and his wife, Margaret, of The Windmill House, Cambridge Road. The 7th. Suffolks were a Kitchener battalion formed at Bury St.Edmunds and Fred enlisted at Ipswich going to France in May 1915.

From June 16th. the 7th. Suffolks were on a tour of trench duty in the area of Ploegsteert Wood. One man was wounded on his way up to the line - the first casualty the battalion suffered. The first fatality occurred on the 22nd. June. They were changing places in and out of the line every six days with the 9th. Essex Regiment for a period of six weeks. Even when they were in support there was work to be done.

Working parties were called upon to handle bricks, fill sandbags or digging in barbed wire.

On July 18th., an officer Lt. Harold P Bamkin and a Private H Armsby were killed while on patrol duty in no-man's land. Fred and two other privates of the same patrol went out and brought back the two bodies. Today they are buried in the (Calvaire) Military Cemetery, Ploegsteert.

The battalion left this quiet, rural sector on September 26th., before going onto the soon-to-be infamous, industrial area of Loos. On March 11th. 1916, the London Gazette carried the following citation announcing the award of the D.C.M to Fred and his comrades. *" For conspicuous gallantry. He formed one of a party which went out to tap an enemy wire. The officer in charge was wounded and Private Davies displayed great bravery in assisting him back to the trenches, subsequently returning to the assistance of another man of the party who had also been wounded. Heavy rifle fire was going on all the time."*

Tragically, by this time Fred was already dead, killed bomb throwing on October 17th. just after the 'official' end of the battle of Loos in the area known as the Quarries. There were two trenches known as 'The Hairpin' and these were part of the Suffolks regular front-line duties in the Hulluch-Givenchy sector. Much bombing, mining, trench mortar fire and gas was experienced and here Fred died. His body was never recovered and his name is one of 20,693 carved in stone on the Loos Memorial.

News of his death was not reported in Saffron Walden until May 19th. 1916. His D.C.M, but not his other medals, is in private hands.

Also in the 7th. Suffolks was a twenty-year old officer, Charles Sorley who was to be shot in the head and killed during the battle of Loos, four days before Fred Davies. His name appears on the same panel on the Loos Memorial. In Sorley's kit was found a number of poems which were published in 1916 and went through four editions. He had no illusions about the horror of death in his poem, *" When You See Millions of the Mouthless Dead,"*

> *'...scanning all the o'er crowded mass, should you*
> *Perceive one face that you loved heretofore,*
> *It is a spook. None wears the face you knew.*
> *Great death has made all his for evermore.'*

Death in the trenches was no respecter of age and the youngest soldier to die, so far from Saffron Walden was to be added to the roll.

PRIVATE GEORGE **KING** (10619) 9TH. ESSEX REGIMENT, KILLED IN ACTION 18TH. OCTOBER 1915, AGED 19. COMMEMORATED ON THE LOOS MEMORIAL TO THE MISSING, FRANCE, PANELS 85 TO 87.

George was the son of Walter and Alice King of 6 Upper Square, Castle Street. After schooling he was employed by the Anglo-American Oil Company at their Railway Sidings in Saffron Walden until the war broke out and he enlisted immediately.

In late September 1915, George and his friends arrived at Loos, described in the regimental history as their, *" first view of a modern battlefield."* The weather was atrocious and the scene horrifying, *" ..bodies of men lay strewn about. Dead horses, lim-*

bers smashed to pieces and indescribable muddle and odour remain in the memory. "

The front-line trench was a mere mud-logged ditch, so this had to be improved and over 400 men toiled, under enfilading fire to build a new trench on the western side of the Chalkpit. On October 18th. it was decided to seize the whole of the enemy trench on the south-western face of the Quarries. As George was in the grenade section he was part of one of the squads deputed for this task. The enemy fought desperately, but resisting strongly were driven back along the trench where near their objective a barricade was erected and the trench - later called Essex Trench - was consolidated. Casualties, however, were heavy and George was counted amongst the missing.

It was not until March 1916 that news filtered home of George's fate, but his body was never recovered from the constantly bombarded battlefield.

The following day another young man " with the much-tried Essex, " was to suffer in an almost identical scenario with similar consequences.

PRIVATE SAMUEL CHARLES **START** (10641) 9TH. ESSEX REGIMENT, KILLED IN ACTION 19TH. OCTOBER 1915, AGED 19. COMMEMORATED ON THE LOOS MEMORIAL TO THE MISSING, FRANCE, PANELS 85 TO 87.

Charles Start as he was known lived with his parents in Castle Street and enlisted at the age of eighteen at Chelmsford. Training took place at Shorncliffe and Aldershot, before he embarked for France on 31st. May 1915, landing at Boulogne as part of 35th. Brigade 12th. Division. He was killed during the latter days of the battle of Loos in the area of the Quarries and the Hohenzollern Redoubt. About the time of his death his parents received a short letter from him, thanking them for a parcel they had sent him. He then said he was busy and had not time to write much. His work was bomb-throwing and that where he was was, *" like hell itself."*

On the Tuesday that Charles died, the 9th. Essex were attacked by the enemy around 4.30 p.m. The battalion history records that, *" The bombing section were entitled to great credit, for they worked themseves to exhaustion.. "* The Germans were repelled by machine-gun fire and rifle fire, but it was not until 22nd. October in a letter from his friend Private Jack Frost, that his parents learnt the harrowing news of their son's death in this action. *" He was killed last Tuesday night, the 19th. I spoke to him a few minutes before it happened. As he passed me he said, " Hulloa, Jack ! " and that was the last time I saw him. I really don't like sending you such bad news, but as we were mates I think it's only right that I should let you know. I don't expect you have heard from him lately, but we have all been the same. We have not been able to write, as we have been so busy. I am in hospital camp myself now, as I got wounded in the head on the night of the 20th. but I do not think it is serious, as I can get about. I am being sent to the base. I know this will be a hard blow for you, but I hope you will try and bear the blow."* Charles' body was never found.

One day later in the same sector with the same battalion of the same regiment a third Saffron Walden soldier disappeared for ever.

PRIVATE HENRY EDWARD **CLARKE** (CLARK) (3/2782) 9TH. ESSEX REGIMENT, KILLED IN ACTION 20TH. OCTOBER 1915. COMMEMORATED ON THE LOOS MEMORIAL TO THE MISSING, FRANCE, FRANCE PANELS 85 TO 87.

Harry Clarke (Clark) was the son of Mr. Simon Clarke of Middle Square, Castle Street. His elder brother Sidney, later joined the same battalion. Harry was a reservist when war erupted over Europe and was thus one of the first from the town to go, leaving for General Service, on 7th. or 8th. November 1914.

In the Loos area, during a bitterly cold October, the battle had officially ended, but death still lurked in the trenches and isolated engagements were a constant occurrence. The German trenches in the Quarries had been taken on October 14th. 1915, but on the Tuesday 19th. and into the following day, Harry's battalion were attacked by three squads of German bombers, accompanied by heavy shelling, and it was at this time, Harry was " blown up." The attack was repulsed, but in the mayhem of this and later battles, no remains were ever found.

1915 saw one more name added to the growing roll of honour (now twenty-five). The war that was to be over by Christmas was now approaching its second celebration of a forlorn " peace on earth ".

PRIVATE BOB **CHANCE** (G/1513) 2ND. ROYAL FUSILIERS, DIED OF WOUNDS 21ST. DECEMBER 1915, AGED 21. BURIED AT PORTIANOS MILITARY CEMETERY, WEST MUDROS, LEMNOS, GREECE, PLOT 3 ROW A GRAVE 287

Bob Chance was the son of Joseph Chance of 25 Castle Street, who had moved from Saffron Walden to 60 Comber Grove, Camberwell. Bob had been to the Boys' British School and was a printer employed by Walter Thompson in the Market Place. He was another keen member of the town football club, and a member of the congregation at the Baptist Church (his name appears on their memorial).

On the opening of hostilities Bob responded quickly to the call to arms and enlisted on 11th. September 1914, leaving Saffron Walden on 7th/8th. November. Perhaps because of his London connections he joined the 2nd. Royal Fusiliers, and spent some months training at Stockingford near Nuneaton as part of 86th. Brigade 29th. Division

In March 1915 the regiment embarked at Avonmouth on the " Alaunia " for Alexandria arriving there on 28th. March. The next stop was Lemnos on April 11th., an island Bob was to return to to die, before journeying to Gallipoli, landing on 25th. April 1915 landing on " X " Beach, before attacking Hill 114 the same day. The 2nd. Battalion were involved in the fighting at Krithia, and Suvla Bay and in one of these engagements Bob was severely wounded.

He was shipped back to the island of Lemnos where there were hospitals in name only. They were usually no more than tents, and the conditions terrible. "Accommodation was primitive...no amenities. The weather was cold; harsh winds and blizzards had to be endured. " A nurse wrote, " We could do little for them except to help them die decently ". Here Bob arrived, having lived with mud or dust, flies, maggots and death on the peninsula, to where there was a scarcity of medical equipment and food. He died four days before Christmas and is one of 352 graves in the military cemetery.

At the time of his death his father was in France himself with a labour (navvy's) battalion. Five weeks later Bob's mother died and two weeks later the expedition to Gallipoli was abandoned at the cost of 28,000 British dead.

In England the end of 1915 was acknowledged with a mood of greater resignation. Britain and Canada were the only participants in the war to still have entirely volunteer armies, but pressure was mounting for conscription which would add at least two million more men to the fighting forces. However in 1916 was to be seen the culmination of this first great volunteer army in the field, Kitchener's New Army, and its eventual annihilation on the downlands of the Somme; an act that heralded the end of the innocence and the for those at home and at the front, the beginnings of the realisation of the old lie - Dulce et Decorum Est.

The year was but two days old when the first new name was added to the lengthening roll, and this brought the tragedy of the war onto the doorstep of the people of Saffron Walden he was the first soldier to die and be buried at home, and his father was a local councillor.

PRIVATE ERNEST HAROLD **GILLING** (2867) 1ST/4TH. HAMPSHIRE REGIMENT, DIED OF ILLNESS, 2ND. JANUARY 1916, AGED 34. BURIED IN SAFFRON WALDEN TOWN CEMETERY, RADWINTER ROAD, ESSEX, PLOT 14 GRAVE 58.

Ernest Gilling was the third son of Alderman John and Ellen Mary Gilling of Market Hill. His father, in addition to his council duties was a chemist and this enabled Ernest and his younger brother, Reginald to attend Saffron Walden Grammar School, where he became school-captain. On leaving school he went into business in Fleet in Hampshire where he was a teacher at the parish church Sunday School and a pre-war territorial.

With the onset of war Ernest enlisted immediately in the 1/4th. Hampshire Regiment at Bustard Camp, Winchester. From England, on 9th. October he was posted to India, arriving after the long sea crossing, on 11th. November. He then went with the Expeditionary Force in March 1915, under General Townshend to the Persian Gulf and Mesopotamia, landing at Basra as part of the 30th. Indian Brigade, 12th. Indian Division. Here fighting the Turks, at some time during the assault on Kut and the advance along the Tigris in September 1915, Ernest contracted malarial fever.

He was transported back to hospital at base in the Persian Gulf, then to India for a month, but as recovery was slow, he was shipped back to the Red Cross hospital at Netley in Hampshire where he died.

On 6th. January 1916 in the afternoon, he was buried in the town cemetery. The inscription on his grave simply reads, " *In Netley Hospital after serving in India and the Persian Gulf.*" Ironically at the time of Ernest's death, his brother, Reginald was also in hospital in Cairo, having been wounded at Gallipoli.

The treatment of serious illness was a major problem exceeded only by that of wounds. The doctors and nurses were fighting death and disease without the benefit of antibiotics such as penicillin; the wounded soldier was at risk, not only from his actual wound where shells caused extensive tissue damage, but from gangrene and tetanus whose organisms thrived in the well-manured fields of France and Flanders.

PRIVATE JOHN **MALLION** (10713) 11TH. ESSEX REGIMENT, DIED OF WOUNDS 9TH. JANUARY 1916, AGED 26. BURIED AT ETAPLES MILITARY CEMETERY, FRANCE, PLOT 6 ROW B GRAVE 9.

John Mallion was the son of William and Sarah Archer of The Butcher's Arms, Sewards End, and he was commonly known as Jack. Little is known of him until in 1914 he enlisted in the Essex Regiment in September at Warley. He then went to Shoreham for training as part of 71st. Brigade 24th. Division. January 1915 saw him in billets in Brighton, before a return to Shoreham and Blackdown, going to France via Boulogne on 11th. October with the 18th. Brigade 6th. Division. As part of the 18th. Brigade 6th. Division the 11th. Essex were heavily involved in the July battles around Hooge.

Sometime at the end of 1915, Jack was severely wounded in the leg by gunshot and was taken to the 23rd. General Hospital where his leg was amputated. Sadly, he never recovered and on January 21st. his parents received a letter from a nurse in ward F 3 to say he had died.

Jack is buried in the adjoining military cemetery with over 11,000 other men from all over the world, friend or foe, all lie together in the comradeship of death.
" I am the enemy you killed, my friend...Let us sleep now..."

Etaples is the biggest British military cemetery in France, but the variety and individuality of all the cemeteries, whatever their size, is what is most memorable. The next casualty from Saffron Walden lies in a much smaller cemetery in the industrial area of northern France, but in common with Jack Mallion and the countless others his headstone is of a standard size, representing equality in death whatever a man's rank or religion. It has an engraved Christian cross (unless the family did not want it, or were Jewish, thus the Star of David) and could have a personal inscription not exceeding sixty-six letters (unfortunately a charge was levied for this and many poor families were deterred). Many of Saffron Walden's dead, thus, have no inscription, including the next fatality.

PRIVATE JOSEPH ERNEST **KETTERIDGE** (3/2682) 9TH. ESSEX REGIMENT, KILLED IN ACTION 15TH. FEBRUARY 1916, AGED 37. BURIED IN VERMELLES BRITISH CEMETERY, FRANCE, PLOT 2 ROW M GRAVE 11.

Joseph Ketteridge was one of five sons of George and Annie Ketteridge who lived at one time in London Road before moving to Great Chesterford where George was a carpenter on the Chesterford Park Estate. Joseph had served in the South African war and then was employed as a plate layer on the Great Eastern Railway (his name appears in the staff magazine roll of honour for October 1914), and remained a reservist. He was married with two children and lived at 8 Thaxted Road.

At the outbreak of war Joseph enlisted in the 3rd. Essex Regiment at Warley, but transferred to the 9th. Essex going to Blenheim Barracks at Aldershot and thence France on 31st. May 1915. All his brothers followed him - Charles into the London Regiment ; James, a sergeant, who was honourably discharged as unfit ; Alfred in the Northamptonshire Regiment and Robert, a lance-corporal in the Royal Fusiliers.

In February 1916 the battalion was to be found in the line near the Quarries which was a chalk pit twenty feet deep and a hundred yards wide, about 3,500 yards north of the Hohenzollern Redoubt, in the so-called battle of the Craters. However, Joseph did not meet his death in the front-line trenches; a letter from Private Elsom, Joseph's friend later explained the circumstances of his death, " *We were behind the lines...Joseph and three other men were killed by a shell.*" Perhaps because of these circumstances his body was laid to rest in the military cemetery at Vermelles, started in August 1915 during the battle of Loos, rather than his name joining the thousands with no known grave on the memorial at Dud Corner. Today Vermelles British Cemetery contains 2145 graves. Joseph's name also appeared on Saffron Walden's Oddfellows Roll of Honour in their long-disappeared Lodge Room.

Sadly, as in Joseph Ketteridge's case being away from the firing-line did not guarantee safety from the ever-searching long range German guns and two weeks later another name appeared on the Roll.

PRIVATE JOSEPH ALBERT **BRAYBROOKE** (PW 187) 18TH. MIDDLESEX REGIMENT, (PIONEERS. THE 1ST. PUBLIC WORKS BATTALION), DIED OF WOUNDS 1ST. MARCH 1916, AGED 36. BURIED IN CAMBRIN CHURCHYARD EXTENSION, FRANCE, ROW J GRAVE 55.

Albert was the fourth son of Joseph and Susannah Braybrooke of Ingleside Place. Soon after the declaration of war all the brothers were to be found in uniform - George, who had been a musician; Horace with the 1/5th. Essex Regiment, saw service in Gallipoli, where he was wounded in the face at Suvla Bay and fought at the Third Battle of Gaza and Frank who joined the 2nd. Essex on mobilisation. Albert also enlisted at Clapton Park and after periods of training at Rayleigh, Clipstone Camp and Salisbury Plain, went to France with the battalion serving as Divisional Pioneers to the 33rd. Division, landing at Le Havre on November 14th. 1915.

Until December the pioneers were at Gorre working on improving water-logged trenches, but were then moved to the area of the La Bassee canal. The work of the Pioneers was dirty, arduous and dangerous, involving making and repairing defences, building machine-gun posts and gun emplacements, laying duck-boards, digging communication trenches and wiring, all under the fire of shell and sniper.

In February, Albert came home on leave for seven days. On leaving he said goodbye to his mother remarking that he felt he would never see her again. Tragically, his premonition was true. On his way back to the trenches, behind the lines, he was killed by a stray shell. He was buried near where he fell, about half a mile from the front line, behind Cambrin Church where the churchyard was extended finally to accommodate over 1300 victims of the war. His brothers all survived the war.

Many Saffron Walden parents were to lose more than one of their sons in the conflict, tearing apart the fabric not only of their close family, but affecting the future of the local community and the country as a whole.

On the Western Front the fighting continued and although the headlines were concerned with the slaughter of Verdun, men continued to die in the infamous Salient of Ypres as well.

SERGEANT HUBERT **CHIPPERFIELD** (S/3637) 10TH. RIFLE BRIGADE, DIED OF WOUNDS 12TH. APRIL 1916, AGED 27. BURIED IN ESSEX FARM CEMETERY, BOESINGHE, BELGIUM, PLOT 2 ROW B GRAVE 1.

Hubert was one of five soldier sons of Thomas and Beatrice Chipperfield of 46 Radwinter Road. Some of the boys had joined at the commencement of the war, but all eventually served and were scattered across the British Army and across the theatres of war - William went with the Essex Regiment to Egypt ; Stanley was a corporal in the North Staffordshire Regiment, later wounded; Reg who after joining the Cambridgeshire Regiment was transferred to the Norfolk Regiment serving in a troubled Ireland and finally, Arnold whose story will be told later.

Hubert was a pupil at the Boys' British School and on leaving went to work initially for Wilkinson's Clothiers in the town. On the outbreak of war, he was working in the clothing department of a London firm where he enlisted in 1914 in the Rifle Brigade. This was a Kitchener battalion formed at Winchester in September 1914. During training Hubert was moved from Blackdown to Witley to Hamilton Camp near Stonehenge, before disembarking at Boulogne as part of the 59th. Brigade, 20th. Division on 21st. July 1915.

Hubert saw action at Pietre before the battalion marched into the area of the Ypres Salient in early 1916. April found Hubert in trenches in the Turco Farm sector, trenches which the regimental history describes as, " *in a state of incredible disrepair...isolated posts, mere sections of trench that by good fortune had escaped annihilation.* " It had snowed, frozen and then thawed, leaving terrible mud and the enemy had been particularly active. Hubert, in these indescribable conditions was badly wounded and taken to a nearby dressing-station where he later died. He was buried in Essex Farm Cemetery, today made famous because it was next to a dressing-station, perhaps where Hubert died, where Colonel John McCrae wrote one of the Great War's most famous poems, " *In Flanders Fields.* "

Hubert's white headstone is one of over 1000 here. His parents paid for the simple inscription, " *Bravely fought, bravely died.* " Later their tragedy, as for so many parents, was to be compounded when their fourth son, Arnold was also to make the supreme sacrifice,

" If ye break faith with us who die we shall not sleep, though poppies grow in Flanders fields. "

One day later, halfway across the world in another theatre of war, another son, another brother and another soldier from Saffron Walden died. The Gallipoli campaign had become a hallmark for failure. Casualties had been immense from bullet, shrapnel and shell, but also from disease and exposure in the unforgiving climate. A conservative estimate of Allied casualties alone is 265,000, of whom 46,000 died of wounds or disease in a campaign that lasted only eight and a half months. Disease claimed Saffron Walden's next victim

Private Reginald Edward John **HOPKINS** (3586) 1st/5th. Essex Regiment, died 13th. April 1916, aged 20. Buried Suez War Cemetery, Egypt, Row D Grave 8.

Reginald was employed by William Cornell and Sons of Hill Street as a basket maker with his father, Stephen John Hopkins. When the 1/5th. Essex Regiment was formed at the Association Buildings, Market Row Chelmsford, on August 4th. 1914, the day war broke out, Reg said his farewells to his father and mother, Fanny who lived at 6 Cates Corner and enlisted immediately. Training took place at Norwich, Colchester and St.Albans, before the battalion sailed for the Dardanelles from Devonport on the " *Grampian* " on 21st. July 1915.

Arriving at the island of Lemnos in the Aegean in August five days were spent in frantic last-minute preparations, before the battalion landed on the peninsula at " A " Beach, Suvla Bay on August 12th. 1915. The battalion was involved in heavy fighting, losing thirty-seven men, before being evacuated back to the island of Mudros on December 4th., thence to Alexandria, Egypt just before Christmas 1915.

At what stage Reg contracted dysentery is not known, but on April 28th. 1916, his parents received confirmation that their son had died on a hospital ship on the Suez Canal two weeks earlier. This was closely followed by a letter from Reg's officer, Lieutenant Thomas N Browett , who described him as, *"a most willing and obliging soldier."* (Lieutenant Thomas N Browett was killed in action on 30th. October 1918 and is buried in Dar-es-Salaam Cemetery, East Africa).

For some, however, foreign service never came, but death did. If shell-fire, bullets, disease, drowning and insanity were not enough, accidents happened in the most innocuous, but no less tragic circumstances.

LANCE-CORPORAL ARTHUR **BRAND** (1282) 2ND/25TH. (COUNTY OF LONDON) CYCLIST BATTALION, THE LONDON REGIMENT, DIED 5TH. JUNE 1916, AGED 26. BURIED IN SAFFRON WALDEN TOWN CEMETERY, RADWINTER ROAD, ESSEX, PLOT 24 ROW G GRAVE 48.

Arthur Brand was the son of Mrs. Brand of Debden Road and attended the Boys' British School. In 1914, he lived at 18 London Road with his wife and young daughter. He was well-known locally as a champion racing cyclist and was employed by the draper, Edward W Trew, 62 High Street, as a commercial traveller. In August 1914, Arthur immediately enlisted at Fulham into the 2/5th. Essex Regiment, which had just been formed. They were immediately sent to man coastal defences in Sussex and were attached to the 1st. London Battalion Headquarters at Lewes. Here Arthur successfully passed a course on musketry and rapidly gained promotion.

In April 1915 the battalion was moved to coastal defences in Norfolk, with the headquarters at Holt, transferring in April 1916 to Bungay. Arthur was stationed at Beccles and it was here the tragic accident occurred.

Arthur was on duty at Bridge House, Gillingham shortly after 9 a.m. on June 5th. when one of the guards patrolling the bridge heard the report of a rifle. Going to the house he found Arthur lying on the floor in a pool of blood. A Doctor Todd and a military doctor were rapidly summoned but could do nothing to avert death a few minutes later. The bullet had entered at the top of the right eye and pierced through the head.

At the inquest it was stated that Arthur was on duty as Sergeant-of-the-Guard and was standing in the guard room reading a morning newspaper. Another soldier picked up a rifle, not knowing it had live ammunition in it and it discharged itself. The soldier was very much distressed, he being a friend of Arthur. The jury returned a verdict of 'accidentally killed.'

Arthur's body was brought back to Saffron Walden, his funeral taking place on June 16th. He rests in a grave with a non-Commonwealth War Grave headstone inscribed, *"In loving memory of Arthur Brand 2/5 County of London Regiment who was accidentally killed by rifle shot while serving his country June 5th. 1916, aged 26 years. In the midst of life we are in death."*

On Saturday July 1st. 1916 at 7.30 a.m. a steady line of British soldiers climbed out of their trenches and walked slowly towards the German lines. By the end of that day there were 60,000 casualties and the first day of the Battle of the Somme was over. In common with every city, town, village and hamlet nationwide it proved the worst day for casualties for Saffron Walden. Four men died and countless more were wounded. It has been estimated that there was a British casualty for every eighteen inches of the front, but cold statistics cannot hint at the waste, the sacrifice.

PRIVATE CHARLES ERNEST **ANDREWS** (17043) 2ND. ESSEX REGIMENT, KILLED IN ACTION 1ST. JULY 1916. BURIED IN SERRE ROAD CEMETERY NO.2, BEAUMONT-HAMEL, FRANCE, PLOT 1 ROW J GRAVE 2.

Very little is known of Charles Andrews except that he was born and lived at Hill Road in Hempstead. His mother, Eliza was housekeeper to a Mr. Thomas Moss of Hill Road and she eventually married him. Charles enlisted in late 1914/early 1915 in Saffron Walden, giving up his job as a farm labourer. When he went to France is not known, but the 2nd. Essex Regiment had arrived at Le Havre in August 1914.

On the night of June 30th. 1916 the battalion assembled and left the village of Bertrancourt for the front-line trenches. The attack was to take place between Gommecourt and Thiepval towards a chain of fortified villages in German hands - Gommecourt, Beaumont-Hamel and Serre. The river Ancre cut the line in two ; the fortified villages up steep slopes and well-nigh impregnable.

At 8.36 a.m. Charles and his comrades left their trenches on the left of the Serre Road, immediately encountering heavy artillery and withering machine-gun fire. They crossed the German lines and moved to the right of Pendant Copse, their eyes fixed on the church spire of Miraumont. Heavy counter-attacks were then made by the Germans, forcing the battalion back to the captured Quadrilateral. So ended their day.

The battalion set off with twenty-four officers and 606 other ranks - a mere two officers and 192 other ranks took what rest they could at the end of that day. Charles Andrews was not one of them. His body was recovered and he lies in the largest cemetery on the Somme, 7139 graves of which 4944 are unidentified.

On the same day with the same battalion and killed in the same action, but with no known grave was a friend of Charles Andrews

PRIVATE GEORGE **CORNELL** (3/1249) 2ND. ESSEX REGIMENT, KILLED IN ACTION 1ST. JULY 1916, AGED 24. COMMEMORATED ON THE THIEPVAL MEMORIAL TO THE MISSING, FRANCE, PANEL 10 D

George Cornell was a reservist, mobilised four days after war was declared on August 8th. 1914. Until then he had lived with his parents at 58 Castle Street, working with his father, Arthur at Alfred Gough, a Maltster in Station Road.

He was sent to France almost at once in October, surviving the battle of Loos and months of trench warfare, although he had to spend some time in 1915 in hospital at Rouen for injuries received from barbed-wire. Christmas 1915, he came home on leave and talked of several narrow escapes he had had. But on his return George's luck ran out.

In the attack on Serre the battalion found themselves isolated, unsupported and running desperately short of ammunition. The Germans placed a barrage on the British front trench and craters caused by the earlier British bombardment afforded protection for the enemy to counter-attack. Even enemy reports praised the obstinacy and courage of the British defence, but the battalion was forced to withdraw and George did not come with them.

Back home news of the huge casualties slowly filtered through and a letter to his mother, from Private J Auger who was in the same company, gave the first news of George's death. Official confirmation followed in late August with those words that caused despair, but left a tantalising hope, " Missing, believed killed." That forlorn hope never materialised and George's body was never found.

Another casualty that day was Sergeant John W Streets, a miner who wrote poetry. He wrote to his publisher just before he died, words that epitomise the citizen army who never came back that day.

" We desire to let them know that in the midst of our keenest sadness for the joy of life we leave behind, we go to meet death grim-lipped, clear-eyed and resolute hearted.'

Amongst the men of the Kitchener battalions " two legions of amateurs " as they were described, who were drawn from all classes of society were the regular soldiers whose resolute hearts were forged through service and experience.

PRIVATE SIDNEY **BARKER** (9708) 1ST. ESSEX REGIMENT, KILLED IN ACTION 1ST. JULY 1916, AGED 23. BURIED AT KNIGHTSBRIDGE CEMETERY, MESNIL-MARTINSART, FRANCE, ROW G GRAVE 2.

When the lamps went out all over Europe, Sidney Barker was with the 1st. Essex in Mauritius. He had been a soldier for four years and was the son of Jane and the late Daniel Barker of 4 Upper Square, Castle Street. The battalion was shipped home and spent three months in England at Harwich and Banbury in training. In March 1915 they embarked for the Dardanelles via Alexandria and Mudros, landing at Gallipoli on April 25th. 1915. Sidney was a machine-gunner, but was wounded by a bullet through the left lung and shoulder blade, as well as in the right hand. He was in hospital for five months but on recovery volunteered to go back to the peninsula where he was again wounded this time in the leg.

Hospitalisation in Egypt saw his battalion leave Gallipoli in January 1916. Sidney was fit enough to join them on their return to France in March. He was regarded as a first-rate shot, which led to his selection as a regimental sniper.

1st. July 1916 saw Sidney and the battalion leave their billets at Louvencourt to form up behind the 87th. Brigade which had a frontage of 1000 yards near Beaumont-Hamel. In the distance was the Serre-Grandcourt ridge with Beaumont-Hamel in the valley below. The first battalions of the 87th. Brigade were badly mauled, but were believed to have reached and be fighting in the enemy's trenches.

At 8.37 a.m. the Essex Regiment on the right was ordered to attack independently from the support or third line trenches. This order was then cancelled and the battalion was told to move up to the front line via a communication trench. The front line was blocked, so they went over from the second line at 10.50 a.m. The 'fire was hellish. '

How hellish became clear to Sidney's mother in a letter received on Sunday 9th. July from a comrade in a Canadian General Hospital, Private J Thayner. ' *Last Saturday morning....Sid was one of the first to go over, he was killed instantly by a bullet...He was my only chum and sniping mate...*' Thayner himself was wounded ten minutes later.

Sid was buried about half a mile behind the front-line at a place where the communication trenches would have started. The local trench was called Knightsbridge. It contains 548 graves and Sid lies in the two rows that contain men of his battalion and from the island of Newfoundland killed on that day.

The final soldier from Saffron Walden killed On July 1st. also held the Distinguished Conduct Medal, but unlike Fred Davies had lived long enough to receive it. However, its award gave the recipient no respite or protection from danger.

CORPORAL JAMES JOHN **HALLS**, D.C.M. (5093) 1ST. RIFLE BRIGADE, KILLED IN ACTION 1ST. JULY 1916, AGED 20. BURIED IN SUCRERIE MILITARY CEMETERY, COLINCAMPS, FRANCE, PLOT 1 ROW GRAVE 16.

James Halls attended, like so many others, the Boys' British School. On leaving he became a telegraph messenger for a short time before enlisting in the Regular Army in London before the war. One of five children James' father had been a former local postman dying of enteric fever whilst with the 2nd. Norfolk Regiment in the South African war. His mother, Elizabeth lived at 13 Museum Street, but James was now married and lived in Johnson's Yard.

The 1st. Rifle Brigade were mobilised at Colchester, spent a few days preparation at Harrow School before being rushed to France at the end of August 1914. In late December James had been slightly wounded in the foot, but in May 1915 he was to be found in trenches near Mousetrap Farm in the Ypres Salient. It was a group of buildings surrounded by water on high ground north of Wieltje overlooking St. Julien and the valley of the Steenbeck. On the 13th. there was intense bombardment and the enemy attacked bidding for control of the remainder of the Frezenberg Ridge.

The Regimental History states,' *Halls of ' B ' Company (and another corporal) were cut off from the company for nine hours by the destruction of our trenches. They had held out in their post and by their accurate shooting had defeated all attempts by the enemy to dig in on the right front.*'

In a letter home, James wrote more modestly and graphically, '*We were in position with a farm on the right known as "Shell-trap.' We were shelled heavily from dawn till 3 p.m. receiving heavy losses, resulting in me and Corporal 'Sonie' (Sunnuck), a Canadian, not killed or wounded. When the shelling stopped the Germans started coming up. 'Sonie' and I crept up the trench and fired on them. Three times this happened. During the day we lost 170 men.*'

For this action both James and Corporal H E Sunnuck were awarded the D.C.M. The London Gazette 5th. August 1915 states, " *For conspicuous gallantry on 13th. May 1915, east of Ypres. When the end of his trench had been blown in, Rifleman Halls remained on the spot with an N.C.O. under heavy fire for nine hours firing on the enemy.* " On receipt of the D.C.M, James was promoted to corporal.

A further letter of August 1915 to his mother shows the character of the man, " *We are now back from the trenches for ten days rest, the first time we have been out of the sound of the guns during nine months I have been out here. This is Sunday and quite a treat to hear the old French bells ringing in the village church, which is about half a mile away. Since I last wrote we have taken part in a charge and captured a length of German trenches and eighty prisoners. Last Sunday we had orders to attack the German trench in front of us, but I hadn't the heart to write and let you know, and I am glad I didn't now, as, thank God, I came out of it quite safe, all but a cut on the face with a small piece of shrapnel, but I scarcely felt that in the excitement.*

Our artillery started the bombardment at 5 o'clock on Tuesday morning and it only lasted an hour, but it was terrible, and at one minute past six we gave a yell, jumped out of our trenches and rushed towards the Germans. By five minutes past six there wasn't a German in their first line trench, except prisoners who were begging for mercy, no doubt thinking we would shoot them straight away, as perhaps they deserved, but that is not our way. We made them work to build up the trench instead, which they were only too eager to do. We lost heavily, especially by bombs and grenades, but our shells must have done terrible work, for the Germans were lying in heaps blown to pieces, but I will not try to explain how horrible it was. I'd like to be able to forget. They left everything behind them, scores of rifles, helmets and equipment etc, and you ought to have seen our boys smoking their cigars, of which we found plenty. They shelled us pretty heavily during the day and tried hard to rush us out of it again, but we stuck it until we were relieved at night very tired and parched, but glad we had done what was wanted of us.

They put some gas shells over during the night, the only way of revenge they can get, but it was no go. It was a sad roll call the morning after we were relieved, but it would have been a lot worse hadn't it been for our artillery keeping them back and stopping them from massing. Don't worry about sending me parcels as long as I can get a smoke nothing else matters.

P.S. I know you will congratulate me, Mother, on having won the D.C.M for something I did in May. I shall probably get a furlough, so look out and cheer up. "

Soon after this James got his home leave, but not in the way he would have wished. He was wounded in the foot and was in hospital in Folkestone for two months, before convalescing at home for three more weeks. He was back in France for the 'Big Push.'

His battalion were to attack the Redan Ridge. They moved off at 7.29 a.m. and were immediately held up by intense fire front the Ridge and the Quadrilateral. Also the enemy wire was uncut, but by 10 a.m. they had entered the German lines. B Company were in the first wave that rushed these trenches and engaged the enemy in close-quarter fighting and bombing, but they were steadily driven back.

Meanwhile, Mrs. Halls had received a postcard from James saying he was all right. Tragically as she read it he was already dead. On entering the German trenches he had been shot in the chest. On July 21st. his family received official confirmation of this from the regimental headquarters.

James Halls is buried in the cemetery where during the days before the battle mass graves had been dug to receive the casualties, little did they envisage the terrible numbers there would be. It is quite possible that he and his battalion had marched past these very graves on their way up to the front-line. Today he lies with over 1100 of his comrades. The inscription chosen by his family reads, *" His memory is as dear today as in the year he passed away. "*

As dusk fell on the first day of the greatest battle the world had ever witnessed, the countless dead and dying lay out in no man's land, few realised that the battle would continue until winter set in on 18th. November 1916. By that time, Saffron Walden, alone had suffered twenty-four more deaths and the roll of honour would now contain the names of over fifty men who would never return.

PRIVATE FRANCIS HENRY **BADMAN** (15930) 7TH. SUFFOLK REGIMENT, KILLED IN ACTION 3RD. JULY 1916, AGED 27. COMMEMORATED ON THIEPVAL MEMORIAL TO THE MISSING, FRANCE, PANELS 1C & 2A

Francis Badman was born and lived at the George Inn in George Street where his father, also George and his mother, Sarah ran the pub. He, like so many of his peers, attended the Boys' British School, but when he got married to Florence Hockley, he moved to Westerfield, Ipswich. Naturally this led to him joining the Suffolk Regiment with whom he went to France in May 1915.

The battalion were not involved in the fateful first two days of the battle, but on Monday 3rd. July, the battalion were moved into support trenches from Henencourt Wood in the early hours of the morning. Their objective at zero hour of 3.15 a.m. was Ovillers and led by the 5th. Royal Berkshire Regiment, they attacked, the first four waves of troops coming under very heavy enemy fire, before clearing their positions as far as the third line. Some of the survivors entered the ruined village, but the advance was brought to a standstill and they had to retire. The battalion was almost destroyed, all the company commanders were killed and casualties were in excess of 450. One of these was Francis Badman.

On July 29th. Mrs. Badman received a letter from the battalion chaplain stating that Francis was presumed a prisoner, but her joy was short-lived. A further letter in early August confirmed he had been missing since the commencement of the big allied advance, but went on to state that Francis had been seen in the trenches by friends on *' an eventful evening,'* but when the roll-call was taken the following morning, he was missing. No trace of him was ever found.

An officer writing his condolences to the family complimented Francis on *' his high efficiency and personal character.'* But it was small consolation for the loss of a son and husband.

The circumstances of Francis' death were repeated over and again over the next few weeks, although the family knew of the next casualty's death only three weeks later and there was no element of doubt.

PRIVATE WILLIAM **DEWBERRY** (24550) 9TH. ESSEX REGIMENT, KILLED IN ACTION 3RD. JULY 1916, AGED 21. COMMEMORATED ON THE THIEPVAL MEMORIAL TO THE MISSING, FRANCE, PANEL 10 D

William Dewberry wrote a field postcard home to his parents at 46 Castle Street a few days before his death. The next information that John William and Sarah Ann

Dewberry received of their third son was a letter informing of his death. He had been in France barely three months.

Before the war, William had been a butler in domestic service, but at the end of 1915, he had enlisted. Training was rigorous, and it was felt that he and his battalion, were not ready to go to France, until just after Easter 1916.

At the opening of the battle, the 9th. Essex were, like the 7th. Suffolks, in reserve at Henencourt Wood, but they proceeded to the front-line the following day. On the morning of Monday July 3rd. at 3.15 a.m., after an intense bombardment intended to destroy the Germans' wire and trench system, the 12th. Eastern Division attacked Ovillers, with the 9th. Essex in support. It was necessary to creep across no man's land, the counter-bombardment and machine-gun fire was so fierce. They had considerable difficulty of getting into the enemy's front-line, casualties were considerable and the attacking troops deteriorated into a series of small groups. Exactly how William died can only be guessed at, but again his body disappeared into the bowels of the battlefield.

Today his name remains, one of 946 comrades from the Essex Regiment, found on the Thiepval Memorial.

One of the most distressing aspects of the Great War for so many families must have been the absence of an actual grave of their loved one. The vast memorial at Thiepval towers 150 feet above this battlefield of the Somme, visible everywhere - its position dictated by the nature of the site and by historical associations. On it are 71,798 names, including fifteen from Saffron Walden.

For those who have a grave the location and the circumstances of their death in this bloody July reflect the intensity of the fighting over a front of such a few miles, the determination to break the well-established German defences at whatever cost and the enemy's equal determination to resist this storm of steel from their well-entrenched deep, concrete dugouts..

PRIVATE WILLIAM FAYER **BOUCH** (G/1514) 9TH. ROYAL FUSILIERS, KILLED IN ACTION 7TH. JULY 1916, AGED 21. BURIED IN OVILLERS MILITARY CEMETERY, OVILLERS-LA-BOISSELLE, FRANCE, PLOT 6 ROW N GRAVE 4.

William Bouch was a Norfolk man, born in King's Lynn, but his parents, William and Emma moved to Saffron Walden living in Pleasant Valley whilst he was young and he attended the Boys' British School before going to work at Mr. Engelmann's Carnation Nurseries. At the commencement of the War, William, the eldest son, joined for General Service and went into the 9th. (Service) Battalion. His brother Cecil joined the King's Own Yorkshire Light Infantry.

France was their destination in May 1915 where William soon distinguished himself as a regimental bomber, being Mentioned in Despatches in September. The task of the 9th. Royal Fusiliers at the onset of the battle of the Somme was to be in support north of Ovillers during the 12th. (Eastern) Division's attacks which were unsuccessful. It was then the turn of William's battalion to try and succeed in attacking Ovillers at daylight on July 7th.

At zero hour of 8.30 a.m, after a four hour bombardment, they attacked in bad weather. The regimental history dryly states, *" few more costly actions were fought in the whole battle of the Somme.'* The battalion kept to the left side of the spur to avoid machine-gun fire from the Leipzig Salient, but they were still exposed to a furious enemy bombardment, sniper and machine-gun fire. To make matters worse the fumes from gas shells blanketed the hollows and craters which became death-traps for the wounded. Finally, the enemy troops opposite them were a crack regiment of the German Army - the Prussian Guard. The Royal Fusiliers' casualties amounted to 225 men, one of whom was William Bouch.

What happened next illustrates the agonising uncertainty for the family at home, clutching at hope, fearing the worst but never having proof until many months later.

On July 29th. William's family received a letter from his Company Sergeant-Major to say he had been wounded. He even joked that a parcel sent to William from home had arrived two days after he had been wounded and the C.S.M had shared it out as there were only three men left in the company! Nothing more was heard until September 2nd. when a telegram came saying he was, 'Missing, believed killed.' That is how things must have stayed until the end of the war when William's remains were found after the Armistice and buried in the nearby cemetery - the dreaded final confirmation of his family's fears.

Today he rests in the old no man's land, one of only twenty-eight percent that are identified. On his grave is the inscription, *" Loved too well to be forgotten.'* Not far from him lies the son of Sir Harry Lauder who wrote the song that typifies the loyalty and courage of these men, *" Keep right on to the end of the road.'*

William's brother, Cecil survived the war, became a Sergeant, winning the Military Medal in October 1917.

Shells, bullets, bombs and gas do not differentiate between ranks, so inevitably we come to the first officer to be killed. Statistics state that 27% of officers died, as against 12% ordinary soldiers, but officers were more easily identifiable so the figures for battle-wound casualties may be more reliable - 47% for officers and 56% for other ranks. The junior subaltern's function in battle was to lead and often these officers were very young - at the battle of Loos eighty-four of the 106 officers who died were under twenty-six years old, they were also often the potential leaders of our society, in politics, in business, in the law and in culture. Their huge losses were reflected in the phrase *'The Lost Generation.'*

LIEUTENANT DONALD FREDERIC GOOLD **JOHNSON**, 2ND. MANCHESTER REGIMENT, DIED OF WOUNDS 15TH. JULY 1916. AGED 26. BURIED IN BOUZINCOURT COMMUNAL CEMETERY EXTENSION, FRANCE, PLOT 1 ROW B GRAVE 8.

Donald Johnson was commissioned in the same regiment as Wilfred Owen, but they had more than that in common, they were both poets. Sadly, they did not meet as Owen did not arrive in France until December 1916.

Donald was born in Saffron Walden in 1890, the youngest son of the town's Congregational minister Reverend Richard and Mrs. Eliza Bennett Johnson of 40 Church Street. He went away to school at Caterham, then became a teacher before going up to Emmanuel College, Cambridge in 1911. He wrote poetry before the war and won the Chancellor's Medal for English Verse in 1914 for a poem entitled, *'The Southern Pole.'* More significantly, he became a Roman Catholic.

At the end of 1914, he intended to pursue a study of Chaucer on a research scholarship, but on the outbreak of war and living in Cambridge he abandoned this idea and as he had been a member of the Officer Training Corps at university, applied for a temporary commission the army on December 8th. 1914. He hoped to join the same unit as his brother and a friend, a Mr. Peake, but this was not to be. On December 4th. 1915 Donald was posted to the 2nd. Manchester Regiment. He went to France on December 7th. 1915, joining his battalion at Etaples. Promotion followed with his being gazetted a temporary lieutenant in April 1916, with effect from the previous February.

In July 1916 the battalion were part of the 14th. Brigade, 32nd. Division assembled in Authuille Wood before attacking the heavily-defended Leipzig Salient which they took and held. After withdrawal from here on 8th-10th. July they were in action on the western side of Ovillers Post where some ground was gained. The regimental history notes that Sausage and Mash Valleys were, " *...littered with the bodies of dead and wounded from the attack which failed...The place was a heap of ruins, and the Boche had a position round the ruins of the church in the shape of a horseshoe."* They then returned to Bouzincourt until the 14th. when they attacked Ovillers again.

On July 15th. a trench had to be held by a bombing party at all costs and the Germans prevented from advancing. Donald without hesitation undertook the task, but bade farewell to his friends, fully certain that he would not return. The party came under heavy fire and twenty-five casualties were sustained forcing them to retire. Donald was one of those casualties.

He was taken to the dressing-station in Bouzincourt where he died from his wounds. In the cemetery where the Commonwealth War Graves Commission (C.W.G.C), *' care for their quiet heritage from day to day, '* the inscription on his headstone says, simply, but poignantly, " *Dearly loved son."* It is the only headstone that has the words, *" Of Saffron Walden "* on it.

What poetic talent was snuffed out that day we can only surmise from one slim volume of verse published posthumously in 1919. In the preface the Master of Emmanuel College declares, '*... he was not a good exam candidate though his teachers were sure he had the root of the matter in him. Literature to him was a part of life, not knowledge to be pursued for gain.'*

His poems have a classical theme ; some were written at the Front, some at home, showing evidence that the small French villages which so delighted him, reminded him of the countryside around Saffron Walden. But there is also the recurring sense of the shortness of life and the waste, as well as the presentiment of death in *" Resurgit, " " Les Pauvres Morts,"* and his sonnet *" Spring 1915 "* which is indeed prophetic

'Next year these shall renew their youth, but thou
No more may'st look upon the bursting flowers
Nor daze thy senses with the breaths of Spring
Silent thou'llt lie throughout the endless hours.'

32

A few days before Donald's death, his parents received a letter from him, swiftly followed by the telegram informing them of his death. This was not the only telegram to come to their home in Church Street. In July 1915, Donald's sister had died in Calcutta. He wote a poem *" H.M.J. "* to her memory, and in 1917, just nine months later, Donald's brother Owen fell at Arras. Their epitaph shall be in Donald's *" Justitia Victrix "* -

'Their glorious names shall be adored
Great was their love and great their worth;
Their fame shall purify the earth,
And honour be their dear reward.'

As public awareness of the casualties involved in 'The Big Push' grew, so often the people at home were lulled into a false, if temporary sense of hope, by a letter or fieldpostcard sent some days before, that for the time being, at least, their loved one was secure.

PRIVATE STANLEY GEORGE **WILSON** (241021) 1ST/5TH. GLOUCESTERSHIRE REGIMENT, KILLED IN ACTION 21ST. JULY 1916, AGED 21. COMMEMORATED ON THIEPVAL MEMORIAL TO THE MISSING, FRANCE, PANELS 5A AND 5B

In early August 1916, Mr. and Mrs. Walter Edward Wilson of 34 Victoria Avenue received a postcard from their second son, Stanley, saying that he had been involved in very heavy fighting, but he had come through it without mishap. One week later came the official communication that he had been missing since July 21st...and not until June 1917 did the comfirmation come that he was dead !

Stanley had been born in Cheltenham, but the family moved to Saffron Walden where after attendance at the Boys' British School, he obtained an apprenticeship as a printer with Hart and Son. On completion of this apprenticeship, Stanley obtained a job as a journeyman printer with Norman Bros. of Bennington Street, Cheltenham.

In the last week of September 1914, he enlisted at Gloucester in 2/5th. Gloucestershire Regiment. His two brothers were also to join the army, Reginald into the Northamptonshire Regiment and Henry, a private in the Royal West Kents.

Stanley started his military service in Essex where the second line Territorial battalions had gone to assemble as part of the 61st..(South Midland) Division. They were used to provide drafts for the front-line battalions in France and Stanley was one of the first to be sent to the 1/5th. Battalion in June 1915. Initially, he saw service in the area of Ploegsteert Wood, before being moved south to occupy a line south of Arras separating Hebuterne from Gommecourt Wood. This was to become the northern end of the Somme battlefield.

In March 1916 Stanley was invalided home with an injury to his knee-cap, septic poisoning caused by the barbed wire. At one time it looked like it might have to be amputated, but he eventually made a complete recovery in Epsom Military Hospital, before returning to France just in time for the big battle.

On July 1st. the battalion were moved a little further south to be ready to take part in the follow-up phase in the Ovillers sector. From here between July 12th. and 17th. they were in support in what was known as the battle of Bazentin Ridge which led to the capture of Ovillers. On the night of Friday the 21st. at 11 p.m. Stanley and the battalion attempted to push the firing-line north-east over the downs beyond Ovillers intending to capture and secure Point 79. ' B ' and ' D ' companies attacked unsuccessfully and were held up by heavy machine-gun fire, Stanley was never seen again.

In addition to Saffron Walden, Stanley's name is to be found on St. Paul's, Cheltenham war memorial and with 1059 other names of the 'Glorious Glosters' on Thiepval.

All over the British Isles communities were counting their dead and wounded, but troops from the Empire were also involved in the battle of the Somme. Ironically, on July 1st. 1916 the only Empire troops destined to take part in the fighting were from the tiny colonies of Newfoundland and Bermuda. But in late July the first Australian involvement on the Somme took place. Many troops in these Empire forces of Australians, Canadians, South Africans and New Zealanders were men from the 'Old Country,' who had gone to seek their fortunes across the world and had now returned to ' help old England in her hour of need.' Seven men from Saffron Walden fought and fell in these uniforms of the Empire. One had perished in Gallipoli, the first was now to die on the soil of France.

PRIVATE VICTOR **SEARLE** (2439) 20TH. INFANTRY BATTALION, AUSTRALIAN IMPERIAL FORCES, KILLED IN ACTION 26TH. JULY 1916, AGED 26. COMMEMORATED ON THE VILLERS-BRETONNEUX MEMORIAL TO THE MISSING, FOUILLOY, FRANCE.

Victor was born in Newport, one of six children of James and Louisa Searle, who later moved to Saffron Walden, first at Mill Lane, then 5 Common Hill and finally to the Rose and Crown Hotel. At the age of nineteen, Victor emigrated to Australia and settled in Wrong, New South Wales, finding employment as a storeman. As news of an early end to the war became more and more unlikely, Victor, in common with many others from the British Isles in the far-flung corners of the Empire, decided to enlist and on August 3rd. 1915 became a private in the 5th. reinforcements to the 20th. Battalion. He was nearly 24 and although only 5 feet 3 inches tall and weighing a mere 8 stones 12 pounds was, eagerly accepted.

He sailed for France, leaving Sydney on the 30th. September and stopping off at Tel-el-Kabir in Egypt in January 1916. A short period of further training ended on March 18th. 1916 with his departure on the troopship 'Ingoma', arriving at Marseilles on March 25th.

Victor's battalion were transported north across France and were heavily involved in the battle of Pozieres Ridge from July 23rd. Three days into the battle Victor was killed. News of his disappearance did not reach Australia until two months later, which led to an enquiry being made by a Mr. Travers of Petersham, New South Wales who had seen Victor's name in the casualty lists. This enquiry led to the bald reply, 'reported missing.'

Victor's personal effects of his kit-bag and a testament were received by his family and a letter arrived in March 1917 to the effect that he had been buried on the battlefield of Pozieres by the chaplain, the Reverend W E Dexter. This proved to be unverified and Victor's grave was never found.

On the crest of a hill with a panoramic view towards the city of Amiens and the valley of the Somme stands the memorial where you will find Victor's name, one of 10,797 Australians, two who hailed from Saffron Walden and who proudly wore the famous slouch-hat of their adopted homeland.

The following day a few miles away in the infamous ' *Devil's Wood* ' - Delville Wood, described as ' *the bloodiest battle hell of 1916,* ' another local soldier died. One who in joining up had exchanged one uniform and strict discipline for another, to fight for his country.

PRIVATE FREDERICK JOHN **BOYCE** (SPTS/1881) 23RD. ROYAL FUSILIERS, KILLED IN ACTION 27TH. JULY 1916, AGED 24. COMMEMORATED ON THE THIEPVAL MEMORIAL TO THE MISSING, FRANCE, PANELS 8C 9A AND 16A.

Fred was the eldest son of Superintendent J E Boyce who was a police officer in the town. After leaving school Fred followed in his father's footsteps and became a policeman at Braintree and then Shoeburyness. Involved in the local community, he was for a time the Honorary Secretary of St. Michael's Bible Class Sports Club in Braintree and on leaving to take up his post in Southend, was highly regarded enough to be presented with a Gladstone bag.

Thus it was no surprise to his parents when Fred enlisted in June 1915 into the newly-formed 1st. Sportsman's Battalion, of the 23rd. Royal Fusiliers at Hornchurch. Training took place at Clipstone Camp, Nottinghamshire before the battalion travelled to France on 17th. November 1915.

July 1916 found Fred and his friends in the area of Bernafay Wood where they had what the regimental history describes as, *'an uncomfortable time,'* before the attack on Thursday July 27th. in an attempt to gain the notorious Delville Wood. Here the ground over which they were to advance was pitted by shell fire, covered by dead bodies from previous attempts, with gas being used and gas-masks not allowed because there was a breeze, supposedly dispersing it. In addition the weather was stiflingly hot!

The battalion formed up in a trench along the edge of the wood with the 1st. King's Royal Rifle Corps and the 1st. Royal Berkshire Regiment in support. The approach was to be covered by an artillery barrage. At 7.10 a.m. the barrage lifted and the Fusiliers attacked. The opposing troops were Brandenburgers, the terrain was terrible. Wood stumps, crashed trees, thick undergrowth made progress both difficult and dangerous, not to mention shell fire, snipers, gas and bombs. The attack was not a success - twelve officers and 276 other ranks were lost in this inferno, including Fred Boyce.

In Saffron Walden, Mr and Mrs. Boyce received, a few days later, their first news in the form of a field-postcard signed in Fred's name from a comrade saying he was wounded, but no other information. This agonising situation was not cleared up until September when confirmation and details of Fred's death emerged, first in a letter from his officer and then in another from his best friend.

Fred was attached to the Lewis-Gun section and his officer wrote, *" I regret that I am unable to give you any definite information as to the present whereabouts of your son. On the morning of the 27th. whilst courageously carrying out his duties, he was wounded in the stomach. However he still carried on in spite of his wound and a little while after he was wounded in the legs. About six hours later he was seen by one of his comrades. Though badly wounded he was still seen living and even then his thoughts were for his gun-team. It was about 4 o 'clock that afternoon that he was last seen and I very much regret that we have not been able to get any further news of him since. His work in the field was splendid. I cannot speak too highly of him. His loss has been keenly felt by the whole section and, in fact, by the whole battalion. It is such men as he who have brought such honour and glory to our battalion in the recent fighting and his deeds will never be forgotten..."*

Less prosaically these sentiments were echoed in a letter from Fred's chum... *" I regret I am unable to tell you much of Fred as I should have liked to have been able to. I was not on his team on the day we attacked so I can only tell you what I have gathered from the men who were near him at the time and those who saw him later. "Billy," as he was known to everyone in the battalion was my best pal. We had everything in common and whenever possible we got together on the same gun-team and naturally I have inquired in every direction for news of him. When we started the attack Fred did great work for which he has been recommended but his luck was out and he was hit while in the German front-line. Always cheerful he is greatly missed in our section. Our loss is great but yours is greater and in your sorrow may you be comforted by the fact that he died a hero and a credit to any army.."*

Two further facts emerged from this. Probably to spare his parents further grief the officer with-held the details that after being wounded in the stomach, a shell burst, killed two of Fred's comrades and blew off his feet. Also, no posthumous decoration was awarded to " Billy " Boyce and his body never located.

Fred is also remembered on the Southend Memorial. A brother also served in the Gordon Highlanders and survived the war.

As the summer progressed so did the killing. In this same sector two more local men, not in the same regiment were to die. Both were involved in the attack of the 2nd. Division.

PRIVATE FREDERICK **HAWES** (19642) 13TH. ESSEX REGIMENT, KILLED IN ACTION 30TH. JULY 1916, AGED 21. BURIED IN BERNAFAY WOOD BRITISH CEMETERY, MONTAUBAN, FRANCE, ROW M GRAVE 74.

Fred Hawes came from Sewards End where his father was a brewer. He worked in Saffron Walden as a chauffeur to Major Martin Nockolds of Castle Hill House, Castle Street, but the excitement of war called and Fred gave up his comfortable occupation enlisting in late 1915 at Warley. He was sent to the 13th. Essex Battalion which had its roots in West Ham. Training took place at Clipstone Camp and the battalion disembarked at Boulogne on November 17th. 1915.

Initially they were in trenches in the Lens area, where Fred received a slight wound before being moved down in late July 1916 to the Somme area as reinforcements in the inappropriately named, Welcome Wood.

On July 25th. the battalion moved forward to a reserve position north of the village of Carnoy. Three days later they were moved again to Breslau Trench at Delville Wood as support before relieving the 17th. Middlesex Regiment on July 29th. in the wood itself. Although the wood was now in Allied hands and had been since July 27th. it was still subject to fierce counter-attack by the Germans and was not in fact fully cleared until 25th. August.

Indeed on Sunday July 30th. the Germans used the dreaded flammenwerfer (flamethrower) in the area of Waterlot Farm, but how Fred Hawes was killed is not known. It was not until late August that the news reached England, perhaps there was some comfort in the knowledge that his body was found and buried in the cemetery on the reverse slope of the Montauban Ridge, near a Dressing Station which was established here. Originally it contained 284 graves, but after the war it was enlarged to take another 638 bodies recovered from the battlefield - over half are 'unknowns.'

The regimental history of the Royal Fusiliers describes this sector as *" perilous "* and so it proved to be for another soldier who forsook the comfort of a good, secure job to serve his country.

LANCE-CORPORAL CHARLES JOHN **MUNK** (E/691) ' C ' COMPANY, 17TH. ROYAL FUSILIERS, KILLED IN ACTION 30TH. JULY 1916, AGED 22. COMMEMORATED ON THE THIEPVAL MEMORIAL TO THE MISSING, FRANCE, PANELS 8C 9A AND 16A.

Charles Munk was born in Littlebury, but at an early age moved to 9 South Road, Saffron Walden with his parents, George and Louisa. His father was the estate carpenter to Miss Gibson. The eldest son, he attended the Boys' British School, after which he secured a promising job as a clerk to the local solicitors, Messrs. Wade and Lyall of 18 Hill Street.

The coming of war and in the fervour of excitement, desperate not to miss the great adventure that would be over by Christmas, Charles and several other men from the town enlisted in London in the 17th. (Service) Battalion (Empire) of the Royal Fusiliers. This battalion was formed on August 31st. 1914 by the British Empire Committee. Training was, initially, at Warlingham, Surrey, before the more serious business took place at Clipstone Camp from June 1915. On 1st. July, the battalion was taken over by the War Office and moved to Tidworth. But on 17th. November 1915, it sailed for Boulogne.

On 3rd. June 1916 a local newspaper carried a letter from Charles entitled, " *A Note from the Germans,* " in which he humorously described his time so far in France.

The 17th. were the first of four Royal Fusilier battalions to enter the battle zone of the Somme. On July 25th. 1916 they took over support lines at Longueval Alley - their first entrance into any battle-zone and what an introduction! On the 27th. ' A ' and ' B ' companies were sent to Delville Wood where they were exposed to tear-gas shells.

The remainder of the battalion still lay south of the Wood but at 2 p.m. they were moved up where they held a strong German counter-attack. Over the next few days they saw service in this sector, the wood finally being cleared of Germans on the 28th. Losses were heavy, three German regiments were completely annihilated, but the counter-attacks continued. The wood was a huge jungle of fallen trees, full of destroyed sections of trench and shell holes full of bodies ; in these conditions on the Sunday, Charles was killed and lost forever.

His friends, Lance-Corporal J Barker and a Corporal Shepherd wrote to his parents in a letter received in August, '*...he went to Holy Communion just before he was* *killed...he was a good soldier doing most of the work and always shared his parcels...they did not know how he died.'*

The image of the slaughter of the Somme is of the infantryman, the " Poor Bloody Infantry, " but the artillery played an equally important role. Each day for a week before the opening of the battle, they had bombarded the enemy positions from 6.25 a.m. until 7.45 a.m. The barrage was the greatest inducer of fear in the troops and its effects devastating. One field gun per ten yards and 'heavies ' every twenty, could rain hell on earth onto troops crouching in their trenches. Of course, the artilleryman was not invulnerable and fierce battles between opposing batteries were commonplace and catastrophic.

GUNNER GEORGE HENRY **MARTIN** (176) 106TH. HOWITZER BATTERY, 6TH. AUSTRALIAN FIELD ARTILLERY, AUSTRALIAN IMPERIAL FORCES, KILLED IN ACTION AUGUST 7TH. 1916, AGED 28. BURIED IN GORDON DUMP CEMETERY, OVILLERS-LA-BOISSELLE, FRANCE, PLOT 1 ROW A GRAVE 34.

George Martin's story comes straight from the pages of the *" Boys Own Paper."* Born in Edmonton, he was the eldest son of Mr. E Martin who moved to 8 Springfield Cottages, Thaxted Road. After leaving school in Saffron Walden aged fourteen, George joined the Royal Navy as an able-seaman, where he endeavoured to continue his education, successfully so, as when serving on H.M.S " *Impregnable ",* he won the ship's prize for Geography and the Royal Society's prize for an essay on cruelty to animals!

When he was twenty, he was invalided out of the Royal Navy with bad teeth and joined the merchant fleet, sailing many times round the globe. While on the S.S. *"Stork"* he was shipwrecked in Hudson's Bay, Canada and had to walk nearly 300 miles over ice and snow to the nearest rail-link.

Perhaps this experience decided George on a less adventurous life and for a while he worked in Canada, but the yearning to move on persisted and he rejoined the Merchant Navy, sailing for Sydney, Australia on the *" Port Jackson. "*

George then came home to Saffron Walden, before returning to Australia on the "*Viemara."* This time he married Muriel and settled down in Jackson Street, Magill, South Australia, having two children and working as a driver for the Magill Brick Company in Adelaide.

War interrupted this peaceful existence and George volunteered on March 27th. 1915 joining the Australian Imperial Forces (A.I.F) with whom he sailed for the Dardanelles and the ill-fated Gallipoli campaign. On 21st. July 1915, he arrived at Lemnos on the *" Port Macquarie."*

On November 5th. he was sent to the Casualty Clearing Station at Suvla with enteric fever which led to pyrexia and necessitated his removal first to the hospital ship, *"Morea"* and then the 1st. Canadian Stationary Hospital at West Mudros, where he stayed until the 16th. when he was discharged for base duties, before returning to the trenches at Suvla on the 23rd.

He survived the flies, the heat, the dysentery and the Turks, being eventually evacuated to Alexandria, Egypt via Mudros in January 1916. On March 10th. 1916, George was transferred to the 22nd. Howitzer Battery at Tel-el-Kabir from the Royal

Australian Naval Bridging Train and was then posted to the 106th. Battery at Zeitoun. Almost immediately on March 19th. he was sent to France aboard *B.8 S.S. Haverford,* disembarking at Marseille on March 25th. Here they entrained for Le Havre where the battery stayed for a week, before moving onto Blaringhem and finally on April 10th through Hazebrouck to Armentieres.

May and June were spent resting and training. As the 106th. Howitzer Battery was now part of 6 Brigade, known as a mobile brigade, its function to rush to where it was needed giving quick support, on July 2nd it was sent straight to the area of Pozieres, on the Somme.

By July 27th, they had taken up position in Sausage Valley, beyond Pozieres, another heavily fortified village on a ridge that had only been captured two days earlier. Here began a week long assault on old German trenches OG1 and 2. The success of this venture resulted in very heavy German bombardments.

In fact, the fighting in this area resulted in more Australians being killed in this sector than in any other part of the Somme battlefield. On August 7th. 1916 George became one of these statistics.

On August 7th, an eleven inch (279.4 mm) shell penetrated C gun-pit and buried the gun. It also exploded all the ammunition, some 200 rounds, killing five men, including George Martin, and four more dying from their wounds. The crater made by the explosion of the ammunition was eleven yards in diameter and ten feet deep.

It was not until September 17th. that his wife received the news. Muriel had had no letter since August 1st. so she contacted the Australian Forces Headquarters in London, who informed her of his death on August Bank Holiday Monday. Finally George's wandering days were over.

Today he is buried in Gordon Dump Cemetery, Ovillers-la Boisselle amidst rolling fields and with ninety-one comrades from across the world, some part of C gun-pit team. His name appears on the memorials of the town of his childhood and, hopefully, in the town of his adoption, Magill. His brother, a shoeing-smith in the Royal Field Artillery survived the war.

Other soldiers born in Saffron Walden had crossed the world to seek their fortune, but many had gone to the corners of the British Isles for the same reason. The onset of war led them to enlist in their local regiments and in the event of their death it can often be found that their names are recorded on more than one war memorial, in this case where their parents lived, Saffron Walden and where they had established their home, North Yorkshire.

PRIVATE CHARLES EDWARD **KETTERIDGE** (28366) 12TH. WEST YORKSHIRE REGIMENT, KILLED IN ACTION 18TH. AUGUST 1916, AGED 27. BURIED IN GUILLEMONT ROAD CEMETERY, GUILLEMONT, FRANCE, PLOT 8 ROW I GRAVE 3.

Edward Ketteridge was the son of Edward and Susan Ketteridge of Saffron Walden, but on his marriage to Annie, he moved to the small village of Ulleskelf, some seven mile south-west of York. In 1915 he enlisted at Selby in the Prince of Wales' Own West Yorkshire Regiment, the 12th. (Service) Battalion one of Kitchener's New Army and part of the 63rd. Brigade, 21st. Division.

In September 1915, the battalion landed at Le Havre becoming part of the 9th. Brigade, 3rd. Division. Early August 1916 saw the battalion in trenches in the Maltz Horn sector under continuous heavy enemy shelling. On the 16th. they were to attack Lonely Trench, described as a " *minor local operation,* " designed to improve the position of the general British line. The 3rd. Division had the responsibility of trying to capture Lonely Trench and Cochrane Alley. They first attacked at 5.30 p.m. on the 16th. capturing the latter, but Lonely Trench proved a much more formidable obstacle as it was held by infantry with machine-guns and was protected by thick barbed-wire. The trench also had a low command, was irregularly sited, difficult to observe and could not, in its most important parts, be bombarded by our heavy artillery, without clearing the British front-line.

On the 17th. at 9.30 p.m. a surprise attack at night with bayonet and bomb was made by the 10th. Royal Welch Fusiliers on the right and the 12th. West Yorks on the left. It proved a costly failure. Exposed to intense machine-gun fire the attackers only got to within a few yards of Lonely Trench suffering 205 casualties, including Edward Ketteridge.

He is buried at the heart of the Somme battlefield amongst illustrious company - the Prime Minister's son, Raymond Asquith killed nearly a month later ; Edward Wyndham Tennant, the poet and William Stanhope Forbes, son of a famous artist in addition to 2251 other graves, more than two thirds unknown. Edward Ketteridge, an ordinary man from the shires has a headstone that simply says, " *Thy Will be Done,* " but in the manner of his death he shares, " *a common gallantry* " with these well-known scions of Edwardian England.

As we have too often seen, the carnage led to many relatives never having a grave to visit, a focal point to assuage their grief. News that a son was ' missing ' did not mean inevitable death - he could be wounded , have lost his memory, be out in no-man's land, be a prisoner-of-war - hope could never be given up until official confirmation was received. For many families this agony of doubt might last to well after the war had ended and many a wife and mother, for the rest of their lives, lived in the belief that one day their loved one would walk in the door. For the next casualty the circumstances of his death have remained a mystery and confirmation of death involved a long, painful process that took over a year.

LANCE-CORPORAL WALTER WILLIAM **TAYLOR** (1641) 51ST. INFANTRY BATTALION, AUSTRALIAN IMPERIAL FORCES, KILLED IN ACTION 3RD. SEPTEMBER 1916, AGED 21. COMMEMORATED ON VILLERS-BRETONNEUX MEMORIAL TO THE MISSING, FOUILLOY, FRANCE.

Walter was born the son of Charles and Clara Taylor in St. Mary's Axe, London, before moving to Saffron Walden at Park Lodge, Abbey Lane, from where he went to school. After completing his education, Walter spent some time at sea in the Merchant Navy with the Newcastle Steamship Company. He also had been a territorial with the 2nd. Essex Regiment but was now time-expired.

After this Walter went to Australia where the outbreak of war found him employed as a bushman. On 5th. January 1915 he enlisted at Blackboy Hall, Western Australia, joining his battalion at Albany. Reinforcements were taken from this and on May 7th. Walter became a member of the 11th. Battalion. Six months later he was in Mudros en route for Gallipoli. Luckily he never got there, as he was discharged from his battalion and used for duty at Imbros until 20th. November when he rejoined it again at Sari Camp, Lemnos.

The evacuation of the peninsula took place in early January 1916 and Walter and his comrades were sent to Alexandria on the 6th. on the H.M.T. " *Lake Michigan* ".

On February 29th. Walter was again transferred to the 51st. Battalion at Serapeum, moving to Tel-el-Kepir on March 1st. Further training under the hot Egyptian sun ended on June 5th, when they boarded the " *Ivernia* " for Marseille, arriving seven days later.

The long train journey up France took Walter to the Somme where he was promoted Lance-Corporal on August 16th. Eighteen days later he disappeared. The battalion on September 3rd. were involved in attacks north-west of Mouquet (Mucky) Farm and his parents, were informed that Walter had been reported ' missing.' No further news was forthcoming until April 23rd. 1917 when a Court of Enquiry was held into Walter's disappearance. Their findings are not known, but on 7th. May Mr. and Mrs. Taylor were officially informed that he had been killed in action. No trace of him was ever found.

Five months before Walter's death, another tragedy had struck the Taylors - his seventeen year old brother, Frederick had died. He is buried in Saffron Walden cemetery and his elder brother, Walter is remembered on the same headstone. Perhaps their parents got some comfort that their younger son at least had a known resting place and had been saved the horror of a battlefield death? After the war, Mr. and Mrs. Taylor moved to Ely.

From the vast outpourings on the Great War, both personal and historical, we are familiar with the bald horrors of death and mutilation on the battlefield, but for the general public at home in 1916 and for some time afterwards, the full details of casualties, of the means, apparatus and manner of death could only be guessed at. Newspaper reports were heavily censored and thoroughly sanitised, soldiers on leave who knew the truth were reluctant to tell, to save people's sensitivities and because they felt that no one would believe them. So when a man was killed, his officer or a comrade would often write a comforting letter home explaining the circumstances of death, assuring their loved ones that death had been quick, heroic and painless..

> *Quietly the Brother Officer went out.*
> *He'd told the poor old dear some gallant lies*
> *That she would nourish all her days, no doubt.*

PRIVATE ALBERT **AUGER** (TF 5867) 1ST/8TH. MIDDLESEX REGIMENT, KILLED IN ACTION 18TH. SEPTEMBER 1916, AGED 24. BURIED IN EUSTON ROAD CEMETERY, COLINCAMPS, FRANCE, PLOT 1 ROW F GRAVE 34.

Albert was one of three soldier sons of the widowed Mrs. Ann Auger of Castle Street. In September 1915 he enlisted in the Essex Yeomanry after leaving his job as a labourer with Thomas Ware. His other brothers had joined the Essex and East Surrey Regiments respectively a year before and were destined to survive the war.

Transferred to the 1/8th. Middlesex Regiment, Albert did not arrive in France until July 15th. 1916 as replacements for the huge casualties from the opening weeks of the battle of the Somme. The battalion were part of the 165th. Brigade, 56th. (1st. London Division) at Souastre. On September 4th. they entrained at St. Riquier for Corbie and from there marched to the Bois des Tallies. On the 10th. they were to be found in trenches in front of Leuze (Lousy) Wood. Over the next few days there were attacks on the German positions on the Ginchy-Morval Road with heavy casualties, before on 14th. the battalion were in support between Wedge Wood and Leuze Wood.

Attacks continued on the 15th. again with heavy losses, until on Monday the 18th. September they were ordered to attack German Wood. At 1.30 p.m. Albert and his comrades were instructed to advance down the north-west side of Bouleaux Wood, where thirty minutes later they were ordered to dig-in. The fighting was desultory, attacking with bayonet and under a constant stream of sniper fire and incessant bomb throwing. On the left of the line it was felt that the enemy's resistance was less obstinate and the troops continually worked themselves towards that flank. By evening the brigade was beginning to establish itself in Middle Copse and the 1/8th. Middlesex were withdrawn in support to Leuze Wood. Casualties had been heavy - 245, including Albert Auger.

Later, a comrade, Private W Ellis wrote to Albert's mother, " ...*he was much liked...his death was instantaneous.* " What truth lay behind that one comforting word - " *instantaneous?* "

Albert is buried in the same grave as another private of the same battalion, the same regiment killed on the same day - space was at a premium. The cemetery is up a lane along which men marched up to the trenches. Also in the cemetery is Sergeant Will Streets, a miner and a poet whose family inscription bears repeating for Albert -
" *I fell, but yielded not my English soul that lives out here beneath the battle's roll.*"

Many regiments not involved in the first day of the Somme battle were hastily brought in as the huge casualties mounted. The 2nd. Royal Sussex Regiment was not directly involved in the fighting until late July, but in their first engagement alone there were 116 casualties. It is no wonder that a feeling of fatalism must have imbued the troops; the knowledge that death was statistically a near-certainty, evidenced by the hundreds of putrefying corpses on the surrounfing battlefield, makes their tenacity, their endurance and their loyalty even more astonishing to our more cynical, modern eyes. By the time the next young man from Saffron Walden was to die, his battalion from July 23rd. until September 9th. had had nearly 1000 casualties but still the attacks continued and the legions of " *the glorious dead* " steadily grew.

SERGEANT JOHN WILLIAM **BAKER** (G/14552) 2ND. ROYAL SUSSEX REGIMENT, KILLED IN ACTION 27TH. SEPTEMBER 1916, AGED 22. COMMEMORATED ON THIEPVAL MEMORIAL TO THE MISSING, FRANCE PANEL 7C.

William Baker was Saffron Walden born and bred, attending the Boys' British School, worshipping at the Baptist church, before going to work at the Carnation Nurseries. He was the eldest son of Mrs. Lucy Baker who lived at 10 Ingleside Place, just off the High Street. He was a pre-war Territorial with the 2/5th. or 3/5th. Essex

Regiment. When the war clouds loomed he enlisted straight away and ended up in the 2nd. Royal Sussex Regiment who were sent to France immediately in August 1914.

Heavily involved in the Somme fighting, William survived the attack on Munster Alley on July 23rd. which even the Official History of the Great War describes as. " ...*standing no chance of success* " because of machine-gun fire - there were 116 casualties ; the attacks on the German trench running westwards across Bazentin-le-Petit from High Wood ; Clark's Trench in Mametz Wood and the ridge between High Wood and Martinpuich - casualties to date a further 480. September 9th. saw further assaults on Wood Lane (casualties 262), before a period of rest and much-needed recuperation for the battered remnants of the battalion.

With such heavy involvement in the fighting, although by no means untypical, the inevitable scenario takes place and William's luck ran out. On September 25th. the battalion took over the Starfish Line in High Wood, the following day attacking Prue Trench. In this battle which lasted two days the battalion suffered a further 161 casualties, including William Baker. In the inferno of the wood, " ...*a battlefield that had to be imagined...in desolation, in horror, in pitifulness, in grimness,* " William's body disappeared and his name is carved with 720 other men of the Royal Sussex Regiment on Thiepval.

An officer recalling High Wood in later life wrote, " *The first time I had seen it was some time previously from a distance in daylight. It was a mass of battered tree-shapes which were as black as though covered with tar, it was not tar but a crawling mass of great fat bluebottle flies, millions of them, millions of them everywhere - you would see them crawling in and out of the holes of empty skulls.* "

News of his death did not reach Ingleside Place until late October. It must have been even more terrible for his mother as William's brother, Alfred, a private in the Royal Fusiliers had just left for France a few days before, another replacement for the Somme. Thankfully, he survived the war.

The Boys' British School in Saffron Walden educated many generations of local boys, educated them for life. Little did anyone realise that three years later on November 11th. 1919, the names of 75 former pupils would be unveiled on the scroll of honour painted by a teacher of the school. These 75 boys saw much in their short lives and even more of death in their allotted span. One day after William Baker died another pupil disappeared on the Somme never to be seen again.

PRIVATE ERNEST WILLIAM **WRIGHT** (G/11948) 7TH. ROYAL WEST SURREY REGIMENT (THE QUEEN'S), KILLED IN ACTION SEPTEMBER 28TH. 1916, AGED 19. COMMEMORATED ON THIEPVAL MEMORIAL TO THE MISSING, FRANCE, PANELS 5D AND 6D

Ernest was the eldest son of James Frank and Florence Annie Wright of 26 East Street. After schooling he obtained a position as a clerk with Woodward & Priday who were local auctioneers, before moving on to work for Messrs William Bell and Sons, established builders of South Road. But in March 1916, Ernest responded to Lord Kitchener's call and joined up. After the period of induction he was sent to France to join his battalion in August who were at rest in the area of St.Omer.

The battalion had been very heavily involved in the initial stages of the Somme battle, indeed in mid-July the strength of the battalion at one time was only 280 fit men ! In early September they were moved to Puchevillers and then to bivouacs in Blighty Valley.

Thursday September 28th. dawned fine and warm, although there were occasional light showers. Ernest's battalion were attached to the 53rd. Brigade as an assaulting battalion ; their assigned task to capture the whole ridge from north-west of Courcelette to the infamous Schwaben Redoubt, a virtual parallelogram of German trenches.

They left Blighty Valley at 10.15 a.m. forming up at noon in the open in their attacking lines. Although their objective had been subjected to a three day preliminary bombardment, they came under heavy shrapnel, machine-gun and long range rifle-fire. At 1 p.m. the barrage crept forward and the lines of men moved off after it, but still they were exposed to heavy fire which checked the attacking waves, inflicting a huge toll of casualties - one officer and forty-five other ranks killed with eighty-seven men missing. Eventually the battalion took and held the southern side of the Redoubt after continuous fighting at close quarters. Ernest was one of the missing.

It was not until August 1917 that Ernest was officially presumed dead. His name is on the same memorial as his old school-fellow, William Baker, comrades in death, as in life.

Few front-line soldiers, if they escaped death, were lucky to survive the war without being wounded, and these wounds which today could often have been easily treated, were often fatal. Wounds to the abdomen were particularly so - a sample of 1000 cases found 510 dying on the battlefield, 460 in the ambulance, twenty-two after the operation. leaving only eight survivors ! The crucial factor was infection. The next telegram received in Sewards End contained the news of the first of three brothers to die, two of whom died from their wounds.

PRIVATE WALTER G **ARCHER** (8754) 70TH. BATTALION, MACHINE GUN CORPS (INFANTRY), DIED OF WOUNDS 2ND. OCTOBER 1916, AGED 24. BURIED IN BECOURT MILITARY CEMETERY, BECORDEL-BECOURT, FRANCE, PLOT 1 ROW W GRAVE 31.

Walter was the second son of John and Eliza Archer of Sewards End. He worked for Mr. C Kettley of Tip Tofts as a labourer until he enlisted, with his younger brother, Charles in the Essex Regiment on June 11th. 1915. He became Private W.G. Archer (19641). In late 1915 or very early 1916 he transferred to the 70th. Brigade Machine Gun Company.

In March 1916 the Brigade disembarked in France becoming part of the 8th. Division, until July 17th. when they rejoined the 23rd. Division. They were evidently well thought of - when the 23rd. Division took Contalmaison in early July, the Divisional Commander was asked what he would like in recognition of the bravery of his formation, he replied that he would like his 70th. Brigade back !

Late September saw Walter in the area of Destremont Farm, a strongly defended group of buildings, described as, " ...*dirty brown slime and mud which was crisscrossed with trenches here and there.* "

On Sunday October 1st. with the 11th. Sherwood Foresters and the 8th. King's Own Yorkshire Light Infantry they were ordered to attack Flers Trench and Flers Support near Le Sars. It was a fine sunny day, a mild 63 F and the clocks had gone back ! The battalion moved forward from the Tangle into their assembly positions in Destremont Trench at 9.15 a.m. The attack was successful, the objective taken and consolidated, but with high casualties from heavy shelling before the attack.

In this engagement Walter was wounded and eventually found by searching stretcher-bearers who took him to a regimental aid-post in a reserve trench dugout or shell hole. Here the medical officer did what he could for Walter, including an injection of morphia before he was transported to a Casualty Clearing Station where the next day he died.

Just before Christmas his parents received a letter from the battalion Chaplain. In it he wrote, " *...he died peacefully and in little pain. He was buried in the soldiers' cemetery.*" Today it is known as Becourt Military Cemetery in an attractive wooded valley along a quiet country lane, containing over 500 graves.

> " *In the little new-made grave-garden*
> *There slept the soldiers of England ;*
> *There the heroes had found their peace.* "

Back home in Fulham hospital the following day another soldier died from his wounds. He was the first Derby Scheme man from Saffron Walden to die. After fifteen months of war the casualties had exceeded everyone's estimates, so men were needed and conscription was openly being talked about. Lord Derby's Scheme retained an element of individual choice, but all men between the ages of nineteen and forty-two had to register - this was estimated to be between three to five million men. The element of choice was that if passed fit they could enlist immediately in a regiment of their choice with the possibility of applying for a commission, or they could wait to be called-up and be sent where the Army chose. There was a six-week period for people to make up their minds and married men were assured they would not be called up until all single men were in the ranks.

PRIVATE DOUGLAS CHARLES **PURSEY** (5778) 23RD. COUNTY OF LONDON REGIMENT, DIED OF WOUNDS 3RD.OCTOBER 1916, AGED 25. BURIED IN SAFFRON WALDEN TOWN CEMETERY, RADWINTER ROAD, ESSEX, PLOT 51 GRAVE 105.

Douglas was the youngest son of Alfred and Emma Pursey of 9 Castle Street. Alfred was church clerk for eleven years and a verger for forty. He was also a carpenter and after leaving the Boys' British School, Douglas followed his father's trade, becoming an apprentice joiner and carpenter with Robert B Parsons, a builder and undertaker of 15 South Rd. His practical skills were matched by his musical ones and he was a trombonist with the Saffron Walden Town Band.

On February 8th. 1916, Douglas joined Lord Derby's scheme, being first attached to the Essex Regiment before being transferred to the London Regiment. In June he was sent to France but the battalion was not involved in 'the big advance.' In early August, Douglas was allowed home on seven days leave as his father was ill, rejoining his pals on August 16th. at St. Riquier.

Mid-September found them in reserve for an attack on High Wood which took place on September 16th. at 9.25 a.m. The battalion encountered heavy fire, in fact companies ' A, ' ' C ' and ' D ' never returned, but the remnants attacked Starfish Line with the 1/24th. London on the 18th., again coming under heavy fire from the northern corner of High Wood, although the objective was taken. Soon afterwards the enemy counter-attacked and the battalion was forced to withdraw 100 yards where they were exposed to severe bombing and involved in hand-to-hand fighting.

At some stage of the fighting of 18th. September, Douglas was severely wounded in the left thigh. From the Casualty Clearing Station he was eventually he was taken to the military hospital at Fulham where septic poisoning set in and his leg had to be amputated. His mother was summoned, but he never regained consciousness after the operation and on October 3rd. at 9 a.m. with his mother at his bedside, he died. By an amazing coincidence, the same day that Douglas was wounded, his elder brother Fred with the Middlesex Regiment, was also wounded, but fortunately survived.

Douglas was buried in Saffron Walden. No firing-party was available, so it was not practical to lay him to rest with full-military honours, but " *all honour possible was given to him.* " The coffin was draped in the Union Jack and carried on a horse-drawn hearse, accompanied by his friends from the Town and Excelsior bands playing at the head of the procession. Today Douglas' grave is to be found with the distinctive white Commonwealth War Graves Commission headstone, not far from three other soldiers who made the final journey to Blighty.

As the Town Band played their doleful marches behind the coffin of Douglas Pursey very few would have believed that just a few days later another band member before the war would also die of wounds in France. The death of this soldier is a prime exam-ple of the involvement of one family in the process of war and its tragic effects on them. There were five sons and one son-in-law serving - two of them died.

PRIVATE FRANK DOUGLAS **DAY** (37271) 26TH. COMPANY, MACHINE GUN CORPS (INFANTRY), DIED OF WOUNDS 13TH. OCTOBER 1916, AGED 22. BURIED IN BECOURT MILITARY CEMETERY, BECORDEL-BECOURT, FRANCE, PLOT 1 ROW X GRAVE 35.

Frank was the fifth son of Arthur and Elizabeth Day of 1 Castle Court, Castle Street. He was a fitter at the Corporation Gas works in Thaxted Road, before transferring to the gasworks at Haverhill. When he joined up in January 1916, one of his brothers had already been lost during the Battle of Neuve-Chapelle in March 1915 - (it has not been possible to identify this brother. His name does not appear on the town's memorials), and three others were already in France with the Royal Fusiliers.

Enlisting in Haverhill in January 1916, Frank became a private in the Suffolk Regiment (23961) before transferring to the Machine Gun Corps and going to France in late July 1916 as a replacement, part of the 9th. (Scottish) Division.

Early October found the company in the area of Albert in positions at Bottom Wood, south-west of Mametz. On October 9th. trenches were taken over in the Flers Line, with a view to an attack being mounted three days later on the Butte de Warlencourt, a chalk-covered mound heavily fortified by the Germans. Fierce machine-gun fire greeted this attack from irregular zig-zagged Snag Trench blocking it, and forcing Frank and his comrades to dig in only 150 yards from their starting-point. Here not only were they exposed to heavy enemy fire, but the British bombardment fell short, incurring further casualties, until they were relieved early the next morning.

During this attack Frank was wounded, taken to Field Dressing Station Number 13 where he succumbed the following day, probably the same mobile hospital in which Walter Archer had died eleven days earlier. Like Walter, Frank was buried in the same nearby cemetery and in the same plot.

Despite the carnage and the intensity of the battle waged since July 1st. the British were still attempting to reach their first day objectives, but now another factor came into the equation - rain and mud. Even though the conditions worsened it was to be over another month before the battle was officially over and still the casualties mounted.

PRIVATE ALBERT THOMAS **KIDMAN** (18963) 11TH. ESSEX REGIMENT, DIED OF WOUNDS 14TH. OCTOBER 1916, AGED 36. BURIED IN ETAPLES MILITARY CEMETERY, FRANCE, PLOT 7 ROW F GRAVE 3A.

Albert was the eldest son of Thomas and Alice Kidman of 1 Pleasant Valley. He was a maltster at Barnard Brothers, married with two children and living at 28 Mill Lane. He also regularly attended the Baptist Church. In late April 1915, Albert enlisted for General Service, as did his four brothers at various later stages; George into the Royal Garrison Artillery; Fred into the Royal Engineers; Harry the 2nd. Royal Fusiliers and Thomas, who whilst under age, got himself accepted in the Machine Gun Corps.

Albert went to France on 30th. August 1915 landing at Boulogne, becoming part of the 6th. Division. In October the battalion was sent as part of the 18th. Brigade in the Ypres sector. It was not until August 1916, that the 11th. Essex were entrained down to the Somme at Mailly-Maillet where they bivouacked south-west of the village in the wood. At some stage in the next few weeks probably in the Hamel sector, Albert was severely wounded by a shell in the back, through the lungs and in the head whilst returning from the firing-line to the rear. The wound was so severe that he was taken to one of the many base hospitals near Etaples.

In early October his wife received a letter from one of Albert's nurses saying he was, " *comfortable, in a clean bed with plenty of food.* " This was finished off with the exhortation, " *...not to worry !* " Almost immediately after reading this news, a telegram arrived summoning her to his bedside, where on October 14th. Albert died. Mrs. Kidman remained in France to see her husband buried with full military honours in the huge cemetery at Etaples.

Albert is remembered on the Baptist Church memorial along with his brother, Harry, who was killed later on. The other three brothers returned, although Fred suffered wounds.

The enthusiasm, patriotism and need for adventure that the early stages of the war engendered led many men to enlist when through age, circumstances or health they need not have. For whatever reason the shell and the bullet were no respecter of person and the loss to many families of a father was in many ways more poignant, more tragic, more far-reaching than the death of the young, single man.

PRIVATE JOSEPH **PEARSON** (19579) 1ST. ESSEX REGIMENT, KILLED IN ACTION 18TH. OCTOBER 1916, AGED 42. COMMEMORATED ON THIEPVAL MEMORIAL TO THE MISSING,

Joseph was the eldest son born to Stephen and Sarah Pearson of 38 Fairycroft Rd. He worked for Mr. A Whitehead and Son, of Church Street as a painter and decorator and was well-known in the town as he distributed the Sunday newspapers. Married to Sarah Ann he lived with his wife and five children in Gold Street.

In 1914 Joseph and his family's simple, but comfortable life changed irrevocably. The Great War broke out and within three months his brother, Charles was dead. This tragedy immediately prompted Joseph, despite his age, to enlist in the Essex Regiment.

In autumn 1915 Joseph was sent to the Mediterranean Expeditionary Force in Egypt, although it does not seem likely that he joined his battalion in Gallipoli. But in March 1916 after the evacuation from the peninsula, the battalion sailed for Marseilles, where they entrained for the Somme.

Heavily involved in the first day attack on Beaumont-Hamel where over 200 casualties were suffered, Joseph saw action until July 27th. when they were transferred to the Ypres sector. In early October they were returned to the Somme for the attack on the village of Guedecourt on the 11th. Guedecourt lay just below a German defensive system, the last but one to be penetrated before Bapaume could be reached from the south. The storming of Hilt Trench with the Newfoundland Regiment and the capture of Grease Trench by some of the Essex men was to be Joseph's last action. On October 18th. attacking Mild Trench, 1000 yards out of the village of Guedecourt, he was killed all objectives were gained. On the 20th. the battalion were relieved. The action was described in a wonderful understatement as " *very costly.* " Joseph's body was never recovered and five more children were fatherless.

Fate had not finished with the Pearson family. Other brothers joined up and in the last days of the war a final telegram dropped through the letter-box at Fairycroft Road with the information that the youngest brother had died from his wounds.

Joseph was the second of three brothers to die and tragically three days later the first of three more brothers and sons was to disappear into the blasted oblivion. Six soldiers in age ranging the exact requirements of the Derby scheme - from 19 to 42 ; serving in five different regiments ; three of whom have no known grave, leaving seven children fatherless and two widows in mourning.

Lance-Corporal William Charles **REED** (70363) 17th. Sherwood Foresters, (Notts and Derby Regiment), killed in action 21st. October 1916. Commemorated on the Thiepval Memorial to the Missing, France, Panels 10C, 10D and 11A.

William was the son of Mrs. Emma Reed, a widow of Bell Cottage, Little Walden. Before the war he had been a milkman employed by Lord Inchcape of Lower Walden with a round in town. The onset of war saw him enlist initially in the Leicestershire Regiment (No. 5967), before transferring to the Sherwood Foresters, into the battalion known as " The Welbeck Rangers ".

In March 1916 the battalion embarked for France as part of the 117th. Brigade, 39th. Division, but they were not involved in the Somme battle until September when they attacked Beaumont-Hamel at 5.10 a.m. on the 3rd. capturing the German front-line.

Casualties were very heavy - 454. October saw the remnants of the battalion in the front-line in the Thiepval sector where an enemy attack by German flamethrowers was repulsed.

From there to Martinsart Wood where they encountered a plague of rats which became more and more numerous before moving onto the North and South Bluffs. Here William, in bitterly cold weather, was engaged in carrying parties to the front-line whilst ' A ' Company attacked south of the River Ancre gaining some ground near the Pope's Nose. At some stage in this conflict William was reported wounded and missing.

It was not until mid-November that his mother officially heard from the regimental headquarters at Lichfield that her son was dead. At almost the same time she was informed that another of her sons, George had been wounded in the face and was recovering in St.George's Hospital, London. He was to get over this wound, only to die a year later near Arras.

On the bare and abrupt hills above the Ancre where William fell, his name is inscribed on one of the piers containing the names of 1459 other 'merry men' of the regiment from the heart of England.

By now the Great War was over two years old. Many of the original British Expeditionary Force were dead, but there were still men left who had enlisted at the beginning or who were pre-war reservists mobilised at the outbreak who rode their luck. Sadly for many this luck or experience could not guarantee survival and the maxim of ' every bullet has its billet ' proved true yet again two days after William Reed's death.

LANCE-CORPORAL ERNEST GEORGE **BACON** (8182) 2ND. ESSEX REGIMENT, KILLED IN ACTION 23RD. OCTOBER 1916, AGED 29. COMMEMORATED ON THIEPVAL MEMORIAL TO THE MISSING, FRANCE, PANEL 10D.

George was the son of Mr. J Bacon of 39 Victoria Avenue. He was married and had three children living at Museum Street. By trade he was a gardener for Miss Gibson at Hill House; he was also a reservist of which at the commencement of the war there were some 145,000. He was immediately mobilised at Chatham, and then to Cromer, Norwich and Harrow for training, before landing in France at Le Havre on August 24th.

Ernest wrote regularly, eager to keep his home contacts fresh in his mind - in March 1915 a friend, Mr. C R Downham received a letter which described the conditions as rough, but exhorting him to keep " *the old game up, "* at The Gate Quoits Club in Thaxted Road. Sadly eighteen months later it was a letter from another friend, Pte. J Auger that brought news of Ernest's death to his wife and family. He had been next to Ernest when he had been hit in the head by a bullet which killed him outright.

On the day of Ernest's death, a Monday, it had rained and was dull and misty. His battalion were to attack enemy patrols to the east of Lesboeufs and Guedecourt. At 2.30 p.m. this attack began, but was immediately met by heavy machine-gun fire. The first four waves of attackers were stopped by the German front-line and only a few managed to cross it. There were 255 casualties, including Ernest Bacon. His body was never found.

No-one could accuse the Bacon family of not ' doing their bit ' for the war effort - apart from Ernest's ' supreme sacrifice ', there were three other brothers serving in France, with a further two in England, including James who had been wounded and invalided out.

November came and despite the huge losses, the lack of real progress made and the deterioration in the weather, still the battle of the Somme rumbled on. Officially, it had only eighteen more days to run, but for Saffron Walden like every city, town, village and hamlet in the country and Empire there was no diminution in the sacrifice. Those eighteen days would claim two more victims and the year of 1916 four more in total.

PRIVATE JESSE **MALLYON** (17109) 8TH. SUFFOLK REGIMENT, KILLED IN ACTION NOVEMBER 1ST. 1916, AGED 23. COMMEMORATED ON THIEPVAL MEMORIAL TO THE MISSING, FRANCE, PIERS 1C AND 2A

Jesse Mallyon was born at Hadstock, one of three sons of William. He grew up and attended school in Ashdon and was a member of the Ashdon Baptist Church. He was a farm labourer at the outbreak of war and had moved to Mitchell Cottages, Little Walden. He joined for General Service in early 1915 in the 18th. Hussars, before going to France around July of that year with the Suffolk Regiment.

The 8th. Battalion had been involved in the Somme battle since its opening day (although they had avoided the slaughter of the first day by being in Brigade reserve), but since then had suffered large casualties at Delville Wood, before being sent to the Armentieres section for six weeks in late July.

On 14th. October the battalion arrived at Albert, going into trenches near Courcelette, before being relieved by the Norfolk on the 21st. The waning days of the battle were spent in and out of Fabeck and Regina trenches, alternating with periods of rest at Albert. Waning the battle may have been but the weather was atrocious - it rained most of October and November, the trenches were appalling with Regina trench knee-deep in clinging mud. Waning the battle may have been but the casualty rates never faltered. On November 1st. Jesse was wounded in a front-line trench. Whilst his wound was being dressed a piece of shell hit him and he died immediately. In the mud his body disappeared like so many.

In addition to being remembered in Saffron Walden, Jesse is commemorated on the memorial of the lovely little Saxon church of Hadstock, his birthplace.

The last battle of the Somme in 1916 is known as the battle of the Ancre, a small, pretty river nestling in attractive wooded country. Here the death-throes of the battle were performed and the name was engraved on many a soldier's memory - *"... yet its stream ran through my heart....as if its rainy tortured blood had swirled into my own."* Here died another young and promising son of the town who although only nineteen was a seasoned soldier, the last casualty of the fabled 'Big Push.'

Perhaps soldier is the wrong term, because he belonged to one of the more anomalous military formations of the Great War - the Royal Naval Division (R.N.D). This was largely Winston Churchill's idea, it was formed of seamen for whom no sea jobs were available. The battalions were named after great commanders - Hawke, Howe,

Nelson, Collingwood, Benbow and so on and they were allowed to remain as naval as possible even if their role became that of the poor bloody infantry.

Thus the R.N.D. had petty-officers instead of sergeants and leading-seamen instead of corporals, and to the ordinary soldier's amazement, they were allowed to grow beards!

ABLE-SEAMAN WILLIAM NORRIS **GUY** (LZ/264) ROYAL NAVAL VOLUNTEER RESERVE, 188TH. BRIGADE, MACHINE-GUN COMPANY, ROYAL NAVAL DIVISION, KILLED IN ACTION 13TH. NOVEMBER 1916, AGED 19. COMMEMORATED ON THIEPVAL MEMORIAL TO THE MISSING, FRANCE, PANEL 1A.

Into the Royal Naval Division, in the early stages of the war, enlisted William Guy who lived with his parents, William, a newsagent and stationer and Sadie Louise, at 6 Cross Street. An only son his background had typically been the Boys' British School followed, perhaps more unusually by the Grammar School where he excelled at sport.

On leaving school he worked in London for the Daily Express until in the first month of the war, eager for excitement he joined up in the London Division. With the R.N.D he sailed for the Dardanelles and Gallipoli, one of the first to go. In that ill-fated campaign, William became an experienced soldier, but his letters home also betray his journalistic experience. At the Suvla Bay landings of May 1915 he was wounded and writes of being, " ...*pipped through the ankle by a Turkish bullet!* "

In addition to this wound he contracted malaria and enteric fever which necessitated evacuation to Egypt and nearly six months in a Cairo hospital. His letters home comment, " *I received my wound last Thursday week almost as soon as an advance was made to take the hill we have been trying to get for a fortnight. The Turks are very dirty fighters adopting all sorts of underhand tricks. We found one of their snipers painted green and concealed in the foliage of a tree. Don't ask what happened to the gent! Most of their officers are German and it is pretty apparent they have to use a little persuasion with the men. In the hands of one German officer we found a short stock with nine leather thongs, nicely knotted!* "

In November 1915, William came home, returning to France in July 1916 at the commencement of the Big Push. He had been recommended for a commission by Lt. Ivan Heald (a well-known Irish writer of the time destined to die himself with the Hood Battalion a month later) and was about to come home and take it. But Fate intervened and William Guy was never to fulfil his potential.

As part of the Hood Battalion 63rd. Royal Naval Division he was involved in the attack on Beaucourt a very strong defensive position in November 1916. Eight naval battalions and four army battalions were ordered to attack the village some mile and a half away. The trenches were indescribably dirty with no deep dug-outs, no traverses and in some places barely knee-deep. The day of the attack dawned foggy and William's battalion was on the right of the advance passing through the enemy's lines at 5 a.m. following the creeping barrage, clearing dug-outs in the railway cutting. Unfortunately, the enemy machine-guns were untouched by the bombardment and at the second line of German trenches William was wounded in the neck and the hand whilst on the parapet.

He was last seen by a comrade making for the English lines holding his neck and with a bandaged hand. For three days his friends searched for him, but all that was found was his pay book, letters and postcards addressed to his parents. He was nineteen years of age and no trace of his body was ever found. The R.N.D suffered 3,500 casualties in the attack on Beaucourt, the heaviest divisional loss of the November attack and the writer, A.P. Herbert who fought there and in Gallipoli, writes in his poem " Beaucourt Revisited " an appropriate epitaph for Able-Seaman William Guy who died a soldier's death

> *" And I said ' There is still the river, and still the stiff, stark trees*
> *to treasure here our story, but there are only these '*
> *But under the white wood crosses the dead men answered low,*
> *' The new men know not Beaucourt, but we are here - we know.' "*

On the same day and not more than eight miles away another young man was killed and never seen again. Like William Guy his name is to be found high above the battlefield of the Somme with 945 other men of the Essex Regiment.

PRIVATE WILLIAM FRANK **START** (43035) 13TH. ESSEX REGIMENT, KILLED IN ACTION 13TH. NOVEMBER 1916, AGED 22. COMMEMORATED ON THE THIEPVAL MEMORIAL TO THE MISSING, FRANCE, PANEL 10D.

William was the third son of Frederick and Elizabeth Start of 97 Castle Street. Before the war he worked for Robson and Company, the mineral water manufacturers in Station Street, as a carman. One of the first to enlist in 1914, William trained in England at Clipstone Camp and Perham Down, Salisbury Plain, before going to France, landing at Boulogne, just before Christmas 1915

The battalion were not involved in the Somme conflict until late July 1916, but this was soon rectified when they saw action in Delville Wood and in the attack on Guillemont. November found them in trenches in the Redan sector, and on the 13th. they were detailed to attack the Quadrilateral, a German strong-point rectangular in shape, 750 yards east of Ginchy on the road to Morval. It was sheltered by clumps of trees, with in front trenches that ran east to west.

The battalion were on the right of the 6th. Brigade attacking from Dog Street to Board Street to capture their first objective. At 5 a.m. there was a heavy artillery strafe, followed at 5.45 a.m. by field-guns and howitzers joining in, then six minutes later at 5.45 a.m. the infantry attack was launched advancing in thick fog with visibility down to thirty yards, by the help of compass bearings. Immediately it was met by hostile machine-gun fire which caused confusion on the front and the flanks. During this confusion William was last seen alive.

It was not until just after Christmas that William's parents received the first news that he was missing and in January in a letter from a friend describing how they were attacking the German trenches and had reached their objective, when William was seen on the parapet, but then not sighted again.

A further letter the following month said *" ...we shook hands and wished each other luck...hopefully he is a prisoner-of-war. "* How long his family fostered that hope, we shall never know, but we do know it was a forlorn and hopeless one. William never returned.

The battle of the Somme ended in appropriate weather, a gale following a rain-drenched night. The last rites showed the gain after four and a half months of a strip of land approximately twenty miles wide by six miles deep at a cost of some 419,654 British and Empire forces - including twenty-eight from Saffron Walden. But although the battle was 'officially ' over, localised attacks and raids continued, as did the unrelentless casualties.

LANCE-CORPORAL T FRANK **ELSOM** (19295) 1ST. ESSEX REGIMENT, DIED OF WOUNDS 21ST. NOVEMBER 1916, AGED 30. BURIED IN GROVE TOWN CEMETERY, MEAULTE, FRANCE, PLOT 2 ROW K GRAVE 22.

Frank was the third son of the late Mr. Jonah Elsom and Mrs. Parish of 1 Chapel Row, Castle Street. He was married with four children and lived at 4 Museum Court and was employed as a labourer by Mr. Samuel Tatham at his lime and whiting manufacturing works in Little Walden Road. In May 1915, Frank and his three brothers all enlisted together, Charles, Arthur and Ernest.

In December 1915, Frank was shipped to Egypt where he joined the remnants of the battalion which had been evacuated on the *" Prince Abbas "* from Gallipoli on January 8th. 1916. It was not until March that the next move to France took place, the battalion arriving in Marseilles. Heavily involved on the opening day of the Somme, when they attacked Beaumont-Hamel, Frank survived this attack which sustained over 200 casualties amongst his comrades, before undergoing a spell in the Ypres sector. Frank's brother, Arthur, was not so fortunate sustaining a wound that necessitated the amputation of his right foot in this action.

On returning to the Somme later in October the battalion took part in the storming of Guedecourt and Hilt Trench with the Newfoundland Regiment. Finally, however, Frank's good fortune ran out. On Monday November 20th. in trenches in Bernafay Wood, he was wounded in the chest and both legs and died the following day at a Casualty Clearing Station which a newly-constructed railway line had brought closer to the fighting area. He is buried, one of 1392 graves. On one headstone nearby is an inscription that Frank's wife and children would surely have echoed, *" If this is Victory, then let God stop all wars. "*

All Frank's brothers returned, including later enlistments, Sam and Walter, but not unscathed - Arthur was crippled for life and Ernest wounded in 1916. These dreadful effects would remain even with the survivors throughout their lives.

Also in Grove Town Cemetery lies the poet and journalist, Leslie Coulson who wrote,
> *" Where war has left its wake of whitened bone,*
> *soft stems of summer grass shall wave again,*
> *and all the blood that war has ever strewn*
> *is but a passing stain."*

As today you walk around the immaculate cemeteries of the Somme this is not difficult to believe, but in the depths of the winter of 1916...?

" The long and sombre procession of cruelty and suffering " claimed one more local victim before the year ended - not from bullet, gas or bomb, but from the atrocious

weather that had curtailed the battle.

PRIVATE WILLIAM DUDLEY **SWAN** (40108) 2ND. ESSEX REGIMENT, DIED 14TH. DECEMBER 1916, AGED 35. BURIED IN PERONNE ROAD CEMETERY, MARICOURT, FRANCE, PLOT 3 ROW D GRAVE 27.

William was the eldest of six children of the late Grey and Sarah Ann Swan of 37 East Street. After leaving school he was employed as a baker for David Miller of London who he had worked for for sixteen years. However, under Lord Derby's Scheme, William joined up in March 1916, going to France on September 7th. 1916. He joined his battalion in the area of Amiens.

In a more enlightened age, poor William would probably not have been expected to be a front-line soldier. He was not a strong man and almost immediately spent six weeks in hospital the result of a poisoned hand and a bad heel. In early December he was discharged and returned to his battalion in the area of Maricourt-Suzanne . The weather was dreadful, the history describes it as, *" Villainous weather, unceasing rain and little shelter. The conditions of the last tour were worse than any previously experienced by the battalion."* Seventy-six men were evacuated to hospital amongst them William Swan and he died from exposure on December 14th.

" To-night, this frost will fasten on this mud and us, shrivelling many hands, puckering foreheads crisp. The burying party, picks and shovels in shaking grasp, pause over half-known faces."

He was buried in a cemetery set up by a Field Ambulance unit where he died, one of 1324 graves. William's mother was to lose another son in 1918 and to receive a third safely home. William is remembered also on Wimbish church memorial and possibly on the memorial in Radwinter churchyard.

January 1917 brought with it little prospect of a swift cessation of the war. On the Western Front there was no new offensive, just the continual round of mud, sniping and shelling. The possibility that America would enter the war increased, but it did little to alleviate the conditions of trench warfare.

" Hell is not fire, that would not be the ultimate in suffering. Hell is mud ! "

GUNNER DAVID JOHN **BARRETT** (122331) ' B ' BATTERY, 78TH. BRIGADE, ROYAL FIELD ARTILLERY, KILLED IN ACTION 22ND. JANUARY 1917. BURIED IN THE GUARDS' CEMETERY, LESBOEUFS, FRANCE, PLOT 8 ROW R GRAVE 2.

David was born in Cambridge and was the son of Arthur Barrett who ran the " Axe and Compasses " in Ashdon Rd. He enlisted in Cambridge and was killed in the area of the Somme. He is buried in the Guards Cemetery in the area captured by the Guards on September 15th. 1916. It is a beautiful cemetery above a sunken road, overlooking Flers and Gueudecourt. No other details of David's life and death are known.

The tide of war moved from the Somme and left it in a period of relative quiet. Relative is an important word - there was still a policy of aggressiveness despite a bleak winter and makeshift trenches - lines had to be rationalised in local attacks, raids planned, anything to constantly harass the enemy and allow him no peace. It was in this atmosphere in February that the next Saffron Walden man died - tragically the second son of this family not to return.

PRIVATE HENRY SIDNEY JAMES **PORTER** (32240) 2ND. ESSEX REGIMENT, KILLED IN ACTION FEBRUARY 8TH. 1917, AGED 37. BURIED IN FINS NEW BRITISH CEMETERY, SOREL-LE-GRAND, FRANCE, PLOT 7 ROW F GRAVE 29.

Henry (always known as Harry) was the son of Mr. and Mrs. George Porter of Debden Road. He was a builder for William Bell and Sons of South Road. He joined the Essex Regiment on October 20th. 1916 and was sent to France at the end of December in the same year.

In early February the battalion were to be found around Bouchavesnes. On February 8th. three companies with one in support were to advance towards the enemy lines, Harry was one of a working-party in support, when he was hit by a shell and killed instantly. It is likely that he was hastily buried where he fell. After the war his body was recovered and reburied in the pleasant, open Fins New British Cemetery, one of 591 recovered in such a way.

The Porter family learnt of Harry's death in early March. Their grief and fears are difficult to imagine - two sons dead and three more still serving, Joseph in the Northumberland Fusiliers, Bertram in the Royal Fusiliers and Ralph in the Royal Naval Air Service. The Fates had not finished with them sadly -of the three remaining sons, two were to come home, but only one was to survive - it is difficult to imagine the ' *scars upon the hearts* ' of their parents.

The river valley of the Ancre was still the focus for an advance by 2 Corps under General Jacob on the southern bank. Over a period of a week, until bad weather intervened various localised attacks successfully drove the Germans back, but still the losses of men echoed the earlier full-scale battles of the area.

PRIVATE WILLIAM **ELLWOOD** (28367) 8TH. EAST SURREY REGIMENT, KILLED IN ACTION 14TH. FEBRUARY 1917. COMMEMORATED ON THIEPVAL MEMORIAL TO THE MISSING, FRANCE, PIERS 6B AND 6C

William was born in Little Walden, the son of Mr. L W Ellwood. Very little is known of his background, although it is probable that he had a brother Charles also destined to also die for his country in the late stages of the war. When he enlisted William lived in Waltham Cross and he joined the Middlesex Regiment at Mill Hill. Later he was transferred to the East Surrey Regiment.

This battalion of the East Surreys had achieved immortal fame on the opening day of the Somme, when under the leadership of Capt. W P (Billie) Nevill, they had dribbled footballs across no-man's land in the heroic, but mistaken belief that the enemy before them had been wiped out. Whether William was with them on that day we do not know, but he could also have seen action with them at the Schwaben Redoubt at the end of September 1916 and the raid on Desire Trench on November 18th. At the end of the year the battalion were in trenches near Ovillers.

In 1917 the East Surreys were part of the 18th. Division in the valley of the Ancre. On February 6th. they were to be found moving on Beaucourt and the following day the village was evacuated. Over the next few days the advance crept towards Baillescourt Farm, before the enemy counter-attacked on the 12th. Bad weather stopped the advance and during this time William was killed. In the depths of this bleak winter his body disappeared into the fertile soil of the Ancre valley.

In late February the Germans retreated to the Hindenburg Line fifteen miles to the east in order to shorten by twenty-five miles the length of line to be defended. In the area between the Germans systematically devastated everything so the Allies would find nothing. The troops were shocked by the devastation.

Our concentration on the Somme over the last few months did not mean that all was quiet on the rest of the Western Front. In the Salient around Ypres a war of constant attrition was still being waged since the Second Battle of Ypres and leading up to the battle of Messines in June.

PRIVATE WILLIAM **ADAMS** (G/15970) 10TH. ROYAL WEST KENT REGIMENT, KILLED IN ACTION 23RD. FEBRUARY 1917, AGED 32. BURIED IN DICKEBUSCH NEW MILITARY CEMETERY, DIKKEBUS, BELGIUM, ROW G GRAVE 13.

William was the eldest son of the late James and Hannah Adams of 3 Thaxted Road. He attended the Boys British School before becoming a bricklayer with J Custerson of Station Street. In June 1916 he left his wife and two children at Mill Lane, Ashdon Road and enlisted. After a few months training he joined his battalion on the Somme in the area of the Pommiers Redoubt. In late October they were moved via Oisemont and Pont-Remy to the notorious Ypres sector.

On Friday, February 23rd..., a friend, Pte. Arthur Malton, who had been at school with William, bumped into him quite by chance, in the trenches. They reminisced of home for a while and Arthur continued with his duties. Going back the following day he found William was gone - he had been killed.

Some two weeks later, in a letter, Mrs. Adams received the news that her children were fatherless and she another Saffron Walden widow. To be nearer her family she moved to Finchingfield.

William is buried well behind the front-lines near the churchyard of Dickebusch. His is one of 623 graves. In his home town in addition to his name on the various memorials is a landmark that is testimony to his and many others local skill - the Water Tower, which he helped build.

The following day back on the Somme another soldier died who had much in common with William Adams. He had attended the same school, although he was six years younger, he had a wife and two children and his grave survived the war.

PRIVATE ARTHUR HORACE **BARKER** (27840) 1ST. ESSEX REGIMENT, KILLED IN ACTION FEBRUARY 24TH. 1917, AGED 26. BURIED IN SAILLY-SAILLISEL BRITISH CEMETERY, FRANCE, PLOT 5 ROW G.

Arthur was born in Buntingford, the son of William Barker who lived in Audley End Village. On leaving the Boys British School he lived for a while at 12 Debden Road, before his marriage to Maud when he moved to Audley End Village where he was employed on the estate.

In early 1917, from February 21st. the battalion were to be found in the Sailly-Saillisel sector, the firing-line being a series of isolated posts, with the Brigade headquarters to be found in the underground catacombs at Combles. This village which had been ' shaved to the ground ' had been captured by the French in 1916, and taken over by the British.

On Saturday February 24th. in these front-line trenches, Arthur was shot by a sniper, the bullet hitting him in the middle of the back and coming out of the neck. Death was instantaneous. It was reported that Arthur was buried near where he fell, the same evening, beneath a wooden cross. Six weeks later his wife and children were informed of his death.

The cemetery was made up after the Armistice of graves recovered from small grave-yards and isolated graves, one of which contained Arthur's remains. It is on a ridge overlooking the battlefield where Arthur fell.

Death in the form of bullet, shell or gas was a constant danger, but the cumulative weight of cold and wet, lice and rats and a poor diet meant illness was also very prevalent. However, to be allowed to enter hospital one had to be a severe case, the ' number nine pill ' (medicine and work) being deemed ineffective. Sadly, many men who were not strong and should not have been exposed to the front-line conditions, or indeed sent home as unfit, were overlooked or ignored.

PRIVATE LEONARD **MOULE** (10591) 9TH. ESSEX REGIMENT, DIED 27TH. FEBRUARY 1917, AGED 28 OR 30. BURIED IN ST. HILAIRE CEMETERY, FREVENT, FRANCE, PLOT 2 ROW C GRAVE 1 .

Leonard was born in Wimbish, the son of the late Thomas Moule of Farmadine Grove. He attended the Boys British School leaving to work for Thomas Myhill and Sons, merchants of Gold Street, as a carman. He was married with a wife, Eve and two children living at 9 Pleasant Valley when war was declared. He was one of the first to enlist at Chelmsford and was placed initially into the 3rd. Battalion of the Essex Regiment at Harwich.

After a period of training at Blenheim Barracks on 15th. June 1915, he journeyed to France, landing at Boulogne with the 9th. Essex Regiment. At Christmas 1916 he returned home on leave and informed his family that during his time in France his health had become so impaired, that he had been taken out of the trenches and placed on regimental transport work.

In early March 1917 a letter was received at Pleasant Valley from the matron of a Stationary Hospital at Frevent, a town of some importance on the Line of Communication, informing Mrs. Moule that her husband had died. He had been taken seriously ill and after two or three days had died in hospital of diabetes.

Leonard's white headstone contains the inscription, " *Rest in Jesus. Blessed is he who dies in the Lord for he shall rest from his labours.* " Today 514 others rest with him in St.Hilaire Cemetery.

The German retreat to the Hindenburg Line, a fortified defence system running from just south of Arras to a point about two miles in front of St.Quentin, and on south-east to the River Aisne, near Soissons, was still in progress at this time and although a strategic withdrawal a fierce rear guard action by the enemy did not give up ground lightly. The Allies advanced after the retreating enemy, but casualties were heavy.

PRIVATE ERNEST HUBERT CHARLES **DOWNHAM** (33936) 10TH. ESSEX REGIMENT, DIED OF WOUNDS 21ST. MARCH 1917, AGED 34. BURIED IN ST. SEVER CEMETERY

EXTENSION, ROUEN, FRANCE, BLOCK O PLOT 8 ROW O GRAVE 6.

Charles, as he seemed to prefer to be known, was the son of Joseph and Eliza Downham. Another pupil at the Boys British School, he worked until he joined up, at Horneybrook Nurseries.

In February 1917 the conditions at the front were harsh - a layer of snow hid the frozen ground, it also " *covered up many horrible sights.* " During this time Charles' battalion were involved in two engagements, an attack on positions south of Miraumont and in early March 1917, the capture of the village of Irles. Between 2 a.m. and 4.30 a.m. the battalion formed up, clad in white mantles as it had snowed. Fortunately, by zero hour, 5.15 a.m. the snow had melted and the mantles were discarded. Considerable resistance was met, but eventually the last ' strong village ' outpost of the Loupart line was wrested from the enemy.

During one of these actions Ernest was wounded. His wife, employed at Saffron Walden Union Hospital, at the end of March received a letter from the Chaplain at one of the eight General Hospitals at Rouen to say her husband had died from wounds received without regaining consciousness on the previous Wednesday.

By September 1916, the cemetery in St. Sever was full, so in order to take the huge numbers of dead from eight General Hospitals, five Stationary Hospitals and one British Red Cross Hospital, an extension was built. Here Charles was laid to rest. Today this extension alone contains 6598 graves.

The Great War for all its participants proved a greater mental test than any previous war and the term ' shell-shock ' came into use. The huge stresses of death on a vast scale, reinforced by mud, lice, the constant uncertainty were cumulative. Bravery was no antidote, men with good war-records like Sassoon and Wilfred Owen suffered, so the blanket ' tag ' of cowardice was totally erroneous. It became yet another harsh and unpleasant fact of trench life.

PRIVATE WILLIAM **START** (3/2684) 11TH. ESSEX REGIMENT, KILLED IN ACTION 24TH. MARCH 1917, AGED 36 . BURIED IN PHILOSOPHE BRITISH CEMETERY, MAZINGARBE, FRANCE, PLOT 1 ROW N GRAVE 17.

William was the father of three and the husband of Elizabeth of 2 Camps Yard, Castle Street. He worked as a horse-keeper for Mr. William Caton, a cow-keeper and farmer of Lofts Lane. On the commencement of hostilities William had joined up, going for training first to Shoreham, then Brighton, back to Shoreham and then to Blackdown in June 1915.

Next step was to France and William arrived on October 1st. 1915 through Boulogne. In December 1915 he became a member of the regimental police. However, at Easter 1916 he was admitted to hospital wounded and with shell-shock. Neither seems to have been diagnosed as severe, because he was not invalided home and was soon back with his battalion.

In December in the area around Bethune, William was slightly wounded, but it did not prevent him from coming home on ten days leave around Christmas. It was the last time his family were to see their father alive. On January 13th. 1917 he rejoined his battalion in the trenches near Mazingarbe.

On a day in early April a letter from the regimental Chaplain arrived at Camps Yard. It informed Mrs. Start that her husband had been killed in action whilst attacking the enemy's positions. A piece of shell had hit him killing him instantly.

Today the British Cemetery at Philosophe is surrounded by rather grim housing estates and the occasional slag-heap. It was an industrial area then as it has become again, but these less than salubrious surroundings cannot detract from the bravery, fortitude and determination of the 2000 soldiers who lie here, not least William Start.

Our attention now shifts to just inside the border of Palestine, where the British attacked the Turkish positions at Gaza. The British outnumbered the Turkish defenders by two to one, but the city held out. One of the reasons for the Turkish fortitude was the assistance they had received from German reconnaissance planes.

PRIVATE ERNEST **DOWNHAM** (276492) 6TH. ESSEX REGIMENT, KILLED IN ACTION 26TH. MARCH 1917, AGED 31. COMMEMORATED ON THE JERUSALEM MEMORIAL TO THE MISSING, PALESTINE, PANELS 33 TO 39.

Ernest was the son of Mr. Charles and Mrs. Mary Downham of 40 Victoria Avenue. He attended the Boys British School before joining the Prudential Insurance Company as an agent in Bishops Stortford where he lived in New Town Road. Single, in March 1916 he enlisted at Bedford into the Bedfordshire Regiment (Number 6361). He was then transferred to the Essex Regiment (7379) before ending up in ' C ' Company of the 6th. Battalion.

This battalion had seen service in Gallipoli, before going to Alexandria, Egypt in December 1915. Once the Sinai peninsula had been cleared of all Turkish forces a limited offensive was launched into Palestine at Gaza and Beersheba. The first attempt at Gaza commenced on March 26th. when Ernest's battalion were to attack due north between Ali el Muntar and a bare sand hill called the Rabbit Warren. The attack commenced on Monday at 4.30 p.m., but the Turks had cleverly sited their machine-guns and their defences were skilfully designed. The *" bullets seemed like rain."*

During this attack Ernest fell. News came in late April that he was wounded. Then in July that he was missing and wounded and finally to his sister, Mrs. A Green of 1 Prospect Place in August that he was officially missing, and a British Red Cross Enquiry dated 1st. August also reported him, ' wounded and missing.' Tragically these reports should have read missing and dead.

Today the name of Ernest Downham, a modern Crusader, is on the Jerusalem Memorial to the Missing, and he is remembered on the 6th. Essex Regimental window and plaque in West Ham parish church.

In France on April 9th. began the new offensive, a battle that on a daily casualty rate was more lethal and costly than the infamous Somme or Passchendaele. It lasted thirty nine days and has been described as *" the most savage infantry battle of the war. "* On this Easter Monday British and Canadian forces launched simultaneous offensives at Arras and at Vimy Ridge using the new tactic of 'creeping' barrages. On this first day two young men from Saffron Walden met their deaths and the battle as a whole claimed a total of eleven local men.

CORPORAL ALFRED WILLIAM **COX** (9782) 9TH. ESSEX REGIMENT, KILLED IN ACTION APRIL

9TH. 1917. COMMEMORATED ON THE ARRAS MEMORIAL TO THE MISSING, FRANCE, BAY 7.

Alfred was the eldest son of Mr. and Mrs. William Cox of 4 Debden Road. He was born in Littlebury and attended the Boys British School and the Baptist church. He was a well-known local runner and footballer who spent six years in the Army in East Africa before working locally for Robson and Company. On mobilisation he was posted to the 1st. battalion and went with them to Gallipoli landing at ' W ' Beach on April 24th. 1915.

Alfred's service on the Peninsula was not without incident. During an advance against Turkish positions in the Twelve Tree Copse sector he was wounded and took shelter in a dug-out . The enemy counter-attacked and the battalion were forced to retire in ' stiff and confused fighting.' On June 12th. he was reported missing - a week before his parents had received a letter in which he said he was, *"..still A1...but was having a rough time. Keep heart. "* A month later the ground was retaken and Alfred was found alive in the same dug-out where he had survived on his hard rations. He then rejoined his regiment.

On January 7th. 1916 a much-depleted battalion left Gallipoli for Mudros on the *"Prince Abbas "* and then Egypt. In March 1916 the battalion sailed for France and at some stage Albert was transferred to the 9th. Battalion with whom he was wounded during the early stages of the Battle of the Somme. Recovering from this Alfred was wounded again slightly in March 1917, but was fit enough to participate in the Spring offensive.

On the opening day of the attack, the battalion were initially held in reserve in the network of cellars under the city of Arras. At 12.15 p.m. they passed through the 36th. and 37th. Brigades gaining the Feuchy Chapel Redoubt. However, enemy action hindered most of the attack and the battalion progress was stopped by Church Work and uncut wire raked by German machine-guns. In this attack Alfred fell and his body never recovered. For his parents in Debden Road this second letter informing them that Alfred was missing, believed killed had no happy sequel.

On the same day the poet Edward Thomas died. One poem contains these lines that could have been written for Alfred Cox,

" And where now at last he sleeps more sound in France - that, too, he secret keeps. "

The huge Arras Memorial near the Citadel contains the names of 35,698 dead including 766 from the Essex Regiment and 638 from the Suffolks. A Suffolk officer from Saffron Walden died that day too, but his body was found and buried not far away. He was the second son to die in just nine months, another life of promise and expectation snuffed out.

SECOND-LIEUTENANT OWEN BENNETT GOOLD **JOHNSON**, 11TH. SUFFOLK REGIMENT, KILLED IN ACTION APRIL 9TH. 1917, AGED 28. BURIED IN ROCLINCOURT VALLEY CEMETERY, FRANCE, PLOT 4 ROW A GRAVE 5

Owen Johnson was one of three sons of the Reverend R Alexander Johnson, who but for the war would have followed his father (and his eldest brother, the Reverend Lewis G Johnson with the YMCA in France) and been ordained into the ministry. A graduate of Sidney Sussex College, Cambridge, obtaining his degree in 1915, he was a very keen musician, a member of the choir at the parish church and an occasional organist both in church and his college chapel.

In October 1914, Owen joined the university Officer Training Corps as a private, applying for a temporary commission on June 18th. 1915, preferrably in the Norfolk, Suffolk or 15th. Manchester Regiments. Owen was gazetted to the 11th. Suffolk Regiment and left England on July 13th. 1916 from Folkestone to Boulogne to join his battalion in the field on July 24th. 1916 at Henencourt Wood where the survivors were recovering from the disastrous attack on July 1st. in the area of Becourt Wood and the Lochnagar Crater; serving with them until November 18th. when he was posted to the 2nd. Army school for a period of training until December 17th. He then came home for twelve days' leave until January 8th. 1917. Sadly, this was the last time he would see his family.

On April 8th.1917, Easter Monday, during what is known as the First Battle of the Scarpe, the Suffolks were moved to assembly positions, half a mile south-east of the village of Roclincourt. The next morning at 4.30 a.m. the artillery let off an opening salvo and 600 men and twenty officers advanced to attack the first German system of trenches. This advance was checked by hostile machine-gun fire, but the first goal was reached, ' A ' company reporting that the Black Line had been captured without loss. After 8 a.m. the battalion headquarters was able to move to the German second line. When this Blue Line was occupied, the position was able to be consolidated and reorganised. In heavy snow, despite the battalion's success, 150 other ranks and two officers were killed - one being Owen Goold Johnson.

A week later the news reached his parents in Saffron Walden. This was the third tragedy of the war to test their faith. In addition, to the death of their youngest son, their daughter had died in Calcutta in July 1915.

A further painful reminder of their loss came in a letter in May 1920. Owen had originally been buried in Kite Crater, Fampoux, but

"...in accordance with the agreement with the French and Belgian governments to remove all scattered graves and small cemeteries containing less than forty graves, also certain other cemeteries which were situated in places unsuitable for permanent retention, it has been found necessary to exhume the bodies in certain areas....you may rest assured that the work of re-burial has been carried out carefully and reverently, special arrangements having been made for the appropriate religious service to be held."

Owen thus today lies in an isolated cemetery amidst the farmed fields of northern France with 543 other allied soldiers. In the parish church, where he sung and played to his God, on the chancel arch is a brass plate simply stating, *" We thank our God upon every remembrance of him."*

Most of the soldiers killed in the Great War died as infantry, but two days after Owen Johnson was struck down and in the same vicinity of Arras, there took place the most romantic and inspirational of all military manoeuvres, the cavalry charge. Romantic it may have been, but it showed the naiveity of those who believed that man and horse was a fair match for machine-gun and shellfire.

Private George Joshua **BASSETT** (80444) ' B ' Squadron, the Essex Yeomanry, killed in action on April 11th. 1917, aged 25. Commemorated on the Arras Memorial to the Missing, France, Bay 1.

George Bassett was born in Wimbish and was employed as a grocer's carman. On October 28th. 1914, he enlisted and in May 1915 was shown to be serving with the Territorial Force. On June 8th.1915 he was sent to France where the Yeomanry were holding part of captured German lines south east of Loos.

1916 was a quiet year for the Essex Yeomen, spending some time in the Hohenzollern Redoubt and later digging graves and collecting battlefield detritus on the Somme. However, on Wednesday April 9th. 1917, the major objective was to capture the German strongpoint of the village of Monchy-le-Preux. Although considerable progress was initially made it was not until 8.30 a.m. on April 11th. in appalling weather, that the Essex Yeomanry (with the 10th.Hussars and the Royal Horse Guards) took off to capture a position north east of the village. An eye-witness described the scene, *" The most wonderful sight was the charge of the cavalry....they passed me on the trot and just as they got level broke into the charge. They thundered past me ...with their swords and lances all in line, while every gun in Germany fired at them....Gaps appeared in the lines and I saw riderless horses, for a while they went and then crashed into the village, which they took and held. "*

Casualties were great among the horses, from a machine-gun barrage from the north and an artillery box-barrage which decimated the concentration of dismounted horses (indeed after this action 600 replacement mounts were asked for).

Once in the village the Essex Yeomanry had to relieve the 37th. Division and dug in on the eastern outskirts. Here they were exposed to enemy bombardment and and shellfire for eighteen hours, before being relieved. Some 500 men were hit, but only eighteen other ranks were killed in this engagement, among them George Bassett. His body was never found, but an appropriate epitaph comes from the enemy who witnessed it. The German view of the cavalry charge was that it was *" ...great and heroic, and they were proud of an opponent who dared to carry it out. "*

At the request of three of Haig's generals the Arras offensive was called off four days later. But to relieve the growing German pressure on the French, Haig reluctantly agreed to a new offensive east of Arras - the Second Battle of the Scarpe - which was to commence on St.George's Day, April 23rd. 1917. On that first day two more men from Saffron Walden were to fall.

Private Charles Henry **ARCHER** (19643) 1st. Essex Regiment, killed in action April 23rd.1917, aged 23. Buried at Feuchy Chapel British Cemetery, Wancourt, France, Plot 1 Row C Grave 24.

Charles Archer was the son of Mr. and Mrs. John Archer of Sewards End. At the outbreak of war he was employed as a horsekeeper and lived in Pleasant Valley. He enlisted in June 1915 at Warley, and went to France where he was involved in the attack on Beaumont-Hamel on July 1st. 1916 and Delville Wood in early October. During this time his brother, Walter, who had enlisted with him on the same day, died from his wounds on another part of the Somme battlefield. However, on November 25th. in the vicinity of Trones Wood it was Charles' misfortune to be wounded.

On recovery, Charles returned to his battalion which was heavily involved in the fighting at Monchy-le-Preux. On April 19th. the survivors took over the support line in trenches at Orange Hill near Feuchy Chapel, with the Royal Newfoundland Regiment - affectionately known as the 'Newfoundessex.' While here they supplied parties for the usual post battle fatigues such as burying the dead and salvaging equipment as well as bringing supplies forward. Enemy artillery was very active all the time, and on Monday, April 23rd. the Brigade was involved in heavy fighting north of the Cambrai road at Machine Gun Wood and String Trench. At the end of the day the battalion was relieved, but Charles Archer was not with them.

Charles is buried near the Cambrai road in the vicinity where he fell. The cemetery contains over 1000 men who mainly fell in the Battles of the Scarpe. A third brother, Albert, was to die before 1917 ended.

The other soldier to be killed on this day was also one of three brothers, fortunately two of them survived. Not for his family the small consolation of a known grave, but a commemoration on a memorial and an agonising wait for confirmation of a loved one's death - it was some five months later that the news was relayed to his wife and family.

PRIVATE FRANK **COE** (G/37054) 1ST. ROYAL WEST SURREY REGIMENT (THE QUEENS), KILLED IN ACTION APRIL 23RD. 1917, AGED 29. COMMEMORATED ON THE ARRAS MEMORIAL TO THE MISSING, FRANCE, BAY 2.

Frank Coe was one of three sons born to Mr. and Mrs. A J Coe of 46 Debden Road. After leaving school he was an under-gardener at Miss Gibson's Hill House, before going into business with his brother, Herbert in Kenley, Surrey. In 1914, Herbert joined up at Kenley and Frank soon followed, leaving his wife, Gertrude and one child.

Frank survived the battalion's involvement in the battle of the Somme where the honours are a litany of bravery - High Wood, Mametz Wood, Gommecourt to name but a few. However, 1917 saw them in the Arras sector and on April 23rd. 1917 a large-scale frontal attack on the Hindenburg Line was planned. This would be difficult to execute because the front-line was highly fortified and the second line contained concrete machine-gun emplacements of two storeys every fifty yards and barbed wire to a depth of twenty yards. It was the most complete system of dugouts and tunnels.

On April 22nd. at 11.30 p.m. Frank and his comrades assembled in quarries half a mile north-east of Croisilles. They were to advance across 800 yards of open in the dark and attack the Hindenburg Line on a front of 400 yards, south of the River Sensee, and to hold the line. An officer wrote *".. a mad scheme in my opinion! "*

At 3.30 a.m. the following morning the assembled troops moved off to their position of deployment. At 4.15 a.m. they advanced to wait for zero hour at 4.45 a.m. The attack initially went well but the battalion were held up by strong uncut wire, and the creeping artillery barrage went too far forward. Two tanks never arrived and the Germans then counter-attacked, pressurising the advancing front troops, who had run out of bombs, to retire. During this retreat the casualties were heavy, including thirteen or fourteen officers who were killed.

At home the family knew nothing. After Frank's last letter, written before the battle, no more were forthcoming, so eventually enquiries were made to Frank's Commanding Officer. In early September a letter from Frank's Regimental Sergeant Major arrived describing his death, *"...he was hit in the chest by shrapnel whilst advancing. Asked where he was hit, he replied, ' Tell my wife...' then no more."* He continued that he cannot say where Frank is buried as he had to continue the advance.

Frank's body was never recovered and is name is recorded as one of 442 from the Queens Regiment on the Arras Memorial. His wife later moved to 13 Chapel Street, Tring, Hertfordshire.

April 1917 ranks as the second worst month of the Great War for fatalities from Saffron Walden and the day after Frank Coe's death, another young man was killed and disappeared into the mud of the Arras battlefields a victim not only of a German shell or bullet, but ironically of brotherly love and family duty.

PRIVATE HARRY ARTHUR **KIDMAN** (G/17631) 2ND. ROYAL FUSILIERS, KILLED IN ACTION APRIL 24TH.1917, AGED 27. COMMEMORATED ON THE ARRAS MEMORIAL TO THE MISSING, FRANCE, BAY 3.

Harry was the son of Mr. and Mrs. Thomas Kidman of 1 Pleasant Valley. After attending the Boys' British School, he obtained employment at Bell and Sons. The coming of the Great War led to an enthusistic rush to join before the 'great adventure' was over and Harry's younger brother, Thomas, was impetuously no exception. On hearing of his enlistment, Harry dutifully also volunteered to accompany him and ' keep an eye on him.'

Harry embarked on March 16th.1915 for Gallipoli, landing at 'X' Beach, Helles on April 25th.1915. He saw action at Krithia, Suvla and Scimitar Hill, survived Turkish bullets, bombs, dysentery and flies, until evacuation on December 7th./8th. to Mudros. After a period of recovery, the battalion went to France, where Harry endured the Somme battlefields of Beaumont-Hamel and Combles.

In April 1917, Harry found himself in the Arras area, again to the east of Monchy where the 2nd. Royal Fusiliers gained ground on April 23rd. This attack was not completely successful, so it was decided that it should be resumed the following day. At 4 p.m. on April 24th. from Shrapnel Trench, the battalion advanced on a three company front to the west of the Bois du Vert. It met intense machine-gun fire for which it paid heavily in casualties, among them Harry Kidman.

In another letter home, his friend, Private Cornell, informed the family of Harry's death. Six months later, Harry's elder brother, Albert was to die, but ironically, Thomas, the reason why Harry enlisted, was to survive !

Harry's remains like so many of his comrades were never recovered, and he also is remembered with 1,421 other Royal Fusiliers on the Arras Memorial.

When you consider the life expectancy of the infantryman in the Great War it is remarkable, but saddening that so many survived the rigours of Gallipoli, the slaughter of the Somme, only for death to catch up with them on the battlefields of the Scarpe. Another such battle-hardened soldier died the day after Harry Kidman, from wounds received two days before.

CORPORAL STANLEY WILLIAM **DOWNHAM** (21436) 88TH. COMPANY, MACHINE GUN CORPS (INFANTRY), DIED OF WOUNDS APRIL 25TH.1917, AGED 25. BURIED IN DUISANS BRITISH CEMETERY, ETRUN, FRANCE, PLOT 2 ROW K GRAVE 1.

Stanley was the eldest son of Mr. and Mrs. William G Downham of 15 Mount Pleasant. He was educated at the Boys British School and on leaving joined the Great Eastern Railway as a bricklayer. When the war clouds gathered he was one of the first to enlist on September 11th. 1914 into the 1st. Essex Regiment. The first tragedy of war was soon to blight the family as Stanley's brother George was killed on October 21st.

With the 1st. Essex as No. 13126 he was sent to Gallipoli, landing at ' W ' Beach, Cape Helles on 25th.April 1915. The 1st. Essex were involved at Krithia, Suvla Bay and Scimitar Hill, before being evacuated from the same beach on the peninsula on January 7th. 1916.

After a brief sojourn in Mudros, Stanley went to Egypt where the 88th. Brigade Machine Gun Company was formed on February 21st. 1916, thus he was a ' founder member, with other ex- Essex Regiment men comprising a section of the Company.' On March 16th. 1916, the Brigade sailed for Marseilles, where it was part of the 'Incomparable' 29th. Division.

In August 1916, Stanley was reported wounded, but had recovered enough to come on home leave at Christmas, before returning to take part in the Scarpe battles. In early May news came that on April 23rd. he had been badly wounded when a shell burst near him taking off his left foot. He was taken to a Casualty Clearing Station, but only lived for a short time. In the same letter home his officer described him as, "..an excellent N.C.O."

Both brothers are remembered on the Baptist church memorial, and a third son, although wounded in Egypt, survived to return home. Stanley rests in a large cemetery of 3295 burials, near to where he died to the west of Arras.

Because of the relatively basic medical help available, particularly the lack of anti-biotics, no blood transfusions, brain surgery in its infancy, the chances of survival of the wounded even if they did reach a casualty clearing were not good, a wound would go septic in six hours, and the following day another soldier succumbed to his wounds.

PRIVATE ERNEST **MANSFIELD** (G/20282) 4TH. MIDDLESEX REGIMENT, DIED OF WOUNDS APRIL 26TH. 1917, AGED 35. BURIED IN AUBIGNY COMMUNAL CEMETERY EXTENSION, AUBIGNY-EN-ARTOIS, FRANCE, PLOT 2 ROW G GRAVE 37.

Ernest Mansfield was the son of Mr. and Mrs. James and Jane Mansfield of Long Row, Thaxted Road. After school he became a milkman, before changing to a railway porter at the Great Eastern station in Saffron Walden. He was married and lived with his wife and children at 4 Thaxted Road.

We do not know when Ernest received his mortal wounds but at the opening of the First Battle of the Scarpe the 4th. Middlesex were in the area of Lone Copse Valley, east of Orange Hill. On April 10th. at 10.30 a.m. they were ordered to advance on Lone Copse Valley through a hail of machine-gun fire and artillery from the direction of Fampoux. Only half a company reached their objective.

For the next few days the battalion were continually under hostile fire making any movement very difficult, although they managed to advance under a heavy barrage to Monchy on April 11th. positions which they consolidated until relieved on the 13th. On April 23rd. they were holding the Hyderabad Redoubt and an oblique line with the right facing almost north (in Clyde Trench) and the left facing east (in a portion of Harrow Trench). At zero hour, 4.45 a.m. the battalion advanced, the weather was dull and smoke obscured their first objective, but by 6.30 a.m. they had reached a line 200 yards east of the Roeux - Gavrelle road. However, murderous enfilade fire from both flanks forced the advancing men to take shelter where from noon to 9 p.m. they consolidated the position under shell and machine-gun fire.

At some time during these few days Ernest was wounded in the back. He was taken to Casualty Clearing Station 30, but never recovered. On Thursday May 10th. Mrs. Mansfield received the awful news.

Ernest is buried next to the French civilian cemetery on the hill overlooking Aubigny where there were a number of Clearing Stations. Nearly 3000 graves in the cemetery are ample evidence that even in these miniature, mobile hospitals life expectancy depended on the seriousness of the wound.

For the soldier whose wound was too serious to be treated at these Casualty Clearing Stations, the next stop was at a Base Hospital, such as Etaples or Rouen, or a hospital in England. Even this did not guarantee survival as the story of the next Saffron Walden soldier to die amply, but tragically shows.

LANCE-CORPORAL JOSEPH JOHN **PORTER** (44429) 25TH. NORTHUMBERLAND FUSILIERS, (3RD. TYNESIDE IRISH), DIED OF WOUNDS APRIL 29TH. 1917, AGED 34. BURIED IN SAFFRON WALDEN TOWN CEMETERY, RADWINTER ROAD, ESSEX, PLOT 51 GRAVE 104.

Joseph Porter was one of four sons born to Mr. and Mrs. George Porter of 15 Debden Road. After school he found employment as a carpenter and joiner with the local builder J Custerson and after some time with Bell & Sons. He was married with one child and lived at 7 East Street. He was, also, well known in the district as a half-mile runner.

When war broke out Joseph, like two of his three other brothers, enlisted in the Essex Regiment as Private 28819. However, after the first day of the Battle of the Somme when they were virtually annhilated, he was transferred to fill the gaps in the Tyneside Irish, a 'Pals' battalion of the Northumberland Fusiliers.

On April 9th. 1917 Joseph and his battalion were part of the 34th. Division who formed the left hand side of the mighty punch at the German positions to the north east of Arras. The ultimate objective was the Green Line on the bare crest of Point du Jour Ridge. The Tyneside Irish were in support, and when the leading battalions were held up by heavy machine-gun fire, they were ordered forward. Confusion reined as Joseph and his comrades found themselves pinned down as well. The sole cause of this mayhem was a single machine gun that had survived the British barrage. In this cacophony of exploding shell, clouds of dust and flying bullets, Joseph was hit in the stomach. Stretcher-bearers recovered him and he started the long, and painful journey back to hospital in England.

Joseph was transferred to hospital in Halifax, where on April 27th. his mother and wife arrived at his bedside, but as with so many wounds infection had set in and on the Sunday, Joseph died. It is impossible to imagine how harrowing his death must have been to his wife, let alone Joseph's mother - it was her third son to die, and cruel fate would soon remove her fourth. Perhaps, some small comfort was gained by her prescence at his bedside ?

Joseph's body was brought back to Saffron Walden and buried in the town cemetery. Sadly, it is not blessed with a Commonwealth War Grave Commission white headstone, and is in a sorry state of neglect. However it is just possible to decipher the inscription, " *Lce-Cpl.Joseph John Porter died of wounds received in France 29th.April 1917 aged 33. In loving memory of my dear husband (Mary).*" Today, Mary lies with her husband, after having been a widow for forty-seven years.

In France the Arras offensive, after the bitter fighting of April 23rd. and the following days had lost its momentum, but not for long - there was no alternative to further action, which despite the tiredness of the troops and the reticence of their commanders to continue, was stepped up again near Roeux on April 28th. 1917. Two days later another local man made the ultimate sacrifice.

PRIVATE GEORGE HENRY **HOWARD** (26959) 9TH. ESSEX REGIMENT, KILLED IN ACTION APRIL 30TH. 1917, AGED 29. COMMEMORATED ON THE ARRAS MEMORIAL TO THE MISSING, FRANCE, BAY 7.

George Howard was the only son of Harry William and Martha Howard of 3 Alpha Place. He attended the Boys British School before obtaining employment as a telegraph messenger at the Saffron Walden Post Office. This led to becoming a postman around the local villages.

In March 1916, George enlisted and after training joined his battalion in France in July 1916 on the Somme in the Albert - Bouzincourt line. Involved in the attack on Skyline Trench in early August, the battalion were transferred to the Arras section for a short while before returning to the Somme on the Gueudecourt (Gird Trench) sector until late October when they went back to Arras yet again.

On the 9th.April 1917 in the opening stages on the battle, George's Division - the 34th. - had captured Observation Ridge, but with this new initiative they found themselves between the River Scarpe and Monchy, attacking an enemy who in undamaged trenches let off a veritable hurricane of machine-gun fire, driving the men back to their original start lines. Here they remained awaiting a further offensive.

In Alpha Place on the 10th. May a letter was recieved from two of George's comrades informing his parents that during this 'quiet ' spell, two days after the aborted attack, George had been killed. Once again the writer, out of feelings for their sorrow, informed the grieving parents that it had been ' instantaneous.'

On May 3rd. the further offensive came. It was ill-conceived and doomed to failure. Known as the Third Battle of the Scarpe, the forces attacked over a front of sixteen miles. One historian called the day, *" the blackest of the war.*" It cerainly proved so for one Saffron Walden family.

LANCE-CORPORAL BERTRAM ALFRED **PORTER** (G/1511) 4TH. ROYAL FUSILIERS,

KILLED IN ACTION MAY 3RD. 1917. COMMEMORATED ON THE ARRAS MEMORIAL TO THE MISSING, FRANCE, BAY 3.

As we have seen Mr. and Mrs. George Porter sent off four sons to the Great War. With the conflict in its infancy after two months one was dead, his body never found. The first few months of 1917 saw two more perish, only one finding a known resting place and then exactly four days after sitting and watching her third son die, the unthinkable happened.

Bertram enlisted early in the war, going to France in June 1915. There is some confusion about his service - two sources (The Commonwealth War Graves Commission (C.W.G.C) and Soldiers' Died in the Great War - The Royal Fusiliers) note him as being in the 4th. Battalion ; the Medal Roll gives his battalion as the 9th. which did indeed go to France in 1915.

However, on the 3rd. May both battalions were on the Arras front, not many miles apart. The 9th. Battalion had been ordered to advance across country towards a sunken road running north-west towards Roeux. Their second objective was to be the village of Pelves, once Roeux had fallen. Although (with the 8th. Battalion) there were only 800 men, their frontage was 1000 yards, but they advanced unsupported deep into German territory by 5 a.m. but as it was dark they passed over unseen groups of the enemy who shot them in the back and they were enfiladed by machine-gun fire from the villafe of Roeux, which had not been captured. In this darkness and carnage, the last Porter son, Bertram, disappeared without trace.

"They await the lost that shall never leave the dock;
They await the lost that shall never again come by the train
To the embraces of all these women with dead faces;
They await the lost who lie dead in trench and barrier and foss,
In the dark of the night.....
There is so much pain."

Officially the Battle of Arras ended on May 17th. 1917. It lasted thirty-nine days and claimed approximately 159,000 casualties at a daily rate of 4076 ; a higher daily rate than the Somme, Passchendaele or the Final Offensive. Before that date was to be reached three more local men were to die, but only one from the effects of that battle.

In 1915, French and British troops had landed in Salonica, in order to defend Serbia from Austro-Hungarian attack. Now in May 1917, a big allied offensive was planned for May 8th. and reinforcements were on their way.

PRIVATE ARTHUR GEORGE **COURTNEAY** (T/202595) 4TH. EAST KENT REGIMENT, (THE BUFFS), DROWNED MAY 4TH.1917, AGED 23. COMMEMORATED ON THE SAVONA TOWN CEMETERY MEMORIAL, ITALY.

George Courtneay was the elder son of Mrs. Harriet Courtneay and the late Arthur George Courtneay of 50 Radwinter Road. After attending the Boys' British School George worked firstly for Webb and Brand, nurserymen of 10 East Street ; then in Lord Howard de Walden's gardens at Chirk Castle and latterly for Mr. Engelmann's Horneybrook Nurseries. On the war's commencement George was eager to join up, but he was not a fit man and was medically rejected four times. In 1915, his younger brother Albert Edward enlisted in the Royal Fusiliers, but was reported missing in July 1916.

Whether this spurred George on or not, in December 1916, he was finally passed fit at Warley and on 22nd. January joined up for basic training with the Essex Regiment before transferring to the Buffs. Because of the Balkan situation, he found himself on the H.T. (Hired Transport) *" Transylvania "* on his way to Salonica with reinforcements and garrison troops. The *" Transylvania "* was a 14,315 ton steamer, armed only for defensive purposes. On May 4th. 1917 it was steaming two and a half miles off Cape Vado, in the Gulf of Genoa, when without warning, it was torpedoed by a submarine. It went down rapidly, and thirty-one officers and 382 other ranks, including George Courtneay, drowned. It was the third largest disaster suffered by Great Britain on a single day from U-boat action (the *"Arcadion "* was also torpedoed with the loss of another 277 lives). Some forty survivors made the shore and 2500 were saved by a Japanese destroyer.

Today George's name is on a memorial in the Italian town cemetery of Savona, close by are the graves of some of his comrades whose bodies were washed ashore. His brother Albert returned from a German prisoner-of-war camp in July 1918.

Three days later in Hampshire the last town man wounded in the Battle of Arras succumbed to those wounds with his wife at his bedside.

PRIVATE SIDNEY **CLARKE** (CLARK) (12422) 9TH. ESSEX REGIMENT, DIED OF WOUNDS MAY 7TH. 1917, AGED 35. BURIED IN SAFFRON WALDEN TOWN CEMETERY, RADWINTER ROAD, ESSEX, PLOT 28 GRAVE 80.

Sidney Clarke was the eldest son of Simeon and Amelia Clarke of Middle Square Castle Street. He was married to Annie and had three children, Alice, Sidney and John, living at 13 Ingleside Place. Despite these ties and his age, Sidney was one of the first to enlist, leaving for General Service training in June 1915. On May 31st. 1915, the 9th. Essex had landed at Boulogne and Sidney was to join it later. Sidney's younger brother, Harry was to be 'blown up' at Loos in October 1915.

In early July Sidney was wounded on the Somme, probably in the attack on Ovillers, but after recuperation he rejoined his comrades in the Arras section. However, Sidney was soon to be wounded again through the right thigh and leg either in the attack of April 29th. 1917 when two companies of the battalion succeeded in getting into Rifle Trench repulsing heavy German attacks until driven back by the enemy working its way up New Street with its junction with Rifle Trench or in the huge final throw of the dice on May 3rd.1917.

After treatment in France, Sidney was brought back to England, to Netley Hospital. Here, sadly, he developed lockjaw and died. He was buried on May 12th. in our town cemetery. He has a standard white headstone, with the simple, but poignant inscription, *" Forever in our thoughts."* For many years there was a rose bush by Sidney's headstone.

The perception of death in the Great War is in mud-filled holes, blown to pieces by huge shells being mown down by strategically placed machine-guns as they progressed in unwavering lines across no-man's land in a futile attempt to gain an important advantage. For millions this was the case, but death comes to some in bizarre, luckless circumstances whilst serving their country.

PRIVATE ARTHUR SAMUEL **RUSHFORTH** (SE/6852) ARMY VETERINARY CORPS, DIED MAY 9TH. 1917, AGED 42. BURIED IN GOURNAY-EN-BRAY COMMUNAL CEMETERY, FRANCE.

Arthur Rushworth was the son of William and Martha Rushforth of Debden Road. He had attended the Boys British School and had then served in the South African war, from whence he returned to work for A N Myhill and Sons Ltd. He was married to Mary Ann and had two children.

Arthur enlisted at Colchester and joined the Army Veterinary Corps, attached to a Convalescent Horse Depot. By 1916 the British Expeditionary Force in France were using at least 400,000 horses, either in the cavalry, or as draught and pack animals. These creatures suffered horribly - it is estimated that some 270,000 were killed or destroyed during the war.

The task of the A.V.C was to treat wounded and sick animals, either at the front, or to send them from veterinary evacuation stations to the veterinary hospitals in the rear.

In Saffron Walden on May 12th. Arthur's wife received at 16 London Road, a telegram notifying her that her husband was in hospital in France, dangerously ill. One week later came the notification that he was dead. Whether Arthur was wounded or died from illness is not known, but if it was as a result of enemy fire it is likely that it occurred either near the front-line treating injured horses or from long-distance shelling. Closely following on from this tragic news came a letter from Arthur's lieutenant which conveyed his sorrow at the loss of one who, "*...had worked under me for twelve months...who was a good comrade and a good worker.*" Another letter from the hospital matron recounted how Arthur's funeral was "*... attended by comrades and French soldiers.*"

What is certain is that he was buried with full military honours amidst the huge family vaults of local French families in the old communal cemetery in Gournay-en-Bray, a small town behind the lines. His white, neat headstone, one of several dotted amongst its more austere neighbours, is inscribed with a simple family tribute, " *Peace, perfect peace.*" Still to be found in front of the stone is the chipped enamel plaque once fixed to his original wooden cross, saying   gratefully. " *Soldat Anglais. Mort pour la France.*"

The focus of events on the Western Front now shifted away from northern France to the prolongation of the same ridge north from Vimy in the Belgian sector of Ypres. On June 7th. 1917 erupted the Battle of Messines, the beginning of the Third Battle of Ypres, latterly also known more resonantly and horrifyingly as Passchendaele. But before these events, the day-to-day story of life, and especially death, continued whether in the front line, in reserve or behind the lines.

RIFLEMAN VICTOR ALPHONSE **GALLEY** (652955) 21ST. COUNTY OF LONDON BATTALION, (THE FIRST SURREY RIFLES), KILLED IN ACTION MAY 20TH. 1917, AGED 30. BURIED IN BEDFORD HOUSE CEMETERY ENCLOSURE NO.4, BELGIUM, SPECIAL MEMORIAL 22.

Victor Galley was the fourth of three surviving sons of Mr. and Mrs. Joseph E Galley, a photographer of 3, London Road. His eldest brother, Ernest had died in 1902, after serving with the 2nd. Scots Guards. Although born at Ridgewell, the family had moved to Saffron Walden and Victor had attended the Boys British School. On leaving he had entered the grocery trade and was, at the outbreak of war, the manager of the Home and Colonial Stores in Peckham, South London. In June 1916, Victor was called up and enlisted at Camberwell in the First Surrey Rifles. After receiving training he proceded to Belgium, joining his battalion in the Ypres sector where they had come in late October 1916.

It was a period of relative inactivity, but on the Saturday night of May 19th. at 10 p.m. whilst on sentry duty Victor was shot. His body was carried behind the lines to one of the Dressing Stations or Field Ambulances that were using the Chateau Rosendal where he died some hours later. He now lies somewhere in the huge Bedford House Cemetery on the site of the chateau. The exact location within the cemetery is not known, hence his headstone is a special memorial to one *" believed to be buried near this spot. "*. His inscription reads, *" Their glory shall not be blotted out."* Of the 5067 graves in this cemetery, some 60% are unnamed.

Victor is also remembered on his brother's headstone in Saffron Walden cemetery. Another brother, Lewis, a Grenadier guardsman, although wounded, survived the war.

On June 7th. 1917 under the Messines ridge, nineteen mines with the power of 500 tons, exploded killing at least 10,000 Germans and heard fifteen miles away in Lille. It was the prelude to the Battle of Messines. On June 11th. another Saffron Walden soldier died, but not in Belgium.

PTE.CHARLES **WREN** (G/7919) 13TH. MIDDLESEX REGIMENT, DIED OF WOUNDS JUNE 11TH. 1917, AGED 32. BURIED IN SAFFRON WALDEN TOWN CEMETERY, RADWINTER ROAD, ESSEX, PLOT 50 GRAVE 45.

Charles Wren was the second son of Mrs. G Francis Penning, his step-father being a rope maker of Little Walden Road and later The Pines, Thaxted Road. After education at the Boys' British School, he became fully involved in the local community playing the tenor-horn in the town band, worshipping at the Baptist church and a member of the local Foresters' Court (a Friendly Society), as well as becoming a traveller for his step-father selling stack covers and ropes.

In late 1914, Charles enlisted with his brother, George and several friends at Warley and eventually was posted to the 13th. (Service) Battalion, the Middlesex Regiment. George and most of his friends were to die in 1915, but Charles survived that year, and in August 1916 was on the Somme in the area of Guillemont and Delville Wood. During this period the Official History records that almost 400 of the battalion had become casualties and it seems probable that it was here that Charles was wounded, too, suffering a fractured left leg from a bullet.

The long process of recovery was started and Charles eventually was sent to the Royal Naval Hospital in Southend on August 18th. Here he had several operations and recovered sufficiently enough to be sent to a convalescent home at Mutlow Hill. He then was allowed home, though having to walk with a stick. Unfortunately, his leg started to swell and he was admitted to Saffron Walden General Hospital, before being transferred to Colchester Military Hospital. Here scepticaemia set in and on June 11th. some nine months after being wounded, he died. His body was brought home to

Saffron Walden and buried in the town cemetery on June 14th. His headstone states, *"In loving memory of Pte.Charles Wren 13th. Middlesex Regt. died June 11th. 1917 from wounds received in action aged 31. Time passes away but memory never fades. "* Like the other non - Commonwealth War Graves, the headstone is in a bad state of repair.

Not all the men who served in the infantry were front-line soldiers, some served in Pioneer battalions. These were intended to provide the Royal Engineers with skilled labour and to relieve the infantry from some of its non-combatant duties, such as trench digging and revetting. But in the times of crisis they would give up their picks and shovels and fight alongside the infantry in repelling the enemy. Inevitably, these men were as vulnerable to shell, shrapnel and bullet as any other soldier.

PRIVATE FRANK WILFRED **REED** (31608) 13TH. (FOREST OF DEAN), GLOUCESTERSHIRE REGIMENT, DIED OF WOUNDS JULY 2ND. 1917, AGED 20. BURIED IN LIJSSENTHOEK MILITARY CEMETERY, POPERINGHE, BELGIUM, PLOT 14 ROW C GRAVE 20.

Frank Reed was the second son of Mr. William and Mrs. Y Reed, a baker and grocer of 51 Ashdon Road. On leaving school Frank worked in his father's bakery, but in August 1914, at a public recruiting meeting in the Market Square, he joined up - he was just 17. He was enlisted into the Royal Fusiliers (No.1518) before going to France on May 31st. 1915 as a despatch rider with the Army Cycle Corps. One day while acting as a telephone operator in an advanced dugout, he was buried by a shell explosion which killed several of his comrades, and had to be dug out by a rescue party. Not surprisingly he was invalided home on May 15th. 1916 suffering from shell-shock, spending some time as a patient in the Eastern General Hospital in Cambridge.

On recovery he was briefly transferred to the Royal West Surrey Regt. (Queens), then to the Gloucestershire Regt, returning to France in November 1916 and joining his battalion before they entrained for Poperinghe and the Ypres Salient on November 18th.

This Pioneer battalion was composed of hard pit-men from the Forest of Dean and they were engaged in laying cordwood tracks and light railway lines for XVIII Corps to the Salient to facilitate ammunition and supplies being brought forward. They also were building bridges to cross the Yperlee Canal. Most of this work was done at night, but they were constantly overlooked by the German positions and suffered a steady bombardment especially of fixed points, notably the bridges. The battalion suffered heavy casualties, and on July 2nd. Frank was hit by a trench mortar, badly wounding his left arm and leg. He was rushed to one of the many Casualty Clearing Stations around Poperinghe, but died just as he reached one, at 5.30 a.m.

At home Frank's parents received the telegram informing them of his death, at the same time as his last letter in which he reassured them that he was, *"...in the pink of condition"* ! Further details followed in letters from the regimental chaplain and headquarters.

Frank was buried in the second largest cemetery on the Salient. It contains 10,773 graves and is a tragic cosmopolitan example of the sacrifice with men from all parts of the globe resting alongside over 200 of the enemy. Frank's elder brother, Frederick survived the conflict after service with the Essex Regiment and the Royal Flying Corps.

For a while all was relatively quiet, apart from one tragic incident that took place at the northernmost end of the Western Front, close to the sea on the Belgian coast at Nieuport. Here two men from Essex, friends, were serving with men from Cumberland and Westmoreland, after being transferred to ' fill the gaps ' of earlier battles. Friends in life and comrades in death.

In June 1917, the British XV Corps took over the line from the French and Belgians. It held the line from St.Georges, Ramskapelle to the sea at Nieuport, with the 32nd. Division holding the part of the line from Geleide brook to St. Georges. The area behind the troops here had lent itself to artificial flooding in this low-lying coastal area and the Germans infantry had been ordered not to go beyond the second breastwork, this led to the 97th.Brigade being the only one to be attacked south of Lombartzyde.

The German bombardment began on July 6th. continuing until the 10th. increasing in intensity from 5 a.m. through the morning. Three floating bridges over the Yser mouth were demolished and by 10.15 a.m. all telephone communication had failed. At 11a.m. the bombardment paused for observation, but continued virtually unabated until 8 p.m. when the enemy attacked. During this inferno in what Conan Doyle called,"*..so small an incident in so great a war,*" our Essex comrades were killed, never to be seen again.

PRIVATE CHARLES **KING** (28294) 11TH. BORDER REGIMENT, KILLED IN ACTION JULY 10TH. 1917, AGED 25. COMMEMORATED ON THE NIEUPORT MEMORIAL TO THE MISSING, BELGIUM.

Charles King was the third son of Mr. and Mrs. Frank King of 61 Castle Street. He worked with his father as a builder and was married with two children. He was also well-known as a local runner.

Charles enlisted at the end of 1916 into the Essex Regiment (32719) and survived the battle of Arras, before being transferred to the Border Regiment. It was not until August 1917 that news came through to Charles' family that he was missing in action with three other comrades from Essex, but was not a prisoner-of-war. Charles' family wrote to the Red Cross Society for further information and this was confirmed. There was now an agonizing wait until in December the dreadful news arrived.

Mrs. King received a letter via the Red Cross from one of the three missing comrades, a Private Douglas who was now a prisoner-of-war in Germany. During the heavy bombardment, a man believed to be Charles had been hit on the head by a piece of shell that exploded in his dugout. He had been buried in a small cemetery behind Nieuport under a wooden cross. Pte. Douglas believed the man to be Charles as he was a battalion runner and Charles was an athlete. The spot where Charles was buried had not yet been recovered by British troops so final confirmation could not be made. Of the other two men, one, Pte. Frederick Smith was dead and the other, Pte. Ames of Alpha Place, a prisoner-of-war.

After the war Charles' grave could not be located and his name was added to the list of "*..intolerably nameless names.*"

PRIVATE FREDERICK HENRY **SMITH** (28245) 11TH. BORDER REGIMENT, KILLED IN ACTION JULY 10TH. 1917, AGED 35. COMMEMORATED ON THE NIEUPORT MEMORIAL TO

Frederick Smith was the son of Abraham Smith of Lenard's End and was born in Wimbish, before moving to Saffron Walden. He lived at 3 Freshwell Street and before the war was a nurseryman and a hay-presser for the War Department. He was married to Florence and had five children. When the Second Military Service Act became law on May 16th. 1916 and married men became eligible for conscription, Frederick was called up, along with his friend, Charles King, into the Essex Regiment (33060). His story is tragically the same, although Mrs. Smith's agony of not knowing was more short-lived.

In August 1917, she wrote to her husband's Commanding Officer because she had received no letter for some weeks. The Chaplain replied informing her that he had been killed in action, and an inference made that he had been buried alive. Ironically, since Mrs. Smith had written, she had received official notification that Frederick was missing in action, presumed dead.

Frederick's body was also never found, and his name appears on the same panel as his friend Charles King, one of 566 officers and men killed without trace in the *"...deplorable affair of Nieuport."*

Mrs. Smith, typical of so many war widows, never remarried. She brought up five children on her own, believing to the end of her days, that one day her beloved husband would return.

> *"What if I bring you nothing, sweet,*
> *Nor maybe come home at all ?*
> *Ah, but you'll know, Brave Heart, you'll know*
> *Two things I'll have kept to send*
> *Mine honour for which you bade me go*
> *And my love - my love to the end."*

Away from Belgium, the war of attrition continued to take its daily toll. Illness and wounds once treated and recovered from, men were sent back to replace the growing round of casualties.

PRIVATE HERBERT JOHN **BRAND** (44559) 20TH. MANCHESTER REGIMENT, KILLED IN ACTION JULY 30TH.1917, AGED 22. BURIED IN H.A.C CEMETERY, ECOUST ST. MEIN, FRANCE, PLOT 2 ROW G GRAVE 10.

Herbert Brand was the son of Mr. and Mrs. Harry Brand of 16 Alpha Place, South Road. On leaving school he was employed as a butcher by George H Willett Junior of 44 High Street, until enlisting at Tottenham in September 1914 in the Royal Fusiliers (No. 2571). With the 2nd. Battalion he landed on ' X ' Beach. Helles, Gallipoli on April 25th. 1915.

On May 3rd. Herbert was slightly wounded during the First Battle of Krithia at Fir Tree Wood, but was able to continue until struck down by enteric fever. Recuperation in Egypt and back in England, took a considerable amount of time and he was not passed fit until June 1917. On his return to France he was posted to the 20th. Manchesters, a ' Pals ' battalion decimated in the battles of the Somme. His return was short-lived.

At home in Alpha Place Herbert's parents were celebrating their son's twenty third birthday, when a telegram arrived to say he had been killed.

Herbert is buried in a cemetery on positions captured in April 1917. It contains the remains of 1910 soldiers.

In Flanders, a day later, started the Battle of Pilckem Ridge. It marked the beginning of what is known as Passchendaele - a name synonymous with futility and mud. On this day, though overcast, but quite warm, a soldier from Saffron Walden, but serving with the third Australian Division became another statistic of this *" foul and endless war."*

PRIVATE WALTER WILLAM **ANDREWS** (2005) 41ST. INFANTRY BATTALION, AUSTRALIAN IMPERIAL FORCES, KILLED IN ACTION JULY 31ST. 1917, AGED 26. COMMEMORATED ON THE MENIN GATE MEMORIAL TO THE MISSING, BELGIUM, PANEL 25.

William Andrews was born in Saffron Walden, the son of David and Emma Foster of Sewards End. After leaving school he emigrated to Australia where he obtained work as a stoker and lived in Albion Park, Queensland.

As the demand for more and more men needed to protect the ' Mother Country ' increased, William enlisted on Christmas Eve 1915 in Brisbane. His records show he was 5 feet 6 inches in height, weighed 10 stones 10 lbs, had fair hair, blue eyes and a light complexion. After a period of training, he embarked from Sydney on the "*Megantic*" on May 3rd. 1916 in the 13th. Training battalion for Egypt. On arrival in Egypt nearly six weeks later, more training was undertaken before leaving Alexandria for England on August 6th. Again a long voyage brought William to England before arriving in France from Southampton with the 41st. Battalion on November 24th. 1916.

On Tuesday, July 31st. 1917 dawned the opening day of the battle of Pilckem Ridge, the 41st. Battalion were in reserve. The attack opened at zero hour, 3.50 a.m. to the north-west of Warneton against a series of German outposts. The Windmill and other objectives were taken and the wire of the Warneton Line reached. At 8 p.m. William's battalion was about to relieve the others, when the Germans counter-attacked the Windmill. In this action, William fell.

He was buried at Messines Cross Avenue and in his belongings was found a letter to a Mrs. J H Johnson of Albion Park, leaving his money to her. The ground where William was buried was shelled and fought over again and again and after the Armistice his body could not be found. He is commemorated on the Menin Gate under the inscription, *" In Maiorem dei Gloriam "* amidst 126 of his battalion comrades. His name also appears on the village memorial in Hempstead where his parents lived for a short while.

The success of the Battle of Pilckem Ridge was relative. Haig had envisaged considerable gains far more than the actual mile achieved and that only in places, not at the huge cost in dead and wounded. It was soon after this that, the Belgian government signed an agreement whereby the land on which the British war cemeteries and graves in Belgium had been made was *" conceded in perpetuity "* to Britain. This seemed a tacit recognition of the rising scale of British losses on Belgian soil. A week before this another soldier from our town was enabled to take 'advantage' of this agreement !

PRIVATE ALBERT EDWARD **BASSETT** (21108) 9TH. EAST SURREY REGIMENT, KILLED IN ACTION AUGUST 3RD. 1917, AGED 20. BURIED IN DUHALLOW A.D.S CEMETERY, YPRES, BELGIUM, PLOT 7 ROW D GRAVE 28.

Albert was the youngest son of Mr. and Mrs. Henry Bassett of 28 Castle Street. Before the war he worked at Robsons, before joining up on May 10th. 1916. He was sent to France in December 1916 and at the beginning of the Battle of Pilckem Ridge, with the 24th. Division, the 72nd. Brigade, was part of a defensive flank, attacking on the 31st. July 1917 at 3.50 a.m. For most of this action, Albert's battalion were in reserve near Bodmin Copse. Over the next five days Albert's battalion were relatively quiet, suffering only intermittent shelling, but even intermittent shelling caused casualties.

On Friday August 3rd. in steady rainfall, a shell fell on the post Albert was on duty in. The shell killed him outright. The letter from his officer did not reach his parents until early September, it praised him as *"..an exceedingly good soldier."* At the time of Albert's death, his elder brother Frank was in hospital in Salonica. He, too, was destined not to return home, dying one month before the Armistice.

On August 10th. the British renewed their offensive in the Salient, but another enemy impeded their progress - rain. However, six days later, with the rain ceased, the village of Langemark was taken, although much of the ground was then subsequently lost.

RIFLEMAN WILLIAM JAMES **RIDGEWELL** (5/439) 2ND. RIFLE BRIGADE, KILLED IN ACTION AUGUST 16TH. 1917, AGED 29. COMMEMORATED ON TYNE COT MEMORIAL TO THE MISSING, BELGIUM, PANELS 145 TO 147.

William Ridgewell was the eldest son of Robert and Thurza Ridgewell of 20 Bridge Street. He was married to Charlotte, but had no children. He was formerly a motor mechanic to Joseph Wright, 26 High Street, before becoming a driver first to Lord Howard de Walden and then latterly to Lord Howard's cousin, a Captain Ellis.

On the outbreak of war, William was one of the first to enlist in October 1914, at Minster on the Isle of Sheppey. He went to France in March 1916 and survived the horrors of the Somme, notably the attack on Zenith Trench in October 1916, when the battalion suffered 238 casualties. However, in early July 1917, William received a slight wound in the arm whilst acting as a stretcher bearer which necessitated a stay in hospital of two weeks.

On his return William was thrown into the cauldron of battle that was Passchendaele. On August 13th. the battalion was moved up to Westhoek Ridge, suffering heavy shelling in difficult country. The front line was found to be composed of short lengths of trench and posts on the east side of the Westhoek - Frezenberg road. The next two days were spent under heavy shelling and sniper fire, until zero hour of 4.45 a.m. on Thursday August 16th. when the Vth. Army attacked. William's battalion were in support of the Royal Irish Rifles, their objective the Green Line (which was, in fact, not achieved until July 31st.),and they came under heavy machine-gun fire which forced them back to the line of the Haanebeek. In this attack, the battalion lost ten killed and fifty missing. One of these missing was William Ridgewell.

In early September, in a letter from a friend, this news reached his wife. William's body was never found and his name is on the Tyne Cot Memorial, a name given to a local group of German blockhouses, by men of the Northumberland Fusiliers. His is one of 606 names of men of the Rifle Brigade killed near here. His younger brother, Lewis, seved with the Egyptian Expeditionary Force, and although wounded, survived the war.

The following day another man from the town was seriously wounded. He was taken to one of the many Casualty Clearing Stations set up for the battles of Passchendaele where he died. The cemeteries that grew up around these clearing stations were known, with typical humour by the soldiers as *"Bandage'em, Mending'em and Dosing'em"*, (In reality, Bandaghem, Mendinghem and Dozinghem!). A grim, but appropriate play upon their Flemish names.

PRIVATE FREDERICK **MASCALL** (55838) 14TH. ROYAL WELCH FUSILIERS, DIED OF WOUNDS OCTOBER 18TH. 1917, AGED 36. BURIED IN DOZINGHEM MILITARY CEMETERY, WESTVLETEREN, BELGIUM, PLOT 4 ROW I GRAVE 8.

Fred was born in Radwinter, the son of the late Mr. and Mrs. Alfred Mascall of Little Walden. After schooling he was employed by Mr. J Hawkey of Berden Hall. Married with two children in May 1916, he enlisted in the Essex Regiment (28771), before going to France in January 1917.

Transferring to the Royal Welch Fusiliers, Fred emerged safely from the thick of the fighting on Pilckem Ridge in July and August, but on a relatively quiet, warm summer's day in the trenches, he was severely wounded in the leg and the arm.

News of his death the following day, far away from the thudding of the guns, came to his family in the form of a letter from a nursing sister at the hospital. A more famous Welch Fusilier, Siegfried Sassoon, conveys the thoughts they must have had,

" Light many lamps and gather round his bed.
Lend him your eyes, warm blood, and will to live.
Speak to him; rouse him; you may save him yet."
But sadly, ..death replied;
'I choose him.' So he went,
And there was silence in the summer nights;
Silence and safety; and the veils of sleep. "

Nine days later, in pouring rain, a mile or so away another soldier laid down his life, his only memorial a simple name carved in Portland stone.. What is remarkable and tragic was that he was William Ridgewell's brother-in-law - names together, forever on the same memorial .

PRIVATE ALFRED GEORGE **KING** (260116) 1ST/6TH. ROYAL WARWICKSHIRE REGIMENT, KILLED IN ACTION AUGUST 27TH. 1917, AGED 30. COMMEMORATED ON THE TYNE COT MEMORIAL TO THE MISSING, BELGIUM, PANELS 23 TO 28.

Alfred King lived at 90 High Street . He had attended the Boys British School before working at Saffron Walden Brewery Stores of Watney Combe Reid at 17 High Street. On June 2nd. 1916 he enlisted in the Essex Regiment (No.400282), before being transferred first to the Suffolks (No.28380) and finally to a Territorial battalion of the Royal Warwicks, the 1/6th.

August 1917 saw Alfred in training at Riegersburg Camp, near St. Julien, but on the 26th. the battalion was moved to positions north and south of the St. Julien - Winnipeg Road. The following day they attacked enemy positions at Winnipeg Farm at 1.55 p.m. They were forced to clear the occupied shell holes, and at least one concrete bunker as they went. The troops found it almost impossible to advance due to the state of the ground and concentrated fire from machine-gunners and snipers protected by concrete emplacements at Springfield Farm on the right and Vancouver Farm in the centre. Three officers and twenty-five other ranks were killed, 120 other ranks wounded and fourteen missing.

It was not until December that Mrs. King had any news of Alfred. She was told that with five others he had not been seen since August 27th. and they had been reported killed. The Red Cross Prisoner of War Committee had no news, so it was most likely that the report, therefore, was regretably true and so it proved to be.

The focus of the war was concentrated on a few square miles of a rain-sodden Flanders, but on other fronts it was far from ' all quiet.' Death was random in his selection and not even the experiences of the battle-hardened soldier, nor the protection of deeply-dug, well-revetted trenches made him immune from the horrors of heavy artillery.

PRIVATE EUSTACE ISAAC WILLIAM **SWAN** (12525) 9TH. ESSEX REGIMENT, DIED OF WOUNDS SEPTEMBER 18TH. 1917, AGED 22. BURIED IN MONCHY BRITISH CEMETERY, MONCHY-LE-PREUX, FRANCE, PLOT 1 ROW M GRAVE 3.

Eustace Swan was the second son of Daniel and Elizabeth Swan of Cement Works Cottages, Thaxted Road (later 19 East Street). Born in Wimbish, after school he had become a shepherd with Mr. H C Wells of Frogs Green, Wimbish, before enlisting on August 31st. 1914 in London and after training going to France on May 30th. 1915. His elder, brother, Thomas, and his younger brother, John Stephen also joined and went to France as well as his sister, who was involved in war work.

Eustace saw action at Loos, the Somme, where he took part on the attacks on Ovillers, Skyline Trench and Bayonet Trench, Arras, at Feuchy Chapel and other more minor engagements without receiving a scratch, but his good fortune finally failed.

September saw the battalion still in the Arras sector, when on Tuesday 18th. September a shell fell on part of the front-line trench, wounding Eustace and killing five others. He was hit on the temple and left side, and died, without regaining consciousness within an hour, on his way to a Casualty Clearing Station.

This sad information reached his parents a fortnight later. The writer, Eustace's officer added, "..he was a good, clever, efficient sniper. The whole platoon mourn him...he was buried behind the lines in a military cemetery." Today that cemetery contains 553 other graves - on Eustace's headstone is the inscription, " Until the day breaks." He is also remembered on his parents' gravestone in the town cemetery (his father, Daniel died in June 1918, without seeing the end of the conflict that claimed his son).

Although the Germans were suffering even more severely than the British during the Third Battle of Ypres, the casualty lists grew as in this war of attrition the enemy were pushed back a few yards here, a few yards there. People at home had began to question these casualty lists - by October 5th. 1917, it was estimated there were 162, 768 dead and wounded, a statistic brought to life, by the next Saffron Walden soldier to die.

PRIVATE CHARLES JOHN **HOUSDEN** (48124) 26TH. ROYAL FUSILIERS, DIED OF WOUNDS SEPTEMBER 21ST. 1917, AGED 25. BURIED LARCH WOOD (RAILWAY CUTTING) CEMETERY, ZILLEBEKE, BELGIUM, SPECIAL MEMORIAL A24.

Charles was the third son of Mr. and Mrs. Charles Housden of 13 Thaxted Road. He worked on Harry Coe's Peaslands Farm as a stockman, with his brother, Jack and was single. In January 1916, Charles joined the 1/5th. Essex Regiment, before at some stage being transferred to the 26th. Royal Fusiliers. He was sent out to France in April 1916, and during August, probably in training, was wounded in the chest by gun shot. This necessitated quite a long stay at a Base Hospital.

Eventually, he was passed fit and returned to his battalion on September 18th. 1917. Three days later he was dead. September 20th. saw the commencement of the Battle of the Menin Road Ridge. For once it was not raining, and below the Ypres - Menin Road, the 26th. Royal Fusiliers' objective was the Tower Hamlets spur. They were on the left in support with a front on the road running north from the west of Lower Star Post. Charles and his comrades had to step off the duckboard track to allow the 32nd. Royal Fusiliers to get in front. Stepping into thick mud which clung so tightly made it very difficult to move, however at zero hour, 5.40 a.m. both battalions moved forward so close to their barrage, that the German counter-barrage fell behind them. They did not, however, escape intense machine-gun fire, lying out in the shell holes, the battalion suffered heavy casualties. In less than ten minutes there was only one unwounded officer out of nineteen who had gone forward. Charles was also badly wounded hit in the head. He died soon after in a field ambulance, never saying anything, according to the chaplain who was with him.

Charles lies, under the gaze of the notorious Hill 60, somewhere in this cemetery started in 1915 in a small plantation of larches. His actual grave was lost in the German advance of 1918. His headstone, thus carries the words, " *Believed to be buried in this cemetery.* " His parents chose the inscription, " *Their glory shall not be blotted out.* "

In " *Passchendaele - The Day by Day Account,* " September 24th. 1917 has the following comment. " *Nothing of significance happened on this day.* " It was warm, there was 50 % cloud cover and it did not rain, but men still died.

PRIVATE WILLIAM ALFRED **MARKS** (3/1515) 1ST. ESSEX REGIMENT, KILLED IN ACTION SEPTEMBER 24TH. 1917, AGED 29. COMMEMORATED ON TYNE COT MEMORIAL TO THE MISSING, BELGIUM, PANELS 98 TO 99.

William Marks was the eldest of three sons of William and Harriet Marks of 18 Thaxted Road. Born in Aldershot, he was single, and worked for Mr. Sidney Kettley, a farmer of Wimbish. He was a reservist and was sent to Egypt on December 1st. 1915, as reinforcements for the Gallipoli campaign. However, evacuation from the peninsula had already begun, some Essex men arriving at Imbros on the 20th, and the bulk being embarked for Mudros on January 7th. and 8th. so William and his battalion were sent on to France.

In September 1916, the battalion were in the Ypres sector when William was wounded in the left side. On recovery in 1917 he found them again still in the Ypres salient, having missed their return to the Somme. The 1st. Essex were at Proven on September 20th. and the following day relieved the Grenadier Guards in the front line. ' Y ' company had its right resting on the Staden railway ; ' Z ' on the left were in touch with the Worcestershire Regiment ' X ' in supprt and ' W ' company were in reserve. The Brigade forward headquarters were placed at Saules Farm with the rear headquarters at Michel Farm. In this position the battalion were busy wiring and patrolling, and although the situation was described as 'quiet ' there were still casualties from sniping and gas shells. On September 24th. William became one of these casualties.

His name is carved with 181 other Essex men on the highest point of the Salient with views across the whole country to the English Channel which he crossed to fight, never to return. One "... *whom the fortune of war denied the known and honoured burial given to their comrades in death."*

Third Ypres would continue inexorably for over another month and ' the fortune of war ' would claim three more Saffron Walden 'comrades in death,' before its finale.

LANCE-CORPORAL CHARLES JAMES **SIMPSON** (43311) 2ND. ESSEX REGIMENT, KILLED IN ACTION OCTOBER 10TH. 1917, AGED 24. COMMEMORATED ON TYNE COT MEMORIAL TO THE MISSING, BELGIUM, PANELS 98 TO 99.

Charles was the eldest son of Arthur Simpson, a coachman and gardener to the late mayor of the town, Dr. Atkinson of 1 Park Place, who later moved to Avenue Terrace, Godmanchester. He was born in Saffron Walden and was, at one time, a gardener to Mr. Favill Tuke of Walden Place. In July 1915, Charles joined up. His younger brother was to follow, serving in Palestine and safely returning.

In 1916 Charles went to his battalion in France, and was wounded by a shell. He spent some time convalescing in hospital in Birmingham, returning to France in February 1917. Early October saw Charles beyond Langemark facing the road which ran to the Houthulst Forest from Poelcapelle. October 9th. at the beginning of the Battle of Poelcapelle, with the 2nd. Essex attacking at 5.20 a.m. between Poelcapelle on their right and the Ypres - Staden railway on the left. The first objective was reached and taken at 5.45 a.m. but then the left came under fire from blockhouses from the north-east of Poelcapelle. However, despite this and small-arms fire, a position was established between the first and second objectives an advance of between 400 yards on the right and 600 on the left. Casualties were heavy from the heavily fortified pillboxes.

It is not clear whether Charles was killed on October 9th. or the following day. It is clear that he was shot in the head and, according to a letter from a comrade *"... suffered no pain."* His lieutenant also wrote, describing him as *"...a good N.C.O."*

On October 12th. the British drew close to the ridge at Passchendaele. Heavy rains turned the already churned up battlefield into liquid mud, the wounded often drowning in the morass. The Germans were worried and twelve divisions destined for the Italian front were re-routed to Flanders. On October 13th. the attack was cancelled because of the rain.

PRIVATE CHARLES WILLIAM **GREEN** (63885) 11TH. ROYAL FUSILIERS, KILLED IN

ACTION 23RD. OCTOBER 1917, AGED 31. COMMEMORATED ON THE TYNE COT MEMORIAL TO THE MISSING, BELGIUM, PANELS 28 TO 30.

Charles was the only son of William, a builder, and Harriet Green of Thaxted Road. He attended the Boys British School before working for Wade and Lyall, solicitors for seventeen years, first in Saffron Walden and then commuting daily to Cornhill, London. He was described as a genial, cheerful and popular employee, a view echoed locally as he was a well-known cricketer and footballer for the town teams, particularly noted for his playing partnership at back with Osborne Whitehead (who was killed in 1915). He was single.

Charles had enlisted in early 1916 at Saffron Walden initially into the 2/5th. East Kent Regiment, The Buffs (No. 242063). He had for some months been a bombing instructor at Westbere and Margate, before going to France on September 11th. 1917, with the Royal Fusiliers. During October, the battalion were involved in the battle for Poelcapelle. On October 22nd. a Tuesday of very heavy rain, the 11th. Royal Fusiliers were called upon to hold a position taken by the 10th. Essex which had successfully attacked at 5.35 a.m. the brewery east of Poelcapelle, then Noble's Farm, Meunier House and finally Tracas Farm, until October 24th. On this day or more likely the following day while holding these positions Charles died.

A comrade, Corporal Pilgrim wrote later in December with the tragic details. He, Charles and another soldier were sitting in a trench together waiting to go over the top for a big attack. They went over and ran what seemed to be like two miles when a heavy barrage opened. They sheltered in a shell-hole. Charles was sitting with his arms upon his knees, with his head bowed when a high explosive shell burst above them. Charles and the other soldier were killed instantly by concussion, and Pilgrim was wounded. Neither of the dead men were hit and, in fact, were seen in exactly the same position some time later completely untouched. Pilgrim reiterated again what a great favourite Charles had been with his comrades because of his football prowess. Despite Charles' body being undamaged, it was never recovered.

" And each day one died or another died each week we sent out thousands that returned by hundreds wounded or gassed."

PRIVATE STANLEY **EVENETT** (764061) 28TH. LONDON REGIMENT, (ARTISTS RIFLES), KILLED IN ACTION OCTOBER 30TH.1917, AGED 25. COMMEMORATED ON TYNE COT MEMORIAL TO THE MISSING, BELGIUM, PANEL 153.

Stanley was the second of three sons born to Walter, a cabinet maker and upholsterer, and Eleanor Evenett of 53 Ashdon Road. He attended the Boys' British School, before going to work at initially at Cheffins, the auctioneer and estate agent at 7 Hill Street, before moving to Somerset in 1913. Here he was employed as assistant to Taylor and Hunt, auctioneers of Langport, Yeovil and Ilminster. Living in Langport, Stanley took an active part in the local community he had joined, playing cricket and football, singing with an excellent bass voice in the choir and bell-ringing in the church, playing with the Excelsior band, as well as being a keen angler.

In December 1916 Stanley joined up into the Artists Rifles, originally an Officer Training Corps. His two brothers, the elder, Sidney was a mechanic in the Royal Flying

Corps and the younger, Cecil, the Essex Regiment (he was later medically discharged to a Training Reserve regiment) were also in the services - and in late February 1917 he left for France from Southampton.

In June 1917 the battalion was sent as part of an infantry brigade to the 63rd. Royal Naval Division and Stanley became involved in the Second Battle of Passchendaele. On October 30th. the Division attacked with one brigade at zero hour, 5.50 a.m. The Germans dropped a counter-barrage one hundred yards behind the British barrage catching the attacking troops struggling in the mud (it was raining again) and inflicted severe casualties. The Artists Rifles were caught taking cover in Source Trench which they still held at the end of the day. At some time during this attack Stanley was killed, details of how emerged in a letter to his parents in early November.

The letter came from his best friend who had entrained with him at Southampton in February. In early October the battalion had moved some miles behind " one of the hottest places of the line." Here, in a local town, Stanley, "always thinking of his mother " had bought a lace handkerchief for her which his friend had helped choose. Then two weeks later they were moved to a camp just behind the lines in preparation for an attack. Two days later they went over the top, darting from shell-hole to shell-hole whilst under fire from rifle, heavy artillery and machine-gun. Suddenly, the friend was slightly wounded and saw at the same time, Stanley on the ground to his right hit in the chest, to which he had applied a field dressing. As he watched, Stanley died without saying a word. The friend, after digging in, returned and collected Stanley's belongings. He was " one of the best soldiers. " Stanley's body was never seen again.

Stanley's death was mourned in the two small towns he had connections with - a memorial service being held in Langport. He is also remembered on his parents' gravestone in Saffron Walden town cemetery. He was the last from our town to die at Passchendaele, a battle which remains as a monument to the British ' Tommy.'
" If mortal men could have pulled down reinforced concrete with their naked hands, these men would have done it. "

On November 10th. the battle of Passchendaele officially ended. It was a severe blow to German morale - a German general described it as, " The greatest martyrdom of the World War."

Far from Flanders, half way across the world, in conditions far removed from the mud, the cold and the incessant rain of the Salient, the main British offensive took place against Beersheba, the following day to Stanley's death. An assault by 40,000 Allied troops and its resultant success, known as the Third Battle of Gaza, the first commanded by Allenby, opened the way to Jerusalem. In this action two soldiers, friends from Saffron Walden were to die together.

PRIVATE ERNEST **FINCH** (2501054) 1ST/5TH. ESSEX REGIMENT, KILLED IN ACTION NOVEMBER 2ND. 1917, AGED 20. BURIED IN GAZA WAR CEMETERY, PALESTINE, PLOT 22 ROW C GRAVE 12.

Ernest was the second son of Mr. and Mrs. William Finch of Little Walden. Here they lived on the estate of the late Mr. E H Gibson, later moving to High Hall, Stow Maries. On leaving school, Ernest went to work for Stebbing, Leverett and Son in the Market

Square as a shop porter.

On enlistment Ernest was sent with the Egyptian Expeditionary Force in May 1916 where they extended the Suez Canal defences into the Sinai Desert. By the end of 1916 they had reached El Arish, and eventually the peninsula was cleared of all Turkish forces. On the first day of the First Battle of Gaza March 26th. 1917, Ernest was wounded at Mansura Ridge. The wound proved not to be serious and he was able to rejoin his battalion for the fresh assault in late October.

On October 31st. Allenby left a mere three divisions demonstrating in front of Gaza while moving the bulk of his forces eastward to Beersheba. On November 2nd. Ernest's battalion were ordered to attack and capture the Rafa Redoubt and Zowaid Trench. At 11 p.m. the men were given a good hot square meal with a pint of beer to wash it down. Just after midnight the battalion assembled, and waited whilst the Turkish positions were bombarded until 1 a.m. At 2.55 a.m. they moved off, with ' A ' and ' D ' companies attacking Rafa Redoubt and ' B ' company, with two platoons of ' C ' moving on Zowaid Trench. Both objectives were taken but at the heavy loss of two officers and seventy-three other ranks. The battalion history states, " *The Turks put up a wonderful fight, meeting our men with the bayonet..* " In this action Ernest and his friend, Horace Green were killed.

From the surrounding area, the bodies of the dead were collected and buried in the cemetery at Gaza, Ernest is one of over 3000 who lie there today.

PRIVATE HORACE STANLEY **GREEN** (251353) 1ST/5TH.ESSEX REGIMENT, KILLED IN ACTION NOVEMBER 2ND. 1917, AGED 23. COMMEMORATED ON JERUSALEM MEMORIAL TO THE MISSING, ISRAEL, PANELS 33 TO 39.

Horace was the youngest son of Mrs.Rose (formerly Green) of 5 Prospect Place. He attended the Boys British School before working at Horneybrooke Nurseries. He was one of the first to enlist at Chelmsford on September 2nd. 1914 and went with the Egyptian Expeditionary Force in May 1916. Unlike his friend, Ernest, Horace went through the First Battle of Gaza without a scratch, but hereafter his story is similar.

On November 14th. Horace's mother received a communication from the record office at Warley notifying her of her beloved son's death. In early February 1918 a letter from Horace's captain described how gallantly he had died. Although many bodies were recovered from the fields and ditches around the scene of their victory, Horace's was not one of them.

A verse from the poem, " *The Wadi* " is an apt epitaph,

"You that saw men die,
Wind and Stream! Reply!
After all our pain
Does no trace remain, -
None but flying
Wings, and crying
Fowl, and weeds and water sighing?"

The greatest inducer of fear in the Great War was the shell - it destroyed the body and often the mind of the front-line infantryman. But the artillerymen, themselves, were also vulnerable, a gun position although behind the front-line was a prime target for the enemy batteries.

CORPORAL DANIEL JABEZ **BACON** (23155) 275TH. SIEGE BATTERY, ROYAL GARRISON ARTILLERY, KILLED IN ACTION NOVEMBER 14TH. 1917, AGED 29. BURIED IN THE HUTS CEMETERY, DIKKEBUS, BELGIUM, PLOT 14 ROW C GRAVE 10.

Daniel was the eldest son of Mr. and Mrs. Daniel Bacon of Middle Square, Castle Street. He had been in the Army for thirteen years, nine before the war, including six of them on garrison duty in India. At the outbreak of war, Daniel had been on furlough when he received a telegram to report to Bishop's Stortford in order to rejoin his unit. He had been in France since then with only one convalescent leave at home in March 1916. In fact, Daniel had been wounded twice, coincidentally both times in the right leg, first in October 1915 and then again on 8th.September 1917. This second wound led to him spending some six weeks recovering in an American Hospital in France.

On leaving hospital, Daniel returned to his battery in the Salient as an acting-sergeant where some three weeks later his third wound proved fatal. Whilst in charge of a working party a shell fell close by and he was hit in the head by a splinter dying instantaneously. In a letter home in December his major wrote to Daniel's parents that he was, "*..a hard worker..buried in the military cemetery.*"

Today that cemetery is The Huts, where the burials are composed of 70 % artillery casualties. It was established here after the Third Battle of Ypres as field ambulances were housed here.

Life in the trenches was a constant source of danger and extreme discomfort. Apart from the obvious factors of shell and sniper fire and trench raiding, there was the cold, the mud, vermin and lice, gas and the lack of rest. In addition, with the vast amounts of unexploded armaments, the continual proximity to loaded weaponry, sometimes non-enemy directed accidents occurred.

PRIVATE CHARLES HERBERT **KETTERIDGE** (493186) 13TH. LONDON REGIMENT, (KENSINGTON), DIED NOVEMBER 17TH. 1917, AGED 23. BURIED IN MORCHIES MILITARY CEMETERY, FRANCE, ROW B GRAVE 28.

Charles was the fifth son of Mr. George Ketteridge formerly of London Road and then Great Chesterford. He worked for the Great Eastern Railway. After the outbreak of war all the sons joined up at various times, Joseph into the 9th. Essex Regiment and destined to die in 1916, Frederick, a driver in the Royal Field Artillery, James who became a sergeant but was honourably discharged as medically unfit, Alfred in the Northamptonshire Regiment, Robert a lance-corporal in the Royal Fusiliers and Richard, a driver with the Army Service Corps.

In early 1916 it was Charles' turn, initially enlisting in the Middlesex Regiment (No. 5871) before going to France in August 1917 with the 13th. London Regiment, the Kensingtons, where he took part in September in the attack on Leuze Wood. In early 1917 he received a card from Major-General Hull of his division commending him for his distinguished gallantry on the field during the latter stages of the Somme battle.

During 1917, Charles and his battalion were involved in the Battle of Arras. On Saturday November 17th. Charles was accidentally killed on the battlefield. What this accident was we do not know, but a letter from the War Office, followed by one from Charles' major confirmed this. He is buried in the small military cemetery at Morchies which was begun in April 1917 and contains 178 graves.

On November 20th. 1917, the third great offensive of that year opened - the Battle of Cambrai. Its object that city and beyond. A quarter of a million British soldiers were involved over a six mile front. It was the first time in history that the main impetus of the attack was carried out by tanks. The first day was a success with ground gained five miles, but as the battle progressed this success was not capitalised upon. It also claimed the lives of three men from Saffron Walden.

RIFLEMAN WILLIAM ALBERT **GOODWIN** (41297) 10TH. ROYAL IRISH RIFLES, KILLED IN ACTION NOVEMBER 22ND. 1917, AGED 23. COMMEMORATED ON THE CAMBRAI MEMORIAL TO THE MISSING, LOUVERVAL MILITARY CEMETERY, FRANCE, PANEL 10.

William was the son of the late James Goodwin. He lived with his widowed mother at Long Row, Thaxted Road. He attended the Boys British School and worshipped at the Baptist church. When war broke out, William was employed as a butcher with Charles R Downham in King Street, but enlisted in the Essex Regiment (32222), before later being posted to the Royal Irish Rifles.

On Thursday November 22nd. 1917, the Royal Irish Rifles were both sides of the Canal du Nord pushing towards the village of Moeuvres. Here they encoutered increasing resistance in the outskirts, and they were unable to hold their position due to heavy machine-gun fire and bombing from German trenches to the west. Inevitably, they had to withdraw to a point only half a mile from where they started. William's battalion were supported by a number of tanks, but nests of machine guns kept the infantry back from the tanks. In these circumstances Willam was killed, his body vanishing into the slough of the battlefield.

The crux of the battle became the Bourlon Ridge and the sinister Bourlon Wood. Haig insisted that this had to be taken to consolidate the Cambrai victory, but it proved too much. On November 30th. the Germans counter-attacked and the hoped-for turning point of the war was lost. Of the 44,000 Allied dead there were two more local men.

PRIVATE WILLIAM WALTER **RUSHFORTH** (17115) 7TH. SUFFOLK REGIMENT, KILLED IN ACTION NOVEMBER 30TH.1917, AGED 27. COMMEMORATED ON THE CAMBRAI MEMORIAL TO THE MISSING, LOUVERVAL MILITARY CEMETERY, PANEL 4.

William was born in Little Walden the son of Walter and Eliza Rushforth, who later moved to Cricket Field Lane, Bishop's Stortford. After schooling at the Boys' British School, he worked as a cowman, before enlisting in 1915, being taken initially into the 18th. Hussars, before joining the 7th. Suffolks.

During the Cambrai battle, after being involved in heavy fighting the battalion were relieved and sent back to brigade reserve, moving into a sunken road less than half a mile from the front-line on newly captured ground 500 yards north of Turner's Quarry to Lateau Wood. Headquarters were in the Cheshire Quarry and the situation was intended to be a temporary one as there was no real trench system. It was described as, *" an unsuitable position but the only place available. "*

On Friday November 30th. at 6.45 a.m. heavy enemy shelling commenced, including gas, and almost before there was time to stand to, German storm troopers in huge numbers from the Banteux Ravine and Mersey Street, swarmed around the Suffolk's flanks attacking from all sides. At the same time numbers of low-flying planes wheeled overhead firing machine-guns and dropping bombs. William and his comrades banded together and offered what resistance they could, but the full force of the German attack bursting on them was too much, the position was lost. Casualties were 232 including William Rushforth.

The counter attack continued the following day and British positions were overrun, despite heroic resistance. Near Moeuvres, by the canal at Lock 5, survivors of ' D ' company 13th. Essex Regiment who were trapped and beyond help decided not to surrender, but to fight it out until the end. It is possible that our next casualty was with them.

LANCE-CORPORAL FRANK **BARKER** (3/1481) 13TH. ESSEX REGIMENT, KILLED IN ACTION DECEMBER 1ST. 1917, AGED 22. COMMEMORATED ON THE CAMBRAI MEMORIAL TO THE MISSING, LOUVERVAL MILITARY CEMETERY, FRANCE, PANELS 7 AND 8.

Frank was the youngest son of Mr. and Mrs. Joseph Barker of Castle Street. He worked for John Taylor and Sons at the Chaff Works, Littlebury. It would seem likely that he was a reservist as he was mobilised at the outbreak of war. On August 4th. 1914, he was due at the local magistrates court charged with being drunk and disorderly, but it was noted that he could not appear as he had gone to join the reservists !

Frank was sent to France on January 12th. 1915 with the 2nd. battalion, where he was wounded in the thigh. Recovering from this he returned to his battalion for the Battle of the Somme where in the attack between Beaumont-Hamel and Serre, in the area of the Quadrilateral he was again wounded by bullets, this time in the face. News of this reached home in a letter from one of his friends, Pte. Frederick T Reed. However, recovery was possible and Frank returned to France, this time to the 13th. Battalion which was part of the 6th. Brigade.

On November 30th. and into the following day the Germans cut round the right flank of the 169th. Brigade cutting off a company of the 13th. Essex who fought to the death. On the left flank the Canal du Nord cut into two parts the sector held by the battalion and here casualties were heavy. In one of these actions Frank was killed. His brother Joseph, a private in the Royal Fusiliers, spent seven months in the Red Cross Hospital at Grantham with a shattered ankle, but survived the war.

At Cambrai withdrawal was the order of the day and by December 7th. the British line west of the Canal du Nord was once more what it was on 20th. November. A lieutenant wrote ".. this really is a filthy place. Corpses were touching, laid down along the fire step.. "

PRIVATE GEORGE WALTER **REED** (26951) 13TH. ESSEX REGIMENT, DIED OF WOUNDS DECEMBER 6TH. 1917, AGED 31. BURIED IN ACHIET-LE-GRAND COMMUNAL CEMETERY EXTENSION, FRANCE, PLOT 2 ROW B GRAVE 67.

George (or Walter George as it is carved on his headstone and most official records show) was the eldest son of Thomas and Emma Reed of Bell Cottage Little Walden. He enlisted in Saffron Walden, but little else is known of him, except that he was wounded in the face sometime in October/November 1916, possibly in the attack on the Quadrilateral on November 13th. spending some time in King George's Hospital London to recover. His movements in the battle of Cambrai were similar to those of Frank Barker, but we do not know where or when he was wounded. He is buried under a headstone with the inscription on it, " *In loving memory. Gone, but not forgotten. Mother.* " Of his younger brothers, William was killed in 1916 and Frank was to die early the following year.

Many of the wounded from the Cambrai conflict ended up at one of the base hospitals on the coast at Etaples. Vera Brittain, working as a nurse, wrote about the distressing suffering she witnessed, "*..the only thing one can say is that severe cases don't last long either they die soon or else improve, usually the former.* "

PRIVATE ALBERT **ARCHER** (G/20265) 17th. MIDDLESEX REGIMENT, DIED OF WOUNDS DECEMBER 10TH. 1917, AGED 36. BURIED IN ETAPLES MILITARY CEMETERY, FRANCE, PLOT 31 ROW C GRAVE 15A.

Albert was the son of John and Eliza Archer of Sewards End. He was born in Wimbish and after marriage to Ethel, lived at 4 Station Road with their five children, and working for John W Reed of New Road as a carter.

In 1916, Albert enlisted at Warley and was sent to France on October 4th. In November the battalion was involved in the attack on Redan Ridge, but Albert had suffered an accidental fracture to his arm and was sent home on convalescent leave. He returned to France on September 6th. 1917.

During the Battle of Cambrai, Albert's battalion with the 13th. Essex and 2nd. South Staffs were holding the left flank of the 2nd. Division in the vicinity of Moeuvres. The battalions were cut in two by the Canal du Nord. On Monday, December 10th. the enemy attacked down both sides of the canal, and down trenches of the Hindenburg Line west of the canal. The fighting was intense, particularly at 5 a.m. with the bridges being swept by enemy fire (the only transit across them was by ropes to help the climber), bombing, sniping and close range hand-to-hand fighting.

At the end of the day the 17th. Middlesex were moved back in support to trenches west of the canal and near the Cambrai - Bapaume road. Casualties were severe with forty killed and 138 wounded, including Albert Archer.

On Tuesday 10th. December, Ethel received a telegram informing her that her husband was in hospital dangerously ill with bullet wounds in the back and the leg. Two days later a letter followed to say that Albert had died in the afternoon of the very day the telegram had been sent. This was a devastating blow for the Archer family as Albert's two brothers, Charles and Walter had already been lost.

Albert was buried in the huge cemetery amongst the sand dunes of Etaples. His headstone inscribed, " *Sweetest thoughts for ever linger.* "

Three Christmases before there had been the famed truce, but in 1917 there was little enthusiasm for this to be repeated. It had been a grim year, French Army mutinies, the sacrificial fighting of Passchendaele and the ruined promise of Cambrai. It seemed to soldier and civilian alike as if the war would go on indefinitely, as the casualties never ceased, even in the season of so-called ' goodwill. '

PRIVATE ROWLAND FRANK GEORGE **FAIRCLOTH** (26957) 13TH. ESSEX REGIMENT, DIED OF WOUNDS DECEMBER 25TH. 1917, AGED 23. BURIED AT CABARET ROUGE BRITISH CEMETERY, SOUCHEZ, FRANCE, PLOT 24 ROW A GRAVE 4.

Rowland was the eldest son of Frank and Clara Faircloth, first of Lime Kiln Lane, Little Walden and then of 63 Victoria Avenue. He attended the Boys British School before being apprenticed to William Bell, and then working with his father, a local builder.

On March 1st. 1916, Rowland enlisted in Saffron Walden into the Essex Regiment, going to France soon after where he was transferred to the Suffolk Regiment. In early September 1916, his parents received a field postcard dated August 19th. from a Base Hospital at Rouen stating that he had been wounded and admitted, injury unknown. This was quickly followed by a letter from Rowland stating that he had been wounded in the left side of the neck by shrapnel. He explained that his battalion in the infamous High Wood, on the Somme, had been attacking the enemy positions all day, when retiring to the first-line of trenches a heavy bombardment was put up and he was hit.

On recovery Rowland returned to France, this time to the Essex Regiment, where he took part at Cambrai, .. *"in the gallant action of the Essex Regiment so praised by Haig."* Perhaps as a result of this he was given fourteen days' leave. He came home to Saffron Walden with his rifle, as he had been the only one to return with his weapon after the gallant events of November 30th. One week before Christmas, he returned to his unit and his parents never saw him again.

Nothing was heard from Rowland until in late January 1918, his parents were officially informed that he had been reported missing since Christmas Eve. Soon afterwards confirmation of his death arrived. The circumstances of Rowland's death are unknown, but in April 1918, the news came that he had died of wounds as a prisoner-of-war on Christmas Day, at Fechain, so it is safe to surmise that he was wounded, captured and taken to a German field hospital where he died.

Rowland is buried in the large cemetery at Cabaret-Rouge, his body brought to lie with over 7000 others after the Armistice. On his headstone are the words, *" In the shadow of his wings, peace, sweet peace. "* His younger brother, Frederick, a corporal in the Royal Field Artillery survived the war.

The ' Official History of the War ' for 1917 ends with these words, *"A nation cannot expect great and immediate victories unless it supplies the means, the men and the material. "* But from Saffron Walden alone, forty-nine more men from the town had died, bringing the total to 112 since hostilities broke out, and victory was still not in sight. How many more would be needed for this ' great victory ' ?

The new year of 1918 began quietly, the Western Front and elsewhere, being the scene of spasmodic, desultory fighting, raids and counter raids. The dreaded telegram did not drop through any Saffron Walden letter-box for nearly three months until March 21st. when the temporary lull was exploded in spectacular and devastating fashion.

On March 9th. the Germans commenced a series of artillery bombardments, the pre-

Loos Memorial

Thiepval Memorial to the Missing

Arras Memorial

The Menin Gate

Ploegsteert Memorial

Villers-Bretonneux Australian Memorial

Nieuport Memorial

La Ferte-sous-Jouarre Memorial

Vis-en-Artois Memorial

Pozieres Memorial

Chatham Naval Memorial, Kent

Helles Memorial,Gallipoli, Turkey

Pte. Jesse Mallyon (centre left)

Pte. Walter Archer   Pte. Frederick H. Smith

Pte. William Swan (left), Pte. George G. Swan (centre), Pte. H.F. Swan (right).

Tyne Cot Memorial, Belgium

Dedication of the the war memorial
May 7th 1921

Pte. Sidney Clarke

Cpl. Stanley Downham

Rfn. Tom Smith

2Lt. Dudley W. Hailstone

Pte. Harry Kidman

Lce-Cpl. Arthur Brand

Pte: Albert Kidman (left - about 1886)

Pte. Stanley G.Wilson

Pte. Charles Archer

Lt. Donald FG Johnson

Original French plaque from grave of
Pte. A.S. Rushworth in Gournay-en-Bray
Communal Cemetery, France

Original Cross on grave of
Pte. W. Swan in Peronne
Road Cemetery, France

Original Cross on grave of
Pte. F. Mascall in Dozinghem
Military Cemetery, Belgium

Original Cross on grave of
Pte. E.W. Mansfield in
Aubigny Communal Cemetery
Extension, France

Boys' British School Roll of Service

Pte. G.S. Pearson, St. Sever
Cemetery Extension,
Rouen, France

Lt. A.G.A. Walters, Heilly
Station Cemetery, France

Tpr. A.J. Hailstone, Shrapnel Valley
Cemetery, Turkey

Able Seaman, F.E. Wells,
Gillingham (Woodlands)
Cemetery, Kent

Lt. D.F.G. Johnson,
Bouzincourt Communal
Cemetery Extension,
France

Pte. W.E. Hill, Saffron Walden
Cemetery

2Lt. S. Walker, Friends'
Burial Ground, Saffron
Walden

Pte. F. Marking, Houplines
Communal Cemetery
Extension

Shoeing-Smith Cpl. C.S. Pearson,
Boulogne Eastern Cemetery, France

Pte. A.G. Courtneay, Savona Town Memorial, Italy

Pte. J. Pearson, Thiepval Memorial, France

Leading Seaman A. Perkin, Chatham Naval Memorial, Kent

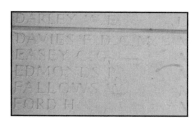

Shoeing-Smith W.H. Saward, La Ferte-sous-Jouarre Memorial, France

Pte. F. Davies, D.C.M., Loos Memorial, France

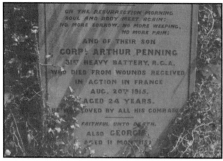

Inscription on the grave of Cpl. A.W. Penning's parents in Saffron Walden cemetery

Pte. C.L. Gardiner, Helles Memorial, Turkey

Becourt Military Cemetery, France

Highland Cemetery, Le Cateau, France

Heilly Station Cemetery, France

Jerusalem (Mount Scopus) War Cemetery, Israel

Hangard Wood Cemetery, France

Gaza War Cemetery, Palestine

1914/15 Star, British War Medal
and Victory Medal

British water bottle found in 1998 near
trenches H12 and H12a held by the Essex
Regiment 12th August 1915, Gallipoli

Boulogne Eastern Cemetery, France

Roll of Honour as it appeared on
fountain in the Market Square

Shrapnel Valley Cemetery, Gallipoli, Turkey

Roll of Honour as it appeared on
fountain in the Market Square (detail)

limimnary phase of the greatest and most essential gamble of the war - victory before the Americans arrived. Zero hour was to be 9.40 a.m. on March 21st. 1918 when three German armies began a massive attack to drive the British from the Somme, the French from the Aisne, threaten Paris and snatch victory - they called it the *"Kaiserschlacht"*, or *"The Kaiser's Battle"*. The full force of the enemy might fell upon the weak divisions of the British Third and Fifth Armies.

ABLE-SEAMAN HORACE WALTER **ERSWELL** (R/5870) ROYAL NAVAL VOLUNTEER RESERVE, " HAWKE " BATTALION, ROYAL NAVAL DIVISION, KILLED IN ACTION MARCH 21ST. 1918, AGED 28. COMMEMORATED ON THE ARRAS MEMORIAL TO THE MISSING, FRANCE, BAY 1.

Horace was one of four sons of Mr. and Mrs. Walter Erswell of 2 Market Row. He attended the Boys British School, before joining the Hawke Battalion R.N.D, probably in late 1917. When the storm broke on March 21st., the Royal Naval Division were dug in on the Flesquieres Ridge manning the vulnerable trenches at the extreme point of the bulge into the German lines. Just over a week previously they had been treated to a mustard-gas bombardment of over 200,000 shells in one day, but that seemed to pale into insignificance to the terrific bombardment that opened the assault at 4.50 a.m.

Horace's battalion was in the line between the 4th. Bedfords and the 2nd. Royal Marines and when the bombardment lifted at certain parts, the enemy were seen to attack. Some sixty men were cut off, killed or captured, but the main line of resistance was not even reached by the enemy. At 10 a.m. suffering heavy casualties from shellfire, the Hawke Battalion were supported by the Drake Battalion, but the heavy fighting continued through the rest of the day, until 4 p.m. when they were withdrawn, in all essentials with their lines intact - but, Horace was not with them.

It is a poignant aspect of this day's battle that there is a high proportion of men with no known graves. Of the 7485 British soldiers killed only 978 have individually identified headstones and Horace is not one of them. In the atmosphere of victory the enemy dead would have been buried in shell-holes or other multiple graves by the Germans.

At virtually the other end of the thirty mile front on the same day another young Saffron Walden soldier died in the ferocious enemy assault. Here the divisions were thinly spread along a line taken over from the French only eight weeks earlier.

PRIVATE FREDERICK GEORGE **WILLS** (27669) 10TH. ESSEX REGIMENT, KILLED IN ACTION MARCH 21ST. 1917, AGED 21. BURIED IN RIBEMONT COMMUNAL CEMETERY EXTENSION (AISNE), FRANCE, ROW A GRAVE 4.

Frederick was the son of Kate Wills of 26 Bridge Street. He was born in Knightsbridge, but his father, Frederick had been killed in the South African war, so the family moved to Saffron Walden. After schooling, he obtained employment as a billiard marker at the Conservative Club until he joined up on March 29th. 1916.

In February 1918, the 18th. Division were moved from the Ypres sector to Lyfontaine. On March 21st. at 4.15 a.m. Frederick and his comrades endured a five hour bombardment - *" to say it was severe would be to use a mild expression. It was wild and mad, "* before the Germans attacked between 7 a.m. and 9.50 a.m. in thick fog. With the visibility being so limited and the troops so thin on the ground, huge gaps were made in the British defences and the enemy infantry stormed through. At 11 a.m. the sun broke through to reveal Lyfontaine had been *" blown to ribbons, "* From then on the enemy advance, concentrated between Moy and La Fere was unstoppable, although pockets of resistance held them up, notably by the 18th. Division. However, at the end of the day much ground had been yielded and 20,000 soldiers had surrendered. In the 18th. Division 182 men were killed, among them Fred Wills.

At home, Mrs. Wills received information that her son had been wounded and was in hospital in France, but then all was silence. Her hopes raised, it was not until January 1919, that a further report came that he had been reported wounded, but was now listed as missing. A further letter in September 1919 from the Army Council finally extinguished any flickering hope that Mrs. Wills still retained - He was last seen wounded making his way to a Casualty Clearing Station and must now be presumed dead.

Fred lies in the beautifully maintained War Graves plot at the back of an anonymous, and rather untidy, French town cemetery with a few of his comrades. Rarely visited, his headstone records, *" To his own the well-beloved his father giveth rest. "*

On the following day the Germans made further advances, but the fighting was just as intense. Although, many British troops were captured, others defended their positions to the last man and whole villages were destroyed in their submission.

PRIVATE FRANK **REED** (118713) 36TH. COMPANY, MACHINE GUN CORPS (INFANTRY), KILLED IN ACTION MARCH 22ND. 1918, AGED 20. COMMEMORATED ON THE POZIERES MEMORIAL TO THE MISSING, FRANCE, PANELS 90 TO 93.

Frank was the youngest of three sons of the late Thomas and Emma Reed of Bell Cottage, Little Walden Road. After enlisting in Saffron Walden, he joined the Royal Army Service Corps (No. 326164), before transferring to the Machine Gun Corps.

March 1918 saw Frank serving with number 2 Section, ' B ' company - the battalion being part of the 36th. (Ulster) Division. It was in the line just south of St. Quentin opposed by a battle-hardened German division veterans of Passchendaele when the battle opened. Over the next two days there were horrendous casualties - the 36th. M.G.C. having the longest list of casualties of any M.G.C battalion. In addition, 128 are listed as missing and amongst them is the name of Frank Reed. Six months later it was defined that he had been killed in action. Frank's name is also carved on the panels of the Pozieres Memorial to the missing of the Fifth Army during this German offensive.

On March 24th. the Germans crossed the Somme and the situation worsened. Two days later at Doullens it was agreed that Marshal Foch would be given overall command of the Allied forces.

PRIVATE SIDNEY (SYDNEY) **BIRD** (43470) 1ST. ROYAL INNISKILLING FUSILIERS, DIED OF WOUNDS MARCH 26TH. 1918, AGED 31. BURIED IN ST. SOUPLET BRITISH CEMETERY, FRANCE, PLOT 1 ROW J GRAVE 26.

Sidney was the only son of William and Emma Bird of 12 Debden Road. His father, William worked for Mr. Osborne Whitehead, the monumental mason of 4 Common Hill. A pupil at the Boys' British School, Sidney then served his apprenticeship as a printer at Harts, before joining a firm in London. In 1915 he married Elizabeth, the daughter of Mr. and Mrs. Day of George Street.

In June 1916, Sidney enlisted at Kensington and after training proceded to France in 1917 with the 13th. London Regt (Kensington) (No 492366). Probably during the Battle of Arras, Sidney was wounded, but not seriously and later at Cambrai in November 1917, again, when a bullet became embedded in his shoulder. This time six weeks' convalescent leave was needed before he returned to France having been transferred to the Royal Inniskilling Fusiliers.

On the second day of Kaiserschlacht, Sidney was wounded and captured. This news reached Saffron Walden in early May, closely followed by information that he had died from those wounds in a German hospital four days later.

St. Souplet Cemetery was begun in late 1918, during the so-called " March to Victory" and Sidney's body was brought here after the Armistice. There are over 700 neat and ordered graves in a tranquil setting on a hillside outside the village which is testimony to the words on Sidney's headstone, " *Peace, perfect, peace.* " His widow, Elizabeth, later re-married becoming Mrs. Dennis and lived at 67 Radwinter Road.

Away from the struggle in France the war at sea continued. Despite success in hunting down and destroying submarines, they were being built and launched almost as rapidly as they were being sunk. Their menace continued to exact a toll on shipping of all types and sizes.

ABLE-SEAMAN ARTHUR JAMES **MEADOWS** (LONDON Z 4982) ROYAL NAVAL VOLUNTEER RESERVE, H.M.S " LADY CORY WRIGHT, " DROWNED MARCH 26TH. 1918. COMMEMORATED ON CHATHAM NAVAL MEMORIAL, KENT, PANEL 31.

Arthur was the only son of Mrs.Emma Jane Meadows of ' *Coniston* ' 63 Ashdon Road, and the late William, a printer. He went to the Boys British School and then Saffron Walden Grammar School before taking up an apprenticeship with William Bell. On February 24th.1916, on reaching his 18th. birthday he immediately joined up into the R.N.V.R, where after three months training at the Crystal Palace, he was sent to Plymouth.

He was assigned to Her Majesty's Mercantile Fleet Auxiliary, " *Lady Cory Wright* ". Built in 1906, as a Cory collier (Cory was one of the major shipping operators on the East Coast), she weighed 2516 tons and steamed along at a steady nine knots. Taken over by the Royal Navy when war was declared she was used as a mine carrier.

On March 26th. she was laying mines fourteen miles south south-west from the Lizard, when she was sunk by a torpedo from a German U-boat. There was only one survivor of the captain and thirty eight crew, sadly it was not Arthur Meadows.

In early April the news of his ' presumed loss ' reached his mother - the element of hope in that simple statement was never realised and Arthur's grave is the ' immensity of the ocean. '

One of the greatest problems of the Great War was communication. This relied on three main methods, the telephone, the wires vulnerable to shell-fire, runners, who carried messages, but all too often disappeared in the inferno of battle and carrier pigeons - wireless was still in its infancy. Inevitably, messages did not get through and tragic mistakes were commonplace, particularly resulting in what the media call ' friendly fire.'

PRIVATE GEORGE WILLIAM **SWAN** (G/21206) 1ST/6TH. EAST KENT REGIMENT, (THE BUFFS), DIED OF WOUNDS MARCH 27TH. 1918, AGED 30. BURIED IN DOULLENS COMMUNAL CEMETERY EXTENSION, FRANCE, PLOT 5 ROW A GRAVE 63.

George Swan was the eldest son of James and Jael Swan of 21 East Street. He was born in Radwinter and attended the Boys British School. Then he became a baker with David Miller of 7 London Road, before joining up in Saffron Walden in April 1916.

Surviving the Battle of Cambrai, where the battalion were in the vicinity of Havrincourt, George, in February 1918, came home on leave and married, Grace Ellen of the General Hospital, Saffron Walden. One month later she was a widow.

The German offensive had, by this time reached the British sectors held to the east of Doullens. The 6th. Buffs were part of the 12th. Division in line with the 63rd. Royal Naval Division in the neighbourhood of Mesnil and Aveluy Wood. Their function was to cover the withdrawal of the 47th. Division, which was achieved without casualties. On Wednesday March 27th. confusion reigned, George was with the Buffs at Mesnil and the R.N.D were at Martinsart, but under the command of the 37th. Brigade. A report came through that the enemy had been seen in the road between Mesnil and Martinsart, putting the R.N.D in danger of being cut off, and that the enemy had gained a foothold in Mesnil itself. This latter report proved accurate and the Buffs ejected the enemy patrol from Mesnil. At the same time the R.N.D attacked Martinsart and met fierce resistance fighting for several hours before it was realised that it was not the enemy holding the village, but the 6th. Buffs, who had advanced there in support, after clearing Mesnil !

There were many casualties of this mistake, among them George Swan who was badly wounded. Taken to one of the many military hospitals in Doullens, he died the same day. He lies with 1782 others under a headstone with a personal family message, *" In loving memory of our dear George from his sorrowing wife, parents and brother".* His brother a corporal with the Royal Field Artillery survived the war.

> *" For some go early, and some go late*
> *(A dying scream on the evening air)*
> *And who is there that believes in fate*
> *As a soul goes out in the sunset flare ? "*

March 28th. saw the dismissal of General Gough, a scapegoat for the debacle of the last few days. It also saw the death of another experienced soldier who had seen foreign service since December 1914, in Gallipoli, on the Somme, Arras, Ypres, but was only nineteen years of age.

CORPORAL SYDNEY GEORGE **HOUSDEN** (280951) 4TH. LONDON REGIMENT, (ROYAL FUSILIERS), KILLED IN ACTION MARCH 28TH. 1918, AGED 19. COMMEMORATED ON THE ARRAS MEMORIAL TO THE MISSING, FRANCE, BAY 9.

Sydney was the eldest son of George William and Susan Maria Housden of 7 Ashdon Road. He was also a Boy Scout with the 1st. Walden group. War was declared on August 4th. 1914 and in October, not to miss the adventure of a life-time, Sydney joined up at Shaftesbury Street, North London. He was aged sixteen years and five months.

On December 23rd. 1914, Sydney started his foreign service in Malta, where he stayed until August when he embarked for Egypt. Here at a camp near Alexandria, training was undertaken until October 8th. when the battalion went to Mudros, before arriving at ' W ' Beach, Cape Helles, Gallipoli on October 15th. around midnight. On October 20th. George was wounded on the march.

On recovery, George went to France on Easter Sunday 1916 where his battalion took part in the attack on Gommecourt, resulting in heavy casualties. Further heavy fighting saw George in action at Leuze Wood, the Quadrilateral, Bouleaux Wood and Hazy Trench. Surviving these he fought through Arras and spent some time in the Ypres salient. On one of his leaves, in early 1918, he took the trouble to give a talk to his old Scout troop, admitting that he had had many narrow escapes.

Once more back in the trenches, the Germans attacked on March 28th. north of the Scarpe where three London battalions were engaged. The main defences were three posts, to the north-west, Oppy Post, facing Oppy, Wood Post and to the south-east, Beatty Post. The first and last of these were overwhelmed almost immediately. Wood Post managed to hold out for an hour before it, too, succumbed. The 1/4th. Londons, a few hundred yards west of Oppy, bore the brunt of the attack, and finally Sydney's good fortune ran out.

The first news of his death reached home in a letter from the chaplain giving brief details. This was followed by another signed by eight of Sydney's friends. It described after a severe bombardment that their lines were attacked by the Germans. Their section of ten were holding a trench behind the front-line, and repulsed the enemy three times, before they eventually managed to push their way through to the right where they enfiladed the section. Sydney kept their spirits up and they were ordered to charge the communication trench at right angles to them. In this attack Sydney was hit in the head by a large shell splinter which pierced his steel helmet. He dropped dead without a murmur. He was *" a gallant soldier. "*

Still Ludendorf's *" Operation Michael "* pressed on. An officer summed up the situation, *" We kept doing counter-attacks, take that wood, lose it, take it again and so on. We kept going backwards and forwards, but it was always one step forward and three back. "*

PRIVATE GEORGE **RICHARDSON** (27090) 2ND. NORTHAMPTONSHIRE REGIMENT, DIED OF WOUNDS MARCH 28TH. 1918, AGED 23. BURIED IN NAMPS-AU-VAL BRITISH CEMETERY, FRANCE, PLOT 1 ROW C GRAVE 15.

George was one of three sons of Daniel and Emma Richardson of 5 Ashdon Road. He attended the Boys' British School and then worked for Horneybrooke Nurseries. On his marriage to Rose, he moved to 20 Mill Lane, with his wife and child before enlisting in July 1916. His brother Arthur had also joined up, destined to die a month before the war ended. Another brother, William fought with the Gloucestershire Regiment and survived.

George was sent to France in November and was involved in the desperate struggle in the Salient, at Pilckem Ridge in July 1917 and Langemark in August 1917. When the great German offensive opened, George was part of the 8th. Division defending the southern part of the river Somme in the area of Nesle and Ham. He was attached to a light trench mortar battery when he was wounded. George was hurriedly transported to a Casualty Clearing Station behind the lines, where he died.

Today he lies in a cemetery started by those Clearing Stations in 1918. Eleven miles south-west of Amiens it contains over 400 graves. On George's are the words, " *Gone, but never forgotten while life lasts.* "

On March 30th. Allied troops successfully recaptured most of Moreuil Wood in a bold counter-attack. This triumph heralded the turn of the tide for the Allies. The enemy had got to within eleven miles of Amiens after twelve consecutive days of fighting. But their impetus was stalled and their losses high.

PRIVATE GEOFFREY **SEARLE** (80966) ESSEX YEOMANRY, KILLED IN ACTION APRIL 1ST. 1918, AGED 22. COMMEMORATED ON THE POZIERES MEMORIAL TO THE MISSING, FRANCE, ADDENDA PANEL.

Geoffrey was the youngest son of Arthur James and Rosetta Searle of 5 Victoria Avenue. He attended the Boys' British School where he was described as *"popular and beloved "*, excelling at cricket and football, as well as being a member of the Peace Boy Scouts.

On 21st. June 1915, he volunteered at the age of seventeen and a half and was soon in France. taking part in 1917 in the thrilling charge of the Yeomanry at Monchy. In 1918 the stunning news came that the Essex Yeomanry were to be dismounted and turned into Corps Cyclists. This greatly dismayed all involved, as their horses were to be handed over.

When the German advance erupted the regiment were at Longpre, but because of the circumstances, they were to be cavalry again. Mounts were found and Geoffrey and his comrades moved off to support the 1st. Cavalry Division in the vicinity of Villers-Bretonneux and Bois de Vaire where they were fighting a rearguard action. They were then allocated a new sector which extended from Warfusee to Hamel, which had been held up to that time by dismounted parties of the 2nd. and 9th. Cavalry Brigades.

On Easter Monday, Geoffrey was sent with two others to take some horses to a Canadian Cavalry Brigade nearby, when two heavy shells fell in their section and nothing was seen of Geoffrey and a Pte. G W Bradley, again. The third man escaped with wounds.

Geoffrey's parents received a letter from his officer in May to say that he was missing, believed killed, " *He was in every way quite one of the best boys in the squadron...always keen to do dangerous work, always the first to volunteer.* " Out of bitter experience he added, " *It is most improbable that he was captured by the enemy.* "

There is a postscript to Geoffrey's tale. His name appears on our town memorials, on the Essex Yeomanry memorial in Chelmsford Cathedral, but not in " *Soldiers' Died in the Great War.* " When I approached the Commonwealth War Graves Commission they had no record of him. I showed them my evidence of his life and death and seventy-seven years later, Geoffrey Searle's name was added to the Pozieres Memorial, where strangely that of Pte. Bradley had been since its inception.

On this same day a few miles to the north, one of the greatest of the war poets, Isaac Rosenberg, died. An image of his contains an essence of the war,

" *Poppies whose roots are in man's veins*
Drop, and are ever dropping "

CAPTAIN HERBERT HAMPDEN **TAYLOR,** ROYAL ARMY MEDICAL CORPS, ATTACHED 4TH. ROYAL FUSILIERS, DIED OF WOUNDS APRIL 3RD. 1918, AGED 35. BURIED IN DOULLENS COMMUNAL CEMETERY EXTENSION NO. 1, FRANCE, PLOT 6 ROW A GRAVE 15.

Herbert was the third son of Louisa Taylor and the late Robert Taylor, a solicitor, of *"Athelney "* Park Farm Road, Bromley, Kent. His connection with Saffron Walden was by adoption, he was employed for some three years before the war as assistant to Dr. Hedley C Bartlett, of Bartlett and Druitt, of 53 High Street.

Herbert joined up at the outbreak of war and was attached as a doctor to the 4th. Royal Fusiliers, which went to France, as part of the 3rd. Division, on August 14th. 1914, landing at Le Havre.

During the Battle of the Somme, the battalion saw action at Delville Wood, in the attack on Guillemont, resulting in large casualties and in the front-line sector at Courcelles. From the bloodbath of the Somme, Herbert's battalion were next engaged in the Battle of Arras, and later in 1917, the hell called Passchendaele , where the Division fought valiantly in the battles of the Menin Road and Polygon Wood.

On March 21st. 1918, the 3rd. Division was back holding part of the line in front of Arras, when the last enemy 'throw' to win the war opened. The beginning of Ludendorf's spring offensive, *" Kaiserschlacht, "* was not focussed on their part of the line until March 28th., when the so-called plan, *" Mars, "* came into action. German troops in nine divisions attacked north of the River Scarpe towards Vimy Ridge, their ultimate goal the port of Boulogne, but they came up against four, perhaps, the finest divisions in the British army, which included the 3rd. Division. The attack was fortunately thwarted Cyril Falls afterwards wrote, *" If this had gone as well as the attack on 21st. March, the war might have been nearly as good as won. "*

Sometime during the great German advance on these positions to the east of Arras, Herbert was wounded. He was taken to a Canadian Stationary Hospital, at Doullens, where he died. Casualties from the German advance were so severe that a terrible strain was put upon, not only, the hospital facilities, but room in the Communal Cemetery. The French Extension (known as No. 1), of the Communal Cemetery was soon full and new ground was occupied on the opposite side (known as Extension No. 2). Today Herbert lies with over 1,000 other men in the original French extension.

On April 5th. Ludendorff called off the *" Michael "* offensive and concentrated on a second thrust *" Georgette "* scheduled for April 9th. on a line south of Armentieres, with the object of threatening the Channel ports. Although, the emphasis of the battle now shifted north, many wounded men from the earlier Picardy offensive ebbed away.

PRIVATE ALBERT EDMUND **BACON** (41848) 4TH. BEDFORDSHIRE REGIMENT, DIED OF WOUNDS APRIL 6TH. 1918, AGED 18. BURIED IN ST. HILAIRE CEMETERY AND EXTENSION, FREVENT, FRANCE, ROW B GRAVE 9.

Albert was the second son of Mr. and Mrs. Daniel Bacon of 3 Middle Square, Castle Street. After leaving school he had worked for the Anchor Brewery stores, but immediately on reaching eighteen in March 1917 had joined up at Warley and was attached to the Bedfords.

The 4th. Bedfords were part of the 63rd. Royal Naval Division and in March 1918, were holding part of the Flesquieres salient, manning the vulnerable trenches at the extreme point of the bulge into the German lines. On March 14th. during the enemy bombardment prior to the " *Kaiser's Battle* " Albert was wounded. He was taken back to a Casualty Clearing Station behind the lines at Frevent where on the Saturday, he died. He had been in France three weeks.

He was buried in the extension to the civilian cemetery, built to cope with the enormous casualties between March and August 1918.

Behind the lines were units of men, called Corps, who performed specialised duties in self-contained units. Although, not front-line troops, these duties were sometimes not without danger and casualties occurred.

LANCE-CORPORAL PERCY JOHN **BEARD** (P/1818) MILITARY FOOT POLICE, MILITARY POLICE CORPS, ATTACHED THE ARGYLL AND SUTHERLAND HIGHLANDERS, KILLED IN ACTION APRIL 13TH.1918, AGED 28. BURIED IN BOVES WEST COMMUNAL CEMETERY EXTENSION, FRANCE, ROW C GRAVE 27.

Percy was born in Grays, Essex, the son of William and Sarah Beard. William was a police officer and was stationed for several years at Saffron Walden. Percy followed in his footsteps and joined the constabulary first at Saffron Walden and then in Great Dunmow ; he also married, Alice Louise Jeffery, the eldest daughter of the late David Jeffery, a shoeing-smith, and settled in the town at 16 Castle Street.

In 1915, Percy exchanged one uniform for another and joined the Corps of Military Police. He was sent first to Ireland for about one year, before returning to England to work at several training centres around the country. In June 1917, he was sent to France.

Details of his death reached his wife in early May 1918 from a captain in the Argyll and Sutherland Highlanders. On Saturday April 13th. he had been killed outright by a shell. He continued *".. he had only been in his command a few days, but was a good man.."*

Percy is buried in the small cemetery extension above the small town of Boves, near Amiens. It contains only seventy graves.

Whilst the German offensive to the north gained dramatic penetration against the First Army in the Lys offensive, on April 20th. the first American troops were in action in the St. Mihiel salient. Also, on this day at the southern edge of the Lys offensive, the one hundredth man from Saffron Walden had been killed, according to a local paper. (this is inaccurate, not all casualties were known at this time, it should have read the one hundred and twenty-fifth.)

PRIVATE GEORGE EDWARD **MOORE** (30198) 1ST. BATTALION MACHINE GUN CORPS (INFANTRY), KILLED IN ACTION APRIL 20TH. 1918, AGED 28. COMMEMORATED ON THE LOOS MEMORIAL TO THE MISSING, FRANCE, PANEL 136.

George was the son of the late Mr. Edward Moore. His mother had re-married Alfred Ernest Wright, a boot and shoe-maker, of 7 Museum Street. After leaving school he became an apprentice printer with Harts, before obtaining work with the Bucks and Berks Free Press at High Wycombe. Whilst here he met and married on Christmas Day 1913 at Hazlemere church, Mildred Alice, and they set up home at The Common, Totteridge, High Wycombe. Here he became active in the choir of St. Andrew's, took part in musical concerts, was manager of the church room, as well as playing cricket and football.

On December 2nd. 1914 George joined up at Oxford into the 3rd. Suffolk Regiment (No. 16793). He was in training with the battalion at Felixstowe until May 3rd. 1915 when he went to France. George was involved in the heavy fighting round Ypres and at Hooge. In July he was gassed and received shrapnel wounds and spent some weeks recovering in Leicester hospital. On recovery he was transferred to the Machine Gun Corps at Grantham and then, Mansfield, returning to France on Easter Monday 1917. On July 20th. 1917, he was buried in a shell explosion and wounded in his back and legs, coming home for a second convalescent leave at a home in Llandudno.

On October 29th. 1917, George returned to France for the final time. In his last letter home he wrote that he expected to get leave home soon, *"...but things are very busy out in France. "* So this proved to be, and in the Battle of Bethune, George, advancing in an attack was killed. The lieutenant of his section who wrote assured his widow there was no pain. His body was never found. A brother, William with the King's Royal Rifle Corps was more lucky, he came home.

The huge casualties of the preceding three and a half years had decimated the officer ranks - 27 % of deaths were officers, as opposed to 18 % other ranks - but it gave the opportunity for the able, educated N.C.O. or even ordinary soldier to rise from the ranks to a commission. The next death from our town was of the tenth ex-Boys' British School pupil so to do.

SECOND-LIEUTENANT ARNOLD HENRY **CHIPPERFIELD**, 12TH. MIDDLESEX REGIMENT, ATTACHED 2ND/2ND. LONDON REGIMENT, (ROYAL FUSILIERS), KILLED IN ACTION APRIL 24TH. 1918, AGED 22. COMMEMORATED ON POZIERES MEMORIAL TO THE MISSING, FRANCE, PANELS 60 AND 61.

Arnold was the fourth son of Thomas William, a business manager, and Beatrice Chipperfield of 46 Radwinter Road, later 57 Buxton Road, Chingford. Educated at the Boys' British School, he then joined a London firm as an accounts clerk. On 9th. September 1914, with thirty-six other employees he enlisted at the East Surrey depot, being posted to the 7th. Lincolnshire Regiment.

It is interesting to note the prevailing optimism of these early days of the war. Arnold's attestation form shows that he had signed for a term of three years or until the war is over. The recruiting-sergeant has added in his own writing, *"...if however the war is over in less than three years you will be discharged with all convenient speed. "*

A period of training led on July 14th. 1915, to Arnold embarking for to France where he was wounded slightly by gunshot in the right arm in February 1916. His stay at 15 Casualty Clearing Station was brief, and five days later he was discharged as fit. By

June 1916 through intelligence and diligence, he had attained the rank of lance-corporal. He fought in the Somme battles and at Arras and in late 1916 was recommended by his Commanding Officer for a commission. He came home to the regiment's depot on December 22nd. before being attached to 4 Officer Cadet battalion at Oxford. On May 29th.1917 was gazetted as a temporary second-lieutenant in the 5th. Middlesex Regiment, being transferred to the Service battalion in October 1917. Just before Christmas, Arnold came home on what was to be his last leave. In March 1918, he was attached to the 2/2nd. London Regiment (Royal Fusiliers), part of the 53rd. Division. On April 24th. the Germans attacked Villers-Bretonneux with the help of thirteen tanks and by 10 a.m. the village had fallen. The Allies responded with their tanks, in what was the first tank versus tank battle in history. However, in this historic action Arnold was lost.

It was the second tragedy to strike the Chipperfield family as their son, Hubert had died in 1916. Three other brothers served and survived - William with the Essex Regiment in Egypt, Stanley a corporal in the North Staffs, although once wounded and the other with the Norfolks in Ireland.

From the same town, the same school, on the same day, in the same area and in the same regiment, another soldier lay down his life. Although a little younger than Arnold, they also share the same fate in death. Both bodies were never found and both their names appear on the same memorial, separated only by their rank.

Private Walter Arthur **CRABB** (G/57767) 2nd. Middlesex Regiment, killed in action April 24th. 1918, aged 18. Commemorated on the Pozieres Memorial to the Missing, France, Panels 60 and 61.

Walter Crabb was born in Islington, the son of Walter and Ella Louisa Crabb of Hounslow. At some time Mr. Crabb's job brought him to Saffron Walden, where he worked for William Bell and Sons, the builders, of South Road and lived at 1 Victoria Gardens. Walter attended the Boys' British School, before enlisting in Hounslow when he was eighteen.

On the night of April 23rd/24th. Walter's battalion as part of the 8th. Division, took over front-line trenches on the Villers-Bretonneux - Lamotte road, just east of the cemetery. It was his first action. At 3.45 a.m. on the 24th. an intense artillery and trench-mortar bombardment began, accompanied by a barrage of lachrymatory gas shells. Lasting two hours, before lifting on the rear lines, these caused many front-line casualties. As the barrage lifted, on the right, the troops were attacked by two hostile tanks firing machine-guns. The tanks were masked by smoke-shells and were able to manoeuvre and enfilade the Middlesex trenches, causing further heavy casualties. A third tank appeared followed by enemy infantry with flame-throwers (flammenwerfer). Nothing could stop the tanks and they passed over the front-line trenches, but a few survivors managed to hide in the railway cutting where they were again heavily shelled. Eventually, they withdrew still under heavy fire to battalion headquarters.

Things were little better on the left. Because of the smoke the tanks and infantry were not seen until they were only twenty yards away. The flammenwerfer was shot down, but the enemy still surged on. The 2nd. Royal Berks formed a defensive flank and the remnants of the battalion eventually also withdrew. In the inferno of shell, gas, smoke and flame, Walter was killed.

On the following day Villers-Bretonneux was recaptured and Ludendorf's final effort to secure Amiens was beginning to falter.

RIFLEMAN ARTHUR WILLIAM **HALLS** (324839) 6TH. LONDON REGIMENT, (RIFLES), KILLED IN ACTION APRIL 25TH. 1918, AGED 24. BURIED IN HANGARD WOOD BRITISH CEMETERY, HANGARD, FRANCE, PLOT 1 ROW D GRAVE 14.

Arthur was one of six brothers who lived at St. Aylett's Cottages, Ashdon. His father was bailiff to Butler's Farm and on leaving school, Arthur joined him as a horsekeeper. On October 24th. with his brother, Ben he enlisted, both joining the Essex Yeomanry, Arthur as No. 1500.

At some stage, both Ben and Arthur were transferred at the same time to the 6th. City of London Battalion (Rifles), known as the " *Cast-Iron Sixth.* " In January 1918, the 1/6th. London and the 2/6th. London were merged and became part of the 174th. Brigade, the 58th. Division. On April 24th. they were in positions south of Villers-Bretonneux and on the extreme right of the British army.

Concealed by fog and aided by tanks the enemy attacked. The 58th. Division and the 8th. bore the full force of the German attack and casualties were significant. Driven back, the fighting continued throughout the day, until at 10 p.m. by moonlight, the 8th., 58th. and the 5th. Australian Divisions endeavoured to counter-attack and regain ground lost earlier that day.

The 8th Division and the 5th. Australian Division attacked Villers-Bretonneux and the 58th., Hangard Wood. Fighting continued over the next two days, until the British line originally held was successfully restored. However, on April 25th., Arthur was killed in the vicinity of Hangard Wood. Today he rests in the small cemetery started in August 1918. There are 141 graves, including a Victoria Cross winner, Pte. J B Croak, from Newfoundland. His inscription is memorable and appropriate, " *Do you wish to show your gratitude ? Kneel down and pray for my soul.* "

Ben Halls, having witnessed his brother's death had only four more months to live, and of the six Halls' brothers only one reached old age.

On April 29th. 1918, thirteen German divisions attacked along a ten mile front. They drove the Allies back, but only a small distance and the offensive was halted - it was a spent force and the gamble had failed. A gamble that caused 50, 000 deaths in three weeks fighting.

RIFLEMAN ARTHUR JOHN **BROWN** (40906) 2ND. RIFLE BRIGADE, DIED OF WOUNDS MAY 4TH. 1918, AGED 18. BURIED IN CROUY BRITISH CEMETERY, FRANCE, PLOT 2 ROW B GRAVE 3.

Arthur was born at Lambourne, Essex, the only son of Arthur Edward and Ellen (Nellie) Elizabeth Brown. Mr. Brown was a police officer at Saffron Walden, before gaining promotion to Inspector at Ongar in 1915. Arthur attended the Boys' British School and then worked for four years as a clerk to Mr. H J Cheffins, auctioneer and estate agents of 7 Hill Street.

In October 1917 on becoming eighteen Arthur enlisted into the Queen's Westminster

Rifles (16th. London Regiment) as No. 557033. On going to France he was transferred to the Rifle Brigade who in April 1918 were to be found in the Hangard - Villers-Bretonneux sector.

On April 20th, the battalion relieved, in the line, portions of the 55th., 56th. Divisions and the 14th. Australian Brigade, and ensconced themselves on a line north of the Villers-Bretonneux - Warfusee highway. On 24th. the Germans attacked and took Villers-Bretonneux and the Rifle Brigade were exposed to a very heavy barrage from 3.45 a.m. On the 26th. April orders were received for Arthur and his comrades to clear the area and establish themselves outside the village to the east and the south. In doing this they met with considerable resistance until the 28th. when they were relieved and marched back to billets.

Casualties were one officer and eighteen other ranks killed and ninety-six wounded. One of these was Arthur Brown who at some time over these four days had been severely wounded in the body, head and legs, after being hit by a shell.

He was taken back to a Casualty Clearing Station, near Crouy, where medical units had come that April where he died on Saturday May 4th. He is buried in the largest cemetery in the area - some 740 graves - in a hillside, rural setting. His inscription reads, " *Only and dearly loved son of Arthur and Nellie Brown. Ongar, Essex.* "

A few weeks earlier, a raid on Zeebrugge had taken place. Blockships were sunk at the entrance to the enemy submarine refuge to entrap them. Propaganda hailed it as a great success, but 200 men died and 400 wounded. The dangers of the ocean were not to be ignored.

CHIEF STEWARD WILLIAM MATTHEW **HEWSON**, M.M.R. H. MERCANTILE MARINE RESERVE, H.M.S " ISONZO, " ACCIDENTALLY DROWNED MAY 7TH. 1918. COMMEMORATED ON THE PLYMOUTH NAVAL MEMORIAL, DEVON, 31.

William was the son of Mrs. Florrie Andrew, a widow, who lived at Melbourne House, 94 Debden Road. He had been in the Merchant Navy since leaving school, and on the outbreak of war was in the Mercantile Marine Reserve. This was a system where if you left the Merchant Navy you could opt for going on the Reserve, or if you had not fulfilled your time, you were put on the Reserve and could be called up in the time of war. When you joined the Merchant Navy you signed up for seven and five years or five and seven years.

William became Chief Steward on the H.M.S. " *Isonzo,*" a merchant ship of 1,728 gross tonnage, built in 1898 and called the " *Isis* " used by its owners P and O, as a mail and shuttle service between Port Said and Brindisi. When the war broke out, the "*Isis*" was in Port Said, the Brindisi service being one of the first to be suspended, before being ordered to Malta to lay up. She reached the island without mishap, though she unwittingly ran through a minefield on the way. From 18th. June 1915, she was requisitioned by the Royal Navy and re-named " *Isis* " as there was already an old cruiser named " *Isonzo,* " utilised as a fleet auxiliary hired for naval service as a fast despatch and fleet messenger ship - she was capable of twenty-two knots in moderate weather.

On May 7th. 1918, " *Isonzo* " was at the Royal Naval Depot, Malta. At 2.30 p.m. on a warm, calm day, a sailing boat, with ten sailors, including William Hewson, left the

100

ship for Calafrana. The ship's log at 10 p.m. that night recorded that the, " *sailing boat not arrived back inquiries made.* " It was not until the following day that it was ascertained that the boat had been involved in an accident in Valetta Harbour which resulted in all ten sailors being drowned among them William Hewson.

In 1914 air warfare had been in its infancy, yet by 1918 plans were in existence to bomb the heart of Germany itself. Military technology had made great steps forward in those eventful years. However, during that time 50,000 airmen had been killed, not least as a result of the rudimentary machines they flew. In 1917 the life expectancy of a pilot on the Western Front was between eleven days and three weeks. Many however never got to see active service, becoming tragic victims of the training involved in becoming a pilot.

SECOND-LIEUTENANT STEPHEN **WALKER,** CAMBRIDGESHIRE REGIMENT AND ROYAL AIR FORCE, DIED MAY 14TH. 1918, AGED 25. BURIED FRIENDS' BURIAL GROUND, SAFFRON WALDEN, ESSEX.

Stephen Walker was the third son of John Edward and Anna Phillis Walker of *"Hazelwood"* Mount Pleasant Road. Born on January 24th. 1893, he attended the Friends' School in Saffron Walden from 1903 to 1904, and other Friends' Schools at Ackworth and Bootham, Yorkshire. After leaving school Stephen trained to be a chartered accountant qualifying in 1916. His father, meanwhile, a schoolmaster had become the Headmaster at Saffron Walden Friends' School.

Also in 1916, Stephen despite his religious beliefs joined up and spent six months in France as a motor despatch rider possibly with the Royal Flying Corps, before being recommended for a commission and returning to England for training with the Suffolk regiment. He underwent a cadet course at Cambridge before being gazetted as a second-lieutenant into the Cambridgshire Regiment, a Territorial force wing of the Suffolks, to whom he was attached for some months.

In the Autumn of 1917, Stephen joined the Royal Air Force to become a pilot. This proceded well and by Tuesday May 14th. 1918, he had completed twenty hours solo and eleven hours dual flight and had just graduated for a further course in Scotland when disaster struck at 6.15 p.m. at Duxford his aircraft crashed and Stephen was killed instantly.

The inquest the following day provided the details of the tragedy. A major in the Royal Air Force gave evidence that he had flown the aircraft involved for thirty minutes previously to Stephen and everything was working well. A lieutenant saw it leave the ground at 5.05 p.m. with Stephen at the controls. Some time later he heard the engine cut out at 500 feet and glide downwards. It was apparent that Stephen was trying to turn the machine when it spun out of control and hit the ground bursting into flames.

The medical evidence, given by a doctor of the R.A.M.C was that Stephen's skull had been badly fractured causing instantaneous death, so mercifully he was dead before the flames engulfed him.

On Friday 17th. May, Stephen was buried in the tranquillity of the Burial Ground behind the Friends' Meeting House in the High Street. His name appears on the memorial in the Friends' School (the only one that is also on the town memorial). One of his brothers, Edmund, a captain in the Cambridgeshire Regiment was awarded the Military Cross at St. Julien in July 1917.

On the headstone of a more famous comrade, Major J T McCudden, V.C. are words fitting to remember Stephen Walker who died so near his home and family,

> " Fly on, dear boy, from this dark world of strife,
> on to the promised land, to eternal life. "

The small village of Morlancourt in France is evidence of the changing fortunes of war. For most of the first part of the conflict it lay well in the Allied rear containing billeting and medical facilities, but in March 1918 the German advance turned it into a front-line position where five days after Stephen Walker's death, another Saffron Walden soldier died, wearing the famous ' Diggers ' slouch hat.

LIEUTENANT ARTHUR GEORGE ALAN **WALTERS** (WATERS), 18TH. BATTALION, AUSTRALIAN IMPERIAL FORCE, KILLED IN ACTION MAY 19TH. 1918, AGED 36. BURIED IN HEILLY STATION CEMETERY, MERICOURT L'ABBE, FRANCE, PLOT 2 ROW H GRAVE 2.

Arthur was the son of Eliza Walters of 47 Radwinter Road, and the late George, a carpenter. In 1911, he emigrated to Australia and became a policeman in Newton, Sydney. In May 1915 he responded to the calls from his 'Mother Country' and enlisted into the 18th. Battalion, 2nd. Reinforcements and in June as private 1769 embarked on the H.M.A.T A61 " Kanowna " for Gallipoli where he landed in August.

Here Arthur distinguished himself being promoted to sergeant on August 23rd. and to Company Sergeant Major in September. After surviving the privations of the peninsula Arthur disembarked at Alexandria via Mudros, before embarking for France in March 1916 and arriving at Marseilles in September, part of urgently needed reinforcements. He had now obtained a commission as a second-lieutenant. In late June he took part in a night raid on enemy trenches, mentioned in the Official History, and it was not long before in December 1916 that he was gazetted as a full lieutenant.

During this period Arthur was detailed for further training at Rollestone and Tidworth, and it is most likely that during this time in England that he was married to Edie. Their time together however was short-lived and in May 1917, he rejoined his battalion at Etaples, resuming duty on June 5th. 1917.

In February 1918, Arthur came home for a fortnight's leave to his wife in Stanley Road, Teddington. It was to be the last time she would see him. His battalion were in the vicinity of Morlancourt attempting to hold back the enemy, when Arthur rejoined them. On the morning of May 19th. Arthur led an attack on the German trenches, but in the resultant bombardment was killed by shell-fire. His, Commanding Officer, wrote of him, " (he)....had up to the time of his death, shewn great dash and bravery. "

Arthur was buried in a cemetery started near three Casualty Clearing Stations and near the railway that constantly ferried the wounded to the coast, and if fortunate, home. His headstone inscription is poignantly personal, " God give me patience and strength, beloved, until we meet again. Edie. "

In France, at long last the Allies counter-attacked when on June 11th., a number of French and American divisions met with some success. But June also saw the advent of a new, and even greater killer than the war - influenza. In India and in Britain, the epidemic that was to kill untold millions began, soon to spread to the Western Front, where another town soldier was to receive wounds that led to illness and death.

PRIVATE WILLIAM **WISKEN** (32348) 1ST. ESSEX REGIMENT, DIED JULY 5TH. 1918, AGED 29. BURIED IN SAFFRON WALDEN TOWN CEMETERY, RADWINTER ROAD, ESSEX, PLOT 24 GRAVE 30.

William was the son of Emily Barker of 16 Mill Lane Ashdon Road. He attended the Boys British School where on leaving he obtained a job as a goods porter at the town station. At some stage, William's mother died and he went to live with an uncle, James at 6 Debden Road. In early 1915, he enlisted and went to France in 1916, fighting at Delville Wood and Guedecourt.

In May, June and July 1918, the battalion were in the area of Bucquoy, mainly assisting in holding the line so although it is not known when William was wounded, it is tragically certain that he developed trench fever and pneumonia and died in hospital in Brighton.

His body was brought back to Saffron Walden and buried on Wednesday July 10th. His inscription reads, simply but eloquently, *" He answered the call. "*

Although the Western Front was experiencing a relatively quiet time before the advance to victory - indeed one regimental history records, *" the whole of July was practically without incident "*- local attacks, raiding parties still resulted in a constant trickle of casualties.

SECOND-LIEUTENANT DUDLEY WILLIAM **HAILSTONE,** 1ST. DUKE OF CORNWALL'S LIGHT INFANTRY, KILLED IN ACTION JULY 7TH. 1918, AGED 21. BURIED IN THIENNES BRITISH CEMETERY, FRANCE, ROW D GRAVE 12.

Dudley was the second son of Oliver and Mary Hailstone. Although born in Witham, when the family moved to Saffron Walden, Dudley attended the Boys British School and Saffron Walden Grammar School where he excelled at sports, cricket and football, of which he was captain and running where he won the school challenge cup in 1913. (Indeed, Sports Day 1913 saw Dudley competing in seven events !). His father was a police superintendant at Saffron Walden who on retirement became Assistant Clerk to the Justices and Joint Clerk to the Tribunal at Brighouse, Yorkshire, living in Southowram, Halifax.

On leaving school Dudley joined the Union Assurance Society, Cornhill, London and lived at Romford, but his career was cut short by the outbreak of war and on September 1st. 1914, aged seventeen, he enlisted in the London Irish Rifles (1/18th. London Regiment). He rose rapidly through the ranks becoming a Lance-Sergeant by the time that the battalion first served in France, where they landed at Le Havre 23rd. June 1916. On 25th. November 1916 they were sent to Salonica. As well as being a first-class shot, winning a silver cup, promotion followed again in April 1917 to Sergeant. In July 1917 he was sent to England to take up a commission at 26th. Training Reserve Brigade cadet school in Berkhampstead. Duly, on December 18th. 1917, he was gazetted a temporary second-lieutenant in the 3rd. D.C.L.I. at Felixstowe. Posted then to the 1st. battalion meant Dudley had to journey to Italy, where they were in Corps

Reserve at Busiago.

On February 3rd. 1918 the battalion took over from 12th. Glosters in a quiet sector in the Piave area, the only event of note being two men slightly wounded by shrapnel. This good fortune was not to last, in April the battalion returned to France. Dudley came home on leave in May, before returning to his comrades in the area of Vieux Berquin and the River Bourre on July 4th. Here in the line local attacks took place up and down it in an attempt to secure the area.

According to a letter later received by his parents from a Captain A Gough, on the night of July 5th/6th. Dudley proceded with his company from La Lacque Camp to the front-line trenches. Here they were employed as a working party to improve the position in front of the trenches when an enemy machine-gun opened fire and he was instantly killed. He spoke no words, suffered no pain and was five days from his twenty-first birthday. Dudley was buried in a neighbouring military cemetery, where he lies today in the shade of the Forest of Nieppe.

Dudley's brother, Kenneth Charles, followed a similar path joining up and attaining the rank of sergeant, before being gazetted as a second-lieutenant in the Hertfordshire Yeomanry. Here the parallel ends - he survived the war.

The effect of the war on every family, particularly the womenfolk, throughout the country continued, not just through the growing numbers of dead, wounded and the maimed, physically and mentally, but the demands on the male population to enlist, either voluntarily or by conscription. Brother followed brother, and even father after son.

PRIVATE BERT WILLIAM **KETTERIDGE** (G/68273) 8TH. ROYAL WEST SURREY REGIMENT, (THE QUEENS), DIED OF WOUNDS JULY 10TH. 1918, AGED 19. BURIED IN BULLY-GRENAY COMMUNAL CEMETERY BRITISH EXTENSION, FRANCE, PLOT 5 ROW F GRAVE 9.

Bert (or Bertie) was the younger son of Mr. and Mrs. Frank William Ketteridge of 1 Westfields, a painter employed for many years by Miss Gibson. He was educated at the Boys British School, before gaining employment as a butcher with Augustus V Britton in Gold Street. He was also a member of the congregation of the Baptist church.

After the outbreak of war, Bert's elder brother, Frank joined the Durham Light Infantry, going to France in December 1917. In September 1917 on attaining the age of eighteen, Bert was called up and was sent to France at Easter 1918. His battalion from May were in the vicinity of Maroc, where they were in receipt of frequent warnings that the enemy were about to attack. These threats never materialised as the battalion spent the whole summer in this, "... *comparatively quiet part of the line.* "

Quiet is a relative term as we have all too frequently seen - there was always desultory shelling and on Tuesday July 9th. Bert was hit, dying the following day. Three weeks previously he had heard that his father, Frank had been called up into the Essex Regiment.

Bert is buried with over 700 others in the British extension to the civilian cemetery. Nearby is a French military plot, allies in death, as in life. Both Bert's father and brother came home to Saffron Walden at the end of hostilities.

August 1918 saw the turn of the tide in the Great War. The Germans were almost played out and at all levels from General to private there was a loss of morale and nerve, as well as a sense of failure. The month also saw the deaths of four more men from Saffron Walden. On August 8th. the Allies opened a new assault - *" the march to victory. "*

SERGEANT ARTHUR GEORGE **BEAVIS** (23206) 2ND. KING'S OWN YORKSHIRE LIGHT INFANTRY, KILLED IN ACTION AUGUST 20TH. 1918, AGED 40. BURIED IN HEATH CEMETERY, HARBONNIERES, FRANCE, PLOT 3 ROW F GRAVE 1.

Arthur was born in Haverhill the second son of George and Mary Ann Beavis, the family later moving to 1 Ingleside Place, Saffron Walden. After school Arthur joined the 12th. Hussars (13975), with whom he served for twelve years. On the outbreak Arthur immediately rejoined at Tottenham, later being posted to the King's Own Yorkshire Light Infantry (K.O.Y.L.I) . His elder brother had enlisted in the Cambridgeshire Regiment with whom he was awarded the Italian Bronze Medal for Valour in September 1916, before becoming a corporal in the Royal Engineers, the Railway Operations Division. In January 1917, he was mentioned in dispatches.

In January 1918, a local newspaper reported brothers meeting on the " field of battle. " The facts were less prosaic. On Christmas Eve 1917, Arthur had just returned from a school of instruction. Three miles away was his brother whom he had not seen for sixteen years. On Christmas Day, to Arthur's surprise and delight his brother found him and they enjoyed a meal together in the headquarters Sergeants' Mess. It was the last time they would see one another.

August 17th., saw Arthur and his battalion being bussed to Harbonnieres to relieve the 17th. A.I.F. An hostile enemy counter-attack was imminent, so they took over a line of trenches just east of Framerville and south of Herleville. At 10.15 a.m. on 19th. August a heavy enemy bombardment was followed by an attack on two posts west of the crucifix. Later that day a counter-attack reoccupied these posts.

The following day, these same posts were attacked again, and amongst the dead were one officer, 2nd. Lieutenant Rendel Powell and Arthur Beavis. The regimental diary records, *"... casualties up to noon, three other ranks killed, seven wounded. About 1 p.m. the enemy put down a heavy strafe on the Crucifix posts which forced ' B ' company to evacuate them for a time. At dusk all was readjusted. We suffered some casualties owing to the barrage.."*

After the war Arthur's body, and that of his officer, were brought with 1860 others to a cemetery formed by the side of the busy, main Amiens - St. Quentin road, not far from where they fell.

Amongst the Allies in August things seemed to be going well ; there was a real sense of optimism that the war would end this year and the headlines in the papers reflected this. Yet for countless families these patriotic words could not hide the daily casualty lists, nor assuage their grief and loss.

PRIVATE THOMAS ARTHUR **CORNELL** (34882) 1ST. ESSEX REGIMENT, KILLED IN ACTION AUGUST 23RD. 1918, AGED 35. COMMEMORATED ON THE VIS-EN-ARTOIS MEMORIAL TO THE MISSING, FRANCE, PANEL 7.

Thomas was the third son of Mr. and Mrs. James Cornell of Debden Road. After leaving school he obtained work as a bricklayer's labourer with the Great Eastern Railway and also got married, living at 26 Thaxted Road with his wife and, later, one child.

In January 1917, Thomas went to France with the Suffolk Regiment (No. 28384) and at some later stage was transferred to the 1st. Essex. In August 1918 the battalion were manning trenches to the north of Achiet-le-Petit. It was planned that there should be a series of strong assaults on practically the whole front of thirty-three miles from the British junction with the French, north of Lihons, to Mercatel near the Hindenburg Line.

Thomas' battalion were to attack near the neighbouring village of Achiet-le-Grand, a strongly held point as it was on a spur to the south. The Essex were on the right of the attack and had to also capture a section of railway cutting and the roads beyond. Friday August 23rd. was one of the hottest days of the year, when at 11 a.m. a creeping barrage opened up. Eight minutes later the soldiers moved forward, attacking in four waves, two companies in the front-line and two in support. They moved as closely as possible to the barrage-line, but the battalion still suffered badly from machine-gun fire. Amongst the dead was Thomas Cornell.

His body never found, he is commemorated in stone with 160 other Essex comrades. Both his brothers returned home, George to his job as a porter at Union House and Albert, from a German prisoner-of-war camp.

On this same day, some hundred miles to the south in a base hospital at Rouen, another soldier from the town lost his fight for life.

SERGEANT GEORGE **FINCH** (325006) 9TH. ESSEX REGIMENT, DIED OF WOUNDS AUGUST 23RD. 1918, AGED 31. BURIED IN ST.SEVER CEMETERY EXTENSION, ROUEN, FRANCE, BLOCK Q PLOT 3 ROW I GRAVE 5.

George was born in Saffron Walden the eldest son of Mr. and Mrs. William Finch who later moved to Little Walden, and thence to High Hall, Stow Maries.

We know little of George's military career, except that he was awarded the Territorial Force War Medal and that the same month his brother, Ernest was killed in Palestine, George was married.

In early August 1918, George and his battalion were involved in the so-called "advance to victory" being in the area between Morlancourt and the river Ancre. On August 10th., the 9th. Essex were sent from the 35th. Brigade to strengthen the 37th. in the centre of the former front-line of the Amiens defences. On August 13th., they advanced assisted by tanks and behind a creeping barrage, but suffered heavy casualties from machine-gun fire which swept the ridge they had to advance up. This fire was so deadly, that the battalion were driven back to the far side of the Bray to Meaulte road. Some time during this period of prolonged conflict, George was seriously wounded. Taken to one of the base hospitals at Rouen, he died and was buried in the huge cemetery extension.

Two days later, Mametz Wood, of which Robert Graves wrote, *" Today I found in Mametz Wood a certain cure for lust of blood, "* was finally captured. Near a copse, far smaller, but as deadly, a little to the south-west, another soldier, in the words of a patriotic little book of poems by a ' Tommy ', *" went west. "*

RIFLEMAN BENJAMIN THOMAS **HALLS** (324846) 6TH. LONDON REGIMENT, (RIFLES),

KILLED IN ACTION AUGUST 25TH. 1918, AGED 22. COMMEMORATED ON THE VIS-EN-ARTOIS MEMORIAL TO THE MISSING, FRANCE, PANEL 10.

A farm labourer before the war, Ben's story is inextricably linked with that of his brother, Arthur, who died in April 1918. The two boys joined the Essex Yeomanry (No. 1494) together on the same day and fought side by side in the " *Cast-Iron Sixth* " until Arthur's death.

In August 1918, Ben was in the region of Franvillers, in Round Wood, re-fitting, reorganising and training, amidst rumours of the impending push. On August 23rd. the battalion was sent to Mirvaux, and the following day to the former British front-line. Thence followed a succession of short moves, culminating at 2 a.m. on the morning of August 25th., Ben and his friends found themselves a mile to the east of Morlancourt.

At 8.30 a.m. the battalion moved on some German positions immediately before a deep depression known, ironically, as " Happy Valley. " At 6 p.m. they moved again in artillery formation to a support position, near a small wood called Trigger Wood, preparing for the attack which was planned for later that evening. However, when night set in it was wet and very dark, the men had great difficulty in reaching the jumping-off position, so the attack was postponed to the morning. Ben never took part in that attack ; at some time during the 25th. he was killed, probably by a stray shell. He was never found.

Continuous attack along the whole of the front-line was Foch's order of the day. In the St. Mihiel salient, the Americans achieved a degree of success, but in the British and French sectors despite the urge to push forward, the enemy still held firm.

SERGEANT REGINALD **GILLING** (206354) 26TH. ROYAL WELCH FUSILIERS, KILLED IN ACTION SEPTEMBER 15TH. 1918, AGED 34. BURIED IN " Y " FARM MILITARY CEMETERY, BOIS GRENIER, FRANCE, ROW M GRAVE 2.

Reginald was the youngest son of John, a chemist and Ellen Mary Gilling of 6 Market Hill. He attended Saffron Walden Grammar School before being articled to an auctioneers and valuers, Bond and Sons, at Ipswich. After this he worked for a Mr. Long at Saxmundham, and latterly on the estate of Mr. Kenneth Clarke of Sudbourne Hall.

On the outbreak of war, Reginald lived in Orford, immediately enlisting in the 1/1st. Suffolk Yeomanry (No. 320163) at Woodbridge. In September 1915 as dismounted troops, the Yeomanry sailed from Liverpool in the " *Olympic* " for Gallipoli, landing at Anzac Beach on September 25th. Here, Reginald was wounded and sent to hospital in Cairo, where he heard the news of his brother, Ernest's death.

After recovery, Reginald became part of the 3rd. Dismounted Brigade guarding the Suez Canal defences until July 1916 when his regiment was sent to France where the Yeomanry became the 15th. Battalion, the Suffolk Regiment. In August 1918 he came home for his first leave after three and a half years active service. It was almost as if the fates were to give his family one last chance to see him. On his return he was transferred to the Royal Welch Fusiliers who were in the vicinity of Lestrem. Here Reginald was killed in unknown circumstances.

He was initially buried in Lestrem cemetery, but at a later date was transferred to "Y" Farm Military Cemetery. His headstone read simply, " *Requiescat in pace.* " He is also remembered on his parents grave in the town cemetery, " *After serving in Gallipoli, Egypt, and Palestine. Interred in Lestrem Cemetery, France.* "

Throughout the war the growing number of prisoners-of-war had naturally increased, so much so that government departments were set up to, and voluntary organisations assisted in, finding out information about them, exchanging wounded and ensuring humane treatment. It is difficult not to believe that for many, of all sides, to be captured unwounded, to be away from the carnage was most welcome. However, it was not always safe, not least from ill-treatment and in 1918, the influenza pandemic. There were also other tragic events.

PRIVATE GEORGE GREY **SWAN** (330186) 1ST/1ST. CAMBRIDGESHIRE REGIMENT, DIED OF WOUNDS SEPTEMBER 23RD. 1918, AGED 30. BURIED IN VALENCIENNES (ST. ROCH) COMMUNAL CEMETERY, FRANCE, PLOT 5 ROW G GRAVE 18.

George was the second of three sons of Grey and Sarah Ann Swan of 3 Radwinter Road. On leaving school he became the manager of the Saffron Walden Co-operative Society store at 48 High Street.

War service was required of all three of the Swan boys ; first, George's elder brother and then in November 1916 enlisting at Warley, George himself - the youngest son, Harry Frederick was to follow with the Essex Yeomanry to France and then Palestine later. Just before George left he married Georgina Minnie, and sadly one month later he heard of his brother, William's death.

George went to France in February 1917 where he suffered from trench fever and had to return to England in late May as a patient in a hospital at Halifax. On returning to France the battalion were in the area of Moislains, during the great German offensive of March 1918, when George was reported missing. This news arrived in a letter from a comrade, Percy Freeman, who thought George might possibly be a prisoner-of-war.

Months of agony followed for his wife and family and it was not until Christmas 1918, after the war had ended that the facts of George's fate were known. it came in the form of a letter from a Private Sullivan of the Lancashire Fusiliers. George had indeed been taken prisoner, where he was working behind the German lines in a hospital garden near Cambrai. Allied bombs had been dropped nearby and George had been wounded in the legs, both being fractures. After one week in the Cambrai hospital, he had been moved to Valenciennes where after three weeks he died from shock. Sullivan, a hospital orderly, assured the family that he had nursed George during this time.

George is buried with nearly 900 prisoners-of-war in the city cemetery of Valenciennes ; a city in German hands for all but a few weeks of the war. His headstone is inscribed, " *This spot is forever England.* "

After the war, his widow Georgina moved to Pen-y-Lan, Cardiff. His remaining brother survived the conflict.

In 1918, 493,562 men joined up, many of them eligible because they had reached the military age of eighteen. For many of these young men, following older brothers, or even fathers, their military service was tragically brief.

PRIVATE SAM **FRANCIS** (G/21549) 1ST. ROYAL WEST KENT REGIMENT, DIED OF

WOUNDS SEPTEMBER 27TH. 1918, AGED 19. BURIED IN H.A.C CEMETERY, ECOUST ST.MEIN, FRANCE, PLOT 8 ROW D GRAVE 5.

Sam was the son of James Gray and Mary Jane Francis of 1 Hodson's Yard, Castle Street. After school he went to work as an assistant at the Saffron Walden Co-operative Bakery in the High Street. He also, lived with his sister, Rhoda, whose husband James, in 1914, was the fourth man from the town to perish in the war, at Prospect House, Castle Street.

On reaching military age, Sam enlisted in the Royal Army Service Corps (R.A.S.C - No. M314409) and on August 19th. 1918 went to France. Transferring to the Royal West Kents, Sam, five and a half weeks later on a Friday, died from his wounds in a field-ambulance.

Along the Western Front, the battle raged ever more fiercely - on September 28th. a massive offensive was launched in the Ypres Salient and the following day the St. Quentin canal was crossed.

PRIVATE CHARLES **ELLWOOD** (G/41079) 1ST. MIDDLESEX REGIMENT, KILLED IN ACTION SEPTEMBER 29TH. 1918. BURIED IN VILLERS HILL BRITISH CEMETERY, VILLERS-GUISLAIN, FRANCE, PLOT 1 ROW C GRAVE 8.

Charles was the son of Mr. L W Elwood and was born in Little Walden. Apart from his brother, William killed in 1917, we have no other family details. At the outbreak of war, he lived in Waltham Cross and enlisted in the Middlesex Regiment at Mill Hill.

In Sptember 1918, the battalion were in support positions in the 98th. Brigade sector, in front of and to the west of Villers-Ghuislain. From September 19th., there was desultory fighting for two or three days, until on the night of 23rd/24th., they relieved the 2nd. Argyll and Sutherland Highlanders on the right of the Brigade front, occupying a line south-east of the village.

On September 26th. Charles and his comrades went to support positions west of Chapel Crossing until the night of 28th/29th. when they relieved the 5th. Cameronians (Scottish Rifles). The attack the following day had the objective of a line running from Derby Post to the eastern end of Villers Hill. Zero hour was 3.30 a.m. and the assault was launched under an intense artillery barrage. Initially, there was early progress, Villers-Guislain was partly cleared, but the enemy filed back into the village and the attack was checked. ' C ' company in the centre met strong opposition at Gloster Road and ' B ' company after capturing 200 of the enemy, found itself surrounded and cut off. By 1 p.m. little progress was reported, although it was thought that ' C ' company had gone forward as far as Villers Ridge.

In this maelstrom Charles was killed. His platoon commander, 2nd. Lieutenant A C Gray wrote to his father, "...*he was killed during an attack on an enemy position..a good willing soldier...I miss him in my platoon. Your son is buried in the company with others who fell on that day and a cross erected over his grave.* "

Today Charles lies in the cemetery on Villers Hill by the Gloster Road where he fell.

October 8th. 1918 proved a day of note - Sergeant Alvin York (then a Corporal) killed twenty-eight Germans, and captured 132 complete with thirty-five machine-guns. He became a national hero and Hollywood feted him in the film with Gary Cooper.

President Wilson rejected the German peace note, indirectly leading to one more month of killing and another Saffron Walden wife became a widow and a child fatherless.

PRIVATE WALTER CHARLES **HOLLAND** (30041) 5TH. ROYAL INNISKILLING FUSILIERS, KILLED IN ACTION OCTOBER 8TH. 1918, AGED 30. BURIED IN BEAUREVOIR BRITISH CEMETERY, FRANCE, ROW G GRAVE 15.

Walter was the second son of Mrs.G Holland. He was born in Wicken Bonhunt and with his brother, Alfred, attended the Boys' British School then he going to work for Horneybrooke Nurseries. He was married to Gertrude Kate with one child and lived at 6 Church Path.

In July 1916 he joined up into the Northamptonshire Regiment (No. 27089), then with many others from the regiment, he was drafted into the ' Skins, as they were known. The battalion spent some time in Salonica where they were involved in extensive operations on the Struma, participating in the battle of Bala-Zir-Jenikeu, where the Bulgars lost some 5000 men. In September 1917, the battalion was shipped to Egypt and Palestine, where they stayed until the middle of June 1918 when they left for France from Alexandria, via Taranto, arriving at Serqueux on June 29th.

The ' Skins were now part of the 66th. Division which they joined at Abancourt, but in October they were in the vicinity of the Siegfried Line, whose final defences, the Beaurevoir Line had been breached, but at immense cost. Part of that cost was to be Walter Holland and, although the circumstances of his death are unknown he rests in a small cemetery created during the great Allied advance of 1918.

We have seen that men from Saffron Walden fought in the uniform of Australia, but one man went even further afield - New Zealand, only to return and die in France. He became part of the myth of the A.N.Z.A.C identity born in the ravines of Gallipoli and come to fruition in the crucible of the Western Front, *"...for the first and only time, they had identified with a cause bigger than themselves and had known what it means to be a man. "*

RIFLEMAN CHARLES THOMAS **SMITH** (75208) 1ST. NEW ZEALAND RIFLE BRIGADE, DIED OF WOUNDS OCTOBER 8TH. 1918, AGED 39. BURIED DELSAUX FARM CEMETERY, BEUGNY, FRANCE, PLOT 1 ROW D GRAVE 28.

Tom came from a large family of the late David Smith who lived at 15 to 19 Debden Road. He emigrated to New Zealand where he became a farmer, working his own piece of land at Kumeur, Kaipara.

In 1918, his sense of guilt that he was safe and far away from danger became to much for him; Tom decided his country needed him more than his farm, so he volunteered and was posted to 'C' company 38th. New Zealand Expeditionary Force Reinforcements.

After initial training Tom embarked on the H.M.N.Z.T. No. 105, *" Rumuera "* at Wellington and after a voyage of eight weeks arrived in Liverpool on July 31st. In England, he spent a further eight weeks with the New Zealand Rifle Brigade (N.Z.R.B) in further training at Brocton, before being shipped to France on September 25th. Before his departure Tom came home to Saffron Walden one last time to say his farewells. At the end of his leave for his short journey to the the station his family hired a handsome coach and horses to transport their hero to the Front.

Here, in Etaples, at the notorious " Bull-Ring, " he was ' toughened up ' for the front-line. He joined 'C' company of his battalion on September 30th. in the vicinity of Cambrai, where the Allied push was in full-swing. On October 8th. he received multiple wounds and died in the 29th. Casualty Clearing Station where he had been taken.

Tom had been in France a mere twelve days ; in the front-line only eight and he was thirteen days away from his fortieth birthday, never again to see the green and rolling hills of his lonely farm.

After the war his only relative, his brother Alfred, received his medals, plaque and scroll, the sole reminders of their hero.

" And having each one given his body to the Commonwealth they received instead thereof a most remarkable sepulchre, not that wherein they are buried so much as the other wherein their glory is laid up on all occasions, both of word and deed, to be remembered for evermore. "

Despite that the war seemed to be nearing its bloody end, October was a bad month for our town - nine men were killed, and the following day two of these met their deaths not ten miles apart. The Hindenburg Line was now completely overrun, and groups of troops and cavalry found themselves in country that had been in enemy hands since August 1914.

PRIVATE ALFRED **ARCHER** (G/20283) 4TH. MIDDLESEX REGIMENT, KILLED IN ACTION OCTOBER 9TH. 1918, AGED 37. BURIED IN NAVES COMMUNAL CEMETERY EXTENSION, FRANCE, PLOT 4 ROW D GRAVE 17.

Alfred was the eldest son of Mr. and Mrs. Alfred Archer, a coal merchant of 74 Radwinter Road. He attended the Boys British School before working for Robson and Company, the mineral water manufacturers of Station Street. He was married to Elizabeth.

Alfred signed up for General Service and in October 1918 was in the area of Haucourt. As part of the 63rd. Brigade, the 4th. Middlesex were to carry on the advance of the 37th. Division first to a line east of the village of Haucourt. At zero hour, 5.30 a.m. on Wednesday, October 9th. the Middlesex were in support of the Lincolnshire Regiment and the Somerset Light Infantry when the advance began. The enemy had fallen back as far as Caudry, and later the 112th. Brigade, passed through the 63rd. in pursuit of the enemy. The regimental history records, *"...little actual fighting done, "* but there was sporadic shelling and machine-gun fire and at some stage Alfred was hit and killed instantaneously. The battalion chaplain later wrote to his family words which may seem incongruous to our late twentieth century agnosticism, *"..it is his gain and he after all received the highest form of promotion ! "*

As an interesting footnote, the Naves community cemetery register published in the mid-1920's notes that by then, Alfred's wife had died. Another broken-hearted widow ?

Some fifteen miles away to the south-east, just north of Le Cateau, scene of one of the magnificent rearguard action by the Old Contemptibles in 1914, is a cemetery only begun some two weeks later by a Royal Garrison artillery unit. It contains nearly 500 graves, a typically cosmopolitan mix, Canadians, Germans and British, and one a regular soldier from Saffron Walden who had fought here in that famous engagement over four years previously.

PRIVATE FRANK **BASSETT** (11275) 5TH. CONNAUGHT RANGERS, KILLED IN ACTION OCTOBER 9TH. 1918, AGED 29. BURIED IN MONTAY-NEUVILLY ROAD CEMETERY, MONTAY, FRANCE, PLOT 1 ROW F GRAVE 16.

Frank, often known as Fred, was the eldest son of Mr. and Mrs. Henry Bassett of 28 Castle Street. At the age of sixteen, Frank had joined the Army into the 2nd. Essex Regiment (No. 8745). On mobilisation in August 1914, Frank was in France on September 14th. 1914. The battle honours for 1914 that Frank was involved in are a litany of courage - Le Cateau, the Retreat from Mons, the Marne, the Aisne, Messines and Armentieres.

In late April 1915 Frank sustained a wound, and another on the Somme in July 1916, probably on his return from convalescence he was posted to the Connaught Rangers who were in Salonica. Although a quiet campaign compared with the Western Front, Frank was buried by a shell and had to be dug out, shaken but unharmed. In September 1917 Frank went to Egypt where whilst recovering in hospital from a bout of malaria, heard the sad news of his younger brother's death. His illness did not prevent him embarking with his battalion for France in late June 1918.

The wheel had come full circle for Frank. He was killed in the same area he had fought over four years previously, and a few weeks from the Armistice. His headstone in the pretty little cemetery reads, " *Never forgotten by those who loved him.* "

The duties of the Royal Engineers or " Sappers " were very diverse. For instance in France in 1916, they were responsible for seventy-seven types of unit, including Tunnelling Companies, camouflage, photographic work,, Light Railways, cable sections, anti-aircraft sections and messenger dogs. Varied there work certainly was, but it was also dangerous.

SAPPER ARTHUR **RICHARDSON** (223443) 129TH. FIELD COMPANY, THE ROYAL ENGINEERS, KILLED IN ACTION OCTOBER 14TH. 1918, AGED 35. BURIED IN ST. AUBERT BRITISH CEMETERY, FRANCE, PLOT 3 ROW A GRAVE 27.

Arthur was the eldest son of Daniel and Emma Richardson, a house decorater and paperhanger of 5 Ashdon Road. He attended the Boys British School before working for a while for the Post Office, then with his father.

Arthur, who was single, enlisted in late 1916 into the Essex Regiment (32379). In March 1918 having transferred to the Royal Engineers he was wounded in the ankle during the great German offensive. On returning in June to duty, during the push forward, he was one of a party putting a pontoon over a river, probably the Selle or the Harpies, under heavy fire when he and a comrade were hit. Arthur died immediately and according to the chaplain was *"..buried in a French cemetery the same afternoon."* It is likely that his body was moved after the Armistice to the newly created (begun two days before Arthur's death), St. Aubert British Cemetery.

The focus of our attention has been away from the Ypres Salient, but here as everywhere on the Western Front, although the Germans were systematically withdrawing, they were not giving in. The more ground they retained the more negotiating aces they held in any peace deal.

LANCE-CORPORAL ARCHIBALD JAMES **WHITEHEAD** (512166) 2ND/14TH. LONDON REGIMENT, (LONDON SCOTTISH), KILLED IN ACTION OCTOBER 15TH. 1918, AGED 30. BURIED IN DERRY HOUSE CEMETERY, WYTSCHAETE, BELGIUM, PLOT 1 ROW F GRAVE 1. James, as he liked to be known, was the fifth son of Mr. and Mrs. Osborne Whitehead, a monumental mason, of 4 Common Hill, Common's Hill (West). Born on April 15th. 1888, he became a pupil at the Boys' British School and then Saffron Walden Grammar School. James was also a treble soloist in the St. Mary's church choir, as well as playing cricket and football for the town. He wanted to be a school-teacher so on completing his education, he served an ' apprenticeship ' at his first old school, before going to St. John's Boys' School, Chelmsford as an assistant.

Passing his exams, James then gained more teaching experience in Grantham, before moving onto college for a year. War interrupted his studies, and in 1915, he volunteered in London. At that time, three of his older brothers were all serving, and his other brother, Osborne was still listed as missing. In addition, Mr. Whitehead died and his mother re-married becoming Mrs. Maria Richardson.

As so often seems to be the case, James came home on leave, three weeks before he was killed by a machine-gun bullet leading his section. His mother received many letters showing the esteem in which James had been held - his sergeant wrote, he was, *"...killed by a machine-gun bullet... I have lost an able and brilliant assistant and the best, staunchest and fearless comrade. "* She also had words of comfort from the chaplain, he was *"... killed in rather a big action with a number of other men, and although I do not know the exact details, I think he died instantly and did not suffer pain...I laid him to rest in a British Cemetery which is now many miles behind the lines and far away from the sound of the guns. "*

In addition, to our town memorials, James' name appears on the Chelmsford Civic Centre Memorial, and was in the Chelmsford Almanac of 1921 in memory of the men who fell, under the Moulsham list.

With James' devoutness, he was also a member of the Chelmsford Church Institute, it is fitting that he received a proper Christian burial, unlike so many who fell in the infamous Salient.

Of males under the age of forty-five, nine per cent died in the war, and it was the quality of these *" flowers of the country "* like James Whitehead, and the next soldier to die that gives such credence to what J B Priestley wrote,

".. the generation ....destroyed between 1914 and 1918, was a great generation, marvellous in its promise. "

LANCE-CORPORAL JOHN **CHAPMAN** (G/16585) 2ND. ROYAL SUSSEX REGIMENT, DIED OF WOUNDS OCTOBER 17TH.1918, AGED 30 BURIED IN BUSIGNY COMMUNAL CEMETERY EXTENSION, FRANCE, PLOT 3 ROW GRAVE 17. John was the second son of Charles and Suzan Eliza Chapman of Audley End. After school he became a gardener at Audley End House, before moving to become head gardener at Greenhurst Park, Capel, Dorking. He was married to Emily and had one child.

John joined up in Brighton on June 16th.1916 and proceded to France in December of that year. In January 1917 he came home on leave, before being involved in the second battle of Passchendaele, and the battles of the Lys in April 1918. On October 16th.,near the Sambre Canal, John was badly wounded, and died early the next day. It was nearly a month later when his wife received the details in his officer's letter. " *They started out at 5 p.m. to take 1500 yards of ground. All went well for 800 yards when a machine-gun opened up on the section John was leading. He fell moaning to the ground and was picked up by stretcher-bearers who took him to a field ambulance, where he died in the early hours of Thursday October 17th... he was very popular.* "

John, a gardener, lies amidst the manicured grass and English flowers in a cemetery, where nearby is a young soldier from Littlebury, Aubrey Hayward, who was killed five days before. He is remembered on his parents' headstone in the town cemetery.

A writer at the time worked out that officer casualties within his regiment were five times those of other ranks, and these deaths greatly moved the ordinary soldier. A special relationship had grown up between the subaltern and his men sharing a common danger. " *Men will forgive anything but lack of courage and devotion.* "

LIEUTENANT ALFRED JOHN **WYATT** 1ST. ATTACHED 8TH. CAMERONIANS (SCOTTISH RIFLES), KILLED IN ACTION OCTOBER 23RD. 1918, AGED 32. BURIED IN HIGHLAND CEMETERY, LE CATEAU, FRANCE, PLOT 8 ROW E GRAVE 7.

Alfred was the eldest son of Alfred and Annie Wyatt of ' The Duke of York ' Inn, 96 High Street. He attended the Boys' British School before joining the Cameronians in 1907 in the ranks. He was eighteen years of age weighing 122 lbs, five feet five in height with grey eyes, a fresh complexion and black hair.

Once in the army, Alfred took as many qualifications as he could, becoming an acting schoolmaster at the Scottish Rifles' depot at Hamilton, Scotland in 1909. Here he rose rapidly through the ranks - lance-corporal in 1908; corporal in 1910; lance-sergeant in 1912 to sergeant in 1914, before being commissioned as a second lieutenant immediately on war's outbreak. This necessitated, as he wrote home that, *"..now I shall have to go over the water.* "

This, for Alfred, meant France embarking from Southampton on April 1st. 1915. He joined the 1st. Battalion in the field on April 14th. 1915. Apart from a two week period of illness in June which necessitated a spell in hospital in Armentieres, he spent nearly six months under continual fire. He also met some old school friends, Sgt. Chipperfield being attached to his company in the trenches for preliminary training and Sapper Kidman of the Royal Engineers who was marching by with his company.

However, his relief from the trenches came on September 25th. at Cuinchy during the battle of Loos, inaccurately described in the propoganda press as, *"..the great advance in France, *" when he was hit by a large piece of shell in his right foot. This was his second narrow escape in a few days, the other being when a shell had landed right by him, but failed to explode. He was taken to 20th. General Hospital at Camiers, before it was decided to evacuate him home and on October 1st. he crossed the Channel on the H.S. *"Dieppe.* " After convalescing in London until a medical board passed him as fit on November 25th. 1915, Alfred was sent to Egypt, attached to the 8th. Battalion. In Egypt he contracted dysentery and was again invalided home.

It took Alfred a long time to get over the debilitating effects of his illness and as assistant adjutant he spent the next two years in Scotland preparing drafts and conducting them over to France. He also got married and in May 1918 became a father.

In early, October he returned to France at Calais to re-join his battalion on October 11th. 1918. Twelve days later he was dead, buried one mile north of Montay. Today he lies in a cemetery to the north of Le Cateau, the town re-occupied after four years of German rule, next to a cemetery of his erstwhile foes. His younger brother, Herbert, a corporal with the Machine Gun Corps, served in Mesopotamia, but survived the war.

As a postscript to Alfred's tale, in December 1918, his widow wrote from her parents-in-law's address to the War Office. She had just received his kit from the ' French frontier ' but several items were missing *"...field glasses, revolver, compass, pocket books and diary (which I am needing to settle a business matter), cord without whistle, safety razor and fittings, watch, fountain pen, trench coat (I now hold the bill for the same being £ 6 19s 6d, he purchased the coat the last day of his leave). I received three or four letters which were found in his pocket.."* How desolate she must have felt that most of her remembrances of him were also lost. She concludes by asking the authorities to look into the matter and what was the necessary action to claim for them. Their reply is not known.

The last man to die in October 1918 had also served in Mesopotamia, but with the Royal Navy, but his death was not from enemy action. October 19th. had seen all German submarines ordered to return to their home bases, and on October 21st the last torpedo was fired from an enemy U-boat, taking eight lives, - to all effects the war at sea was over.

ABLE-SEAMAN FRANK ERNEST **WELLS** (J/12077) ROYAL NAVY, H.M.S " PEMBROKE", DIED OCTOBER 25TH. 1918, AGED 25. BURIED IN GILLINGHAM (WOODLANDS) CEMETERY, KENT, NAVAL PLOT ROW 5 GRAVE 241.

Frank was born on September 30th. 1893, the youngest son of Mrs. Mary Ann Wells, a widow, of 7 Ingleside Place. He attended the Boys British School before enlisting in the Royal Navy in 1911 for twelve years. He had also worked for Mr. E W Trew, the draper, at 62 High Street and before that had been a waiter.

On the outbreak of war he was attached to H.M.S. *"Hibernia "*, a King Edward VIIth. Class battleship which, at Weymouth in 1912, had seen the first launch of an aircraft from a ship under way. After a short period at shore-base, Frank in August 1915, joined H.M.S. *"Alert "*, a screw-sloop, before in December 1915 being transferred to H.M.S *" Cranefly "*, a brand new Fly Class River Gunboat, part of a flotilla concentrated on the River Tigris at Ali Gharbi.

Here they were part of an operation to try and relieve the beleaguered forces closed in by the Turks at Kut al Amara. The Tigris here has numerous bends and large marshy areas facilitating the Turkish defences. The relief force engaged the Turks on January 5th. 1916 with the gunboats chiefly employed in supporting the assault upon the Turkish right. The battle continued with the greatest obstinacy for two days until the enemy withdrew and the British army and the flotilla followed up, reconnoitring the new Turkish positions at Hanna and later bombarding them. However, by the end of

January it was evident that the attack had failed.

In March a new attempt was made, again using the " *Cranefly* " and the rest of the flotilla to bombard the enemy's positons, but no real progress was made. A further attempt was hampered by the Tigris rising and overflowing its banks, and it fell to one of the flotilla, the Julnar, to make the last heroic attempt to reach Kut. Tragically, this failed and on April 29th. the garrison at Kut surrendered.

In May 1916, Frank transferred to the " *Dalhousie* ", a Royal Indian Marine troop-ship. During the next twenty months, Frank saw much service in the Persian Gulf theatre of the war, including the capture of Baghdad, reinforcement of the small agency guard at Bushire, attacks on the Tangistani tribesmen and forcing the Turkish garrison to evacuate Al Bida in August 1917. Service followed in Bahrein, but the exacting circumstances of climate, disease and warfare, began to take their toll on Frank's health and he returned home to England in January 1918, to the H.M.S " *Pembroke* ", described as a ' stone frigate ' i.e. a shore base, out of the Chatham depot, where he gained a reputation as a first-class gunner.

In September 1918 he was sent home for one month on sick leave, having been mentioned for promotion and transfer to a submarine as a gunner. Whether he was not fully recovered from his recent illness we shall never know, but on his return he was immediately struck down by meningitis and died in the Royal Naval hospital in Chatham.

He was buried in the naval plot of the cemetery at Gillingham with full military honours. Here, unusually, some of the headstones in the serried rows are of black stone, but Frank's, is of the standard white Portland.

November came and the armistice negotiations continued, so did the fighting, and inevitably the dying. The final two soldiers from Saffron Walden to die in the war were both nineteen and both died in the same hospital in the cathedral city of Rouen. Today they lie a few rows apart in the same cemetery.

PRIVATE PETER RICHARD **HOUSDEN** (355373) 7TH. LONDON REGIMENT, DIED OF WOUNDS NOVEMBER 1ST. 1918, AGED 19. BURIED IN ST. SEVER CEMETERY EXTENSION, ROUEN, FRANCE, BLOCK S PLOT 2 ROW JJ GRAVE 16.

Peter, always known as Dick, was born and lived in Saffron Walden, the youngest of four brothers, living at 28 Thaxted Road with his parents Peter and Susannah. On leaving the Boys British School he worked for a time as an under-gardener to the late Mrs. E B Gibson of Elm Grove, before moving to Hounslow. In 1917, on reaching military age he enlisted in the 7th. City of London Battalion, affectionately known as, " *The Shiny Seventh.* "

On October 24th. 1918 at 2 a.m. during an enemy attack, Dick was severely wounded in the side and the ankle. After a painful journey by ambulance and train, he arrived at a Base Hospital in Rouen, where he managed to dictate a letter to a ward sister for his parents, stating that he was all right.

They received this on Sunday October 27th., but their relief at the news was short-lived for on the evening of Tuesday November 5th. a second letter arrived saying that Dick had died suddenly on the Friday morning - the gunshot wound in his thigh had haemorrhaged internally.

He was buried on the Saturday with full military honours, his headstone simply stating, *" Until we meet at Jesu's feet. "* His name also appears on the Baptist church memorial.

The war had already touched the Housden family, their eldest son, Harry a gunner in the Royal Field Artillery had been wounded and was in a Leeds hospital ; Frederick, the second son, with the Essex Regiment had been captured at Mons and suffered the privations of a prisoner-of-war camp in Germany for four long years. In addition, George, a bombardier with the Canadian forces, survived unscathed.

But further tragedy was to strike - on the day Dick was buried, his mother was called to Sheffield to be at the bedside of Frederick's dying wife, Beatrice, another victim of influenza.

This is a tale of sacrifice, if nothing else, not just by the men themselves but by those who knew and loved them. Perhaps, the most poignant story of them all is that of the last war-time death and how it affected one typical, ordinary family.

PRIVATE GEORGE STEPHEN **PEARSON** (41875) 1ST/1ST. HERTFORDSHIRE REGIMENT, DIED OF WOUNDS NOVEMBER 5TH. 1918, AGED 19. BURIED IN ST. SEVER CEMETERY EXTENSION, ROUEN, FRANCE, BLOCK S PLOT 3 ROW M GRAVE 11.

George was the youngest of four sons of Stephen and Sarah Pearson of 38 Fairycroft Road. In April 1918 on attaining military age he went to France and was immediately severely wounded in the back and left thigh. Taken to a base hospital, over a period of six months and much pain, he had two operations and died. He had been in France one month when he was wounded.

The bald facts are cruel enough, but they become worse. George's brother, Charles was killed in October 1914, he left a widow and two children. Immediately his elder brother Joseph joined up and disappeared without trace on the Somme in 1916. He left five children fatherless. Finally, three days before George died, perhaps sensing that after so interminable a time her third son would not recover, his grief-stricken mother, Sarah, passed away.

The fourth son, Herbert, serving with the Wiltshire Regiment, survived to come home to what was left of his family.

Just east of Mons, in Belgium, and not far from where the first shots of the Great War were fired, at two minutes to eleven on the eleventh day of the eleventh month in 1918, a German sniper shot and killed a Canadian soldier. He was probably the last of over eight and a half million soldiers to be killed *in* the Great War. Soldiers who died at the rate of 5,600 each day of that dreadful conflict.

In Saffron Walden, as everywhere the end did not bring great rejoicing, too many people had gone, too many were still lost, too many would never recover. The mood is reflected in Hardy's poem,

" Calm fell. From heaven distilled a clemency;
There was peace on earth and silence in the sky
Some could, some could not shake off misery
The Sinister Spirit sneered, " It had to be! "
And again the Spirit of Pity whispered, " Why? "

117

Although the war was over, the deaths caused by it were not ; many a soldier posted missing was not confirmed dead for many months afterwards and many lingered on ill in mind and body for months, or even years. Because of this it was decreed that the official date of the ending of the Great War was to be August 31st. 1921. The roll of honour, thus, had still five more names to be added to it.

PRIVATE HENRY JOHN **BOWTLE** (28771) BEDFORDSHIRE REGIMENT TRANSFERRED TO THE LABOUR CORPS (468257), DIED DECEMBER 5TH. 1918, AGED 23. BURIED IN SAFFRON WALDEN TOWN CEMETERY, RADWINTER ROAD, ESSEX, PLOT 28 GRAVE 121.

Henry was the son of Edward Charles and Ellen Overill Bowtle of 21 Fairycroft. He was educated at the Boys British School (on whose memorial board he appears mysteriously as Sidney) and then enlisted into the Bedfordshire Regiment. In February 1917 the Labour Corps was created employing men on a myriad number of tasks ranging from building gun emplacements to unloading ships. Demand for their skills was great and Henry was transferred becoming No. 468257.

He was employed as a coach painter for the remainder of the war, until just after the Armistice he contracted pneumonia and after eight days illness died in a military hospital in York. His body was brought back to Saffron Walden and the following Wednesday he was buried. His conventional white headstone is inscribed, *" At Rest in God. "*

Inevitably, in the post-war desire to record and honour all who died within the prescribed dates of the Great War, names were unknowingly overlooked. The next soldier's name, although on our town memorials, was unknown to the Commonwealth War Graves Commission (C.W.G.C) and he had no known grave. My research eventually located him in our town cemetery and with the good auspices of the C.W.G.C just before Christmas 1996, a headstone was dedicated by the Reverend Duncan Green, in the prescence of Sir Alan Haselhurst, the Mayoress and Walter Hill's nephew, Peter, seventy-eight years after he died from the lingering effects of gas, *"..obscene as cancer, bitter as the cud. "*

PRIVATE WALTER EDWARD **HILL** 6733 16TH. (THE QUEEN'S) LANCERS, DIED OF WOUNDS APRIL 10TH. 1919, AGED 26. BURIED IN SAFFRON TOWN WALDEN CEMETERY, RADWINTER ROAD, ESSEX, PLOT 28 GRAVE 149.

Walter was the second of three sons of Mr. and Mrs. Walter Hill of 11 Castle Street. He enlisted on August 27th. 1914 just after war was declared and after training arrived in France on December 8th. 1915. At some stage, possibly in the Waverans - Vermelles area in June 1916, he was badly gassed. So severe was it that he had to be honourably discharged on July 6th. 1916.

The rest of Walter's life reflects Owen's powerful poem,

" ..watch the white eyes writhing in his face. "

He was admitted from one hospital to another but his condition gradually declined and after nearly three long years of suffering he died.

On Monday 14th. April 1919, a hand carriage carrying a coffin draped in the Union flag was slowly carried by Walter's brothers, Frank and Arthur, as well as local Comrades of the Great War, along the Radwinter Road and into the town cemetery where it was lowered into the grave containing the remains of Walter's sister, Katherine, who had died in 1901.

The family were unable to afford a headstone and there Walter lay for the intervening years beneath a grassy space. Today a white headstone, " *standard sized representing equality,* " bears his details and the inscriptions, " *Fought with Courage,* " and " *Also Kate Hill died March 21st. 1901, aged 26.* "

Of the many tragedies of the Great War, none proved as ironic or as ill-fated, as to die after the cessation of hostilities in an accident. In this accident the attempted intervention of a former enemy, perhaps proves the shared companionship and experience of the front-line soldier, whatever their nationality.

PRIVATE CHARLES DOUGLAS **MARTIN** (99769) ATTACHED 383 PRISONER-OF-WAR COMPANY, 1ST. KING'S LIVERPOOL REGIMENT, DROWNED JUNE 9TH. 1919, AGED 27. BURIED IN METEREN MILITARY CEMETERY, FRANCE, PLOT 2 ROW H GRAVE 232.

Charles was the son of Thomas and Sarah Martin of 7 Jones Yard, Freshwell Street. At the end of the war, Charles was attached to 383 Prisoner-of-War Company engaged in clearing the debris of the aftermath of war.

About noon on Whit Monday, Charles had gone swimming with a friend, Private Catherall, in a pond, one hundred yards from their camp. Cries of help were suddenly heard from Charles who was attacked by cramp and had got into difficulties. A German prisoner and a strong swimmer, named Bunte, dived in to help, as well as some of the escort, but to no avail, Charles could not be found. Later that evening at 9 p.m. his body was recovered, and Charles was buried two days later in the nearby military cemetery.

The physical and psychological wounds of the war for many would not heal, their suffering a source of almost equal pain and helpless pity for their loved ones who could not help. For some these wound proved too much and death became a longed-for release.

PRIVATE HAROLD GEORGE **CORNELL** (43586) 6TH. NORTHAMPTONSHIRE REGIMENT, DIED OF WOUNDS JUNE 18TH. 1919, AGED 24. BURIED IN SAFFRON WALDEN TOWN CEMETERY, RADWINTER ROAD, ESSEX, PLOT 28.

Harold was the only son of George and Charlotte Cornell of 12, Mount Pleasant. After school he had worked for William Bell and Sons, the builders of South Road, before enlisting in the Essex Regiment, later being transferred to the Northants. He was single.

He had been wounded twice previously and his parents were delighted to see him home on leave in the August of 1918. One month later on his return to the front, he was horrifically shot through the spine. Completely paralysed he was first treated in a French base hospital, then sent to Paddington Hospital where over several months the doctors worked to try and rehabilitate him, but in April 1919 it was decided that the wound was incurable. Harold was transferred to a Richmond home for incurable wounds, where he died peacefully.

Enter Saffron Walden cemetery by the left-hand gate, and under a magnificent tree just in front of the chapel, you will see the solitary white headstone of the one hundred and fifty-ninth - and last man from our town to die in the Great War. One who *'marched away'* but unlike so many of his comrades, rests here at home and not in *'some foreign field.'* His is a story of suffering and great pain, of courage and sacrifice, just like all the others. Lest We Forget.

RIFLEMAN THOMAS JOHN ARTHUR **GRIME** (592746) 18TH. LONDON REGIMENT, (LONDON IRISH RIFLES), DIED OF WOUNDS DECEMBER 12TH. 1919, AGED 24. BURIED IN SAFFRON WALDEN TOWN CEMETERY, RADWINTER ROAD, ESSEX, PLOT 17 GRAVE 42.

Arthur Grime was born in Leytonstone the son of Mrs. Ada Ann and the late Thomas Grime. At some stage Mrs. Grime came to live in Saffron Walden, at 4 New Road, and Arthur went to the Boys British School. After leaving school he went to live in Harrow and obtained employment there.

With the onset of war Arthur enlisted at Marylebone, first in the Middlesex Regiment (No. G/12282) before joining the London Irish Rifles on December 12th. 1915. In June 1916, he went to France and survived the actions at High Wood and Flers Trench. In September 1917, Mrs Grime received the news that Arthur had been wounded four or five times when a shell burst near his dug-out and was in hospital near Windsor. Most of the wounds were superficial, although the wound in his left leg was quite troublesome.

On returning to France, Arthur was wounded for a second time in August 1918. An explosive poisonous bullet shattered his left thigh - the same leg that had been hit before. This time it was much more serious. Over the next sixteen months, Arthur experienced great suffering. He endured nineteen operations all to no avail. On Friday December 12th. the day after the last of these operations in the Kitchener's Military Hospital, Brighton, his pain ceased forever. It was the fourth anniversary of his joining the London Irish Rifles.

His body was brought home on the following Wenesday and was laid in the Roman Catholic church. The following day Arthur was buried beneath a headstone with an inscription, *" Lord, All Pitying, Jesu Blest. Grant him Eternal Rest. "*

Arthur's name does not appear on the Boys' British School memorial board completed on November 11th. 1919 - he was still alive. His mother later moved to Husbands Bosworth, Rugby.

As I come to the end of this page of history I feel a sense of loss, a sense of lingering sorrow, although it all occurred eighty years ago to men that I never knew. But I do know these men, now - men who lived in my road, our town ; men who were far from Classical heroes ; far from supermen ; not perfect or idealised, just caught in a moment of time where they felt they had to do their duty out of patriotism, or fear, love, necessity, under duress - who knows ? I have tried not to romanticise them, war is not romantic, but it is their human story of the men who fought in what was then known as the Great War.

It is also the story of the human suffering it embedded in the fabric of a small East Anglian market-town. For those who lost a loved one, a light had been extinguished, never to be rekindled. For many of those who did return had physical and psychological scars. These could not fade away - they were the legacy of a war that ended only with their deaths or the deaths of those who loved them.

" What can the world hold afterwards worthy of of laughter or tears ? "

Statistics still astound - 743,000 British dead alone, but are meaningless - it is the individual tragic tale that resonates in our mind and the familiar images and echoes of that conflict still reverberate in our consciousness, casting a shadow over eighty years later, and will, perhaps, forever.

" How can we atone for the lost millions and millions of years of life, how atone for those lakes and seas of blood ?... What can we do ? Headstones and wreaths and memorials and speeches and the Cenotaph...no, no, it has got to be something in us...Somehow we must atone to the dead... The reproach is not from them, but in our-selves. "

Richard Aldington - Prologue to ' *Death of a Hero.* '

APPENDIX 1

An incomplete list of men whose names do not appear on our memorial but have a connection with the town. Some were born here and moved away, or resided here when they enlisted. Some of their names appear on local village memorials. There are anomalies, however, why is **Alfred Tredgett's** name not on our memorial? It is possible his family did not want it.

Barker Pte. Charles 11th. Essex Regt. kia 9.1.16 (born & resided Saffron Walden. Name on Newport memorial) - Potijze Burial Ground, Ypres, Belgium, Row V Grave 12.

Bartram Cpl. John James 1st. Essex Regt. dow as a P.O.W, 16.5.17 (resided Saffron Walden. Name on Ashdon memorial) - Niederzwehren Cemetery, Kassel, Germany, Plot 1 Row E Grave 2.

Bass Pte. Ernest Walter 10th. Royal Fusiliers kia 8.10.18 (resided Saffron Walden. Name on Debden memorial) - Bois-des-Angles British Cemetery, Crevecoeur-sur-l'Escaut, France, Plot 1 Row C Grave 36.

Bass Pte. Frederick John 1st. Essex Regt. kia 20.5.17 (born Debden, parents lived Wimbish) - Orange Trench Cemetery, Monchy-le-Preux, France, Row D Grave 1.

Bateman Gnr. George C Bty. 251st. Brigade Royal Field Artillery dow 5.9.18 (born Saffron Walden. Name on Debden memorial) - Chauny Communal Cemetery British Extension, France, Plot 5 Row G Grave 2.

Bennett Pte. Reginald Howard 17th. Royal Fusiliers kia 27.4.16 (born Saffron Walden. Name on Newport Free Grammar school memorial) - Tranchee-de-Mecknes Cem, Aix-Noulette, France, Row C Grave 2

Bird Pte. Edgar Royal Army Service Corps died 21.11.17 (born Saffron Walden) - Hollybrook Memorial, Hampshire

Brooks Rfn. Frederick William 2nd. Kings Royal Rifle Corps kia 25.9.15 (resided Saffron Walden) - Loos Memorial to the Missing, France, Panels 101 to 102.

Brown Pte. Nathaniel Bertram 2nd. Royal Sussex Regt. kia 26.5.15 (born Saffron Walden) - Le Touret Memorial, France, Panels 20 & 21.

Burchell Pte. Owen Stanley 1st. Notts & Derby Regt. (Sherwood Foresters) kia 26.3.18 (parents lived Saffron Walden) - Pozieres Memorial to the Missing, France, Panels 52 to 54.

Byatt Pte. Edward Charles 11th. Royal Fusiliers kia 10.8.17 (resided Saffron Walden. Name on Ashdon memorial as Edwin) - Hooge Crater Cemetery, Zillebeke, Belgium, Plot 6 Row G Grave 8.

Choppen Pte. Victor Cecil 4th. South Staffs Regt. dow 3.9.18 (born Saffron Walden) - Terlincthun British Cemetery, Wimille, France, Plot 16 Row F Grave 10.

Clark Pte. Frederick Allen 8th. East Surrey Regt. kia 22.3.18 (born Saffron Walden) - Chauny Communal Cemetery British Extension, France, Plot 2 Row C Grave 2.

Clayden Pte. Edward 11th. Essex Regt. kia 26.9.15 (born Saffron Walden. Name on Quendon/ Rickling memorial) - Loos Memorial to the Missing, France, Panels 85 to 87.

Copelin Sgt. Joseph Henry 1st/7th. Middlesex Regt. kia 16.8.17 (born Saffron Walden) - Tyne Cot Memorial to the Missing, Belgium, Panels 113 to 115.

Cornell Pte.Charles William 1st. Essex Regt. kia 22.11.17 (born Wimbish. Resided Saffron Walden. Name on Wimbish memorial) - Cambrai Memorial to the Missing, Louverval Military Cemetery, France, Panel 7.

Cornell Pte. William 4th. Middlesex Regt. kia 21.11.14 (born Saffron Walden. Name on Wimbish memorial) - Ploegsteert Memorial to the Missing, Belgium, Panel 8

Cowell Pte. James 15th. Essex Regt. dow 14.8.18 (born Saffron Walden) - Bagneux British Cemetery, Gezaincourt, France, Plot 4 Row C Grave 9.

Davies Pte. Arthur Ley 3rd. Essex Regt. drowned 4.5.17 (born Saffron Walden) - Savona Town Memorial, Italy.

Dove Pte. Walter Henry Greensides 6th. East Kent Regt (Buffs) kia 20.6.18 (resided Saffron Walden) - Harponville Communal Cemetery Extension, France, Row D Grave 1.

English Pte. Maurice Seymour 7th. London Regt. kia 11.4.18 (born Saffron Walden) - Ploegsteert Memorial to the Missing, Belgium, Panel 10.

Francis Pte. John 2nd. Grenadier Guards kia 4.9.14 (born Saffron Walden. Name on Debden memorial) - Guards Grave,Villers-Cotterets, France, Grave 3.

Gent Sgt. Jim Pate 8th. Rifle Brigade kia 3.5.17 (born Saffron Walden) - Arras Memorial to the Missing, France, Bay 9.

Gray Pte. Hugh Gardiner 7th. Royal West Kent Regt. kia 29.10.16 (born Saffron Walden) - Thiepval Memorial, France, Panel 11C.

Green Pte. Charles Walter 14th. Royal Warwickshire Regt. kia 30.4.18 - Granezza British Cemetery, Italy, Plot 1 Row A Grave 3.

Harrington Sgt. Thomas Martin 72nd. Battery Royal Field Artillery kia 15.1.17 (born Saffron Walden) - Cambrin Churchyard Extension, France, Row T Grave 17.

Harrison Pte. Reginald 7th. East Yorks Regt. kia 8.9.17 (wife from Saffron Walden) - Browns Copse Cemetery, Roeux, France, Plot 4 Row B Grave 68.

Harvey Pte. Percy James 7th. Yorkshire Regt. kia 16.10.17 (born Saffron Walden) - Tyne Cot Memorial to the Missing, Belgium, Panels 52 to 54.

Hopwood Pte. Ernest Richard 5th. Wiltshire Regt. died 5.10.18 (born Saffron Walden. Name on Elmdon memorial) - Kirkee Memorial, India, Panel 7.

Howe Pte. John Purseglove 11th. Suffolk Regt. kia 19.4.18 (born Saffron Walden) - Ploegsteert Memorial to the Missing, Belgium, Panel 3.

Jeffrey Pte. Arthur Wright 7th. Oxford & Buckinghamshire Light Infantry kia 9.5.17 (born Saffron Walden) - Doiran Memorial, Greece.

Jeffrey Pte. Ernest Hertfordshire Regt. kia 31.7.17 (resided Saffron Walden. Name on Newport memorial) - Menin Gate Memorial to the Missing, Belgium, Panels 54 & 56.

Jelf 2nd. Lt. Charles Gordon 6th. East Kent Regt. (Buffs) kia 13.10.15 - Vermelles British Cemetery, France, Plot 1 Row E Grave 12. (Mentioned in *" The Bickersteth Diaries. "*).

Jones Pte. Frederick 1st. Dorsetshire Regt. kia 26.11.14 (born Saffron Walden) - Menin Gate Memorial to the Missing, Belgium, Panel 37.

Kent Lce-Cpl. Fred 1st. West Yorkshire Regt. kia 31.3.15 (born Saffron Walden. Name on Ashdon church memorial) - St. Sever Cemetery, Rouen, France, Plot A Row 7 Grave 9.

King Pte. Arthur 2nd. Essex Regt. kia 13.4.17 (born Saffron Walden. Name on Rickling memorial) - Arras Memorial to the Missing, France, Bay 7.

Lanham Lce-Cpl. William Herbert 9th. Essex Regt. kia 3.7.16 (resided Saffron

Walden. Name on Wimbish memorial) - Ovillers Military Cemetery, Ovillers-la-Boisselle, France, Plot 8 Row S Grave 3.

Law Gnr. Walter William C Bty. 149th. Brigade Royal Field Artillery kia 21.10.17 (born Saffron Walden. Name on Elmdon & Wenden Lofts memorial) - Lindenhoek Chalet Military Cemetery, Kemmel, Belgium, Plot 1 Row A Grave 3.

Lilley Pte. Ernest George 3rd. Grenadier Guards kia 27.9.15 (born Saffron Walden) - Maroc British Cemetery, Grenay, France, Plot 1 Row K Grave 44.

Marshall Gnr. Henry James 104th. Siege Battery Royal Garrison Artillery kia 19.8.16 (born Saffron Walden) - Warloy-Baillon Communal Cemetery Extension, France, Plot 7 Row D Grave 6.

Mason Pte. Albert 11th. Suffolk Regt kia 1.7.16 (resided Saffron Walden) - Thiepval Memorial to the Missing, France, Panels 1C & 2A.

Moore Rfn. William 12th. Kings Royal Rifle Corps kia 30.6.16 (born Saffron Walden) - Ypres Reservoir Cemetery, Belgium, Plot 1 Row C Grave 25.

Negus Pte. Albert Charles Royal Field Artillery att. 7/8th. Mountain Battery, Royal Garrison Artillery kia 21.10.18 (born Saffron Walden) - Beirut War Cemetery, Lebanon, Grave 70.

Parish Pte. Cecil 9th. Essex Regt. kia 12.10.15 (resided Saffron Walden. Name on Great Sampford memorial) - Dud Corner Cemetery, Loos, France, Plot 8 Row B Grave 17.

Pitkin Pte. John 26th. Northumberland Fusiliers kia 6.12.17 (born Saffron Walden) - Bucquoy Road Cemetery, Ficheux, France, Plot 2 Row L Grave 7.

Porter Sgt. Charles Royal Army Ordnance Corps died 23.12.15 (born Saffron Walden) - Burscough Bridge (St. John the Baptist) Churchyard, Lancashire, Row E Grave 2114.

Poulter Sgt. William James (M.S.M) Royal Field Artillery 31.10.18 (wife from Saffron Walden. Name on Newport memorial) - Newport Churchyard, Essex.

Purkiss Spr. Arthur 3 Field Survey Co. Royal Engineers kia 3.10.18 (born Saffron Walden. Name on Hempstead memorial) - Chapel Corner Cemetery, Sauchy-Lestree, France, Row C Grave 6.

Purkiss Pte. Willie 11th. Essex Regt. kia 24.3.16 (resided Saffron Walden. Name on

Hempstead memorial) - Lijssenthoek Military Cemetery, Poperinghe, Belgium, Plot 5 Row D Grave 16A.

Richardson Pte. Charles Allen 57th. Battery Royal Field Artillery 22.10.17 (born Saffron Walden) - Tyne Cot Memorial to the Missing, Belgium, Panels 4 to 6.

Richardson Pte. Edward 15th. Durham Light Infantry kia 3.5.17 (born Saffron Walden) - Arras Memorial to the Missing, France, Bay 8.

Richardson Cpl. William Charles 1st. King's Liverpool Regt. kia 22.1.16 (born Saffron Walden) - Bethune Town Cemetery, France, Plot 4 Row H Grave 50.

Richardson Gnr. William James 'L' Battery Royal Horse Artillery kia 1.9.14 (born Saffron Walden. Name on Great Chesterford memorial) - Verberie French National Cemetery, France, Special Memorial.

Ridgewell Pte. Frederick 4th. Bedfordshire Regt. kia 27.9.18 (born Saffron Walden) - Queant Road Cemetery, Buissy, France, Plot 7 Row F Grave 28.

Rowell Sgt. George Edward 15th. Hampshire Regt kia 2.10.18 (born and resided Saffron Walden. Name on Ashdon memorial) - Hooge Crater Cemetery, Zillebeke, Belgium, Plot 14 Row K Grave 10

Rule Pte.Reginald 1st. Hampshire Regt. kia 16.5.15 (born Saffron Walden) - Menin Gate Memorial to the Missing, Belgium, Panel 35

Saunders Pte.William Frank 7th. East Kent Regt. (Buffs) kia 19.9.18 (resided Saffron Walden. Name on Little Chesterford memorial) - Unicorn Cemetery, Vendhuile, France, Plot 1 Row D Grave 8.

Seaman Gnr. Percy C/76 Royal Field Artillery kia 10.7.16 (resided Saffron Walden. Name on Little Chesterford memorial) - Lijssenthoek Military Cemetery, Poperinghe, Belgium, Plot 8 Row C Grave 11A.

Sharp(e) Sgt. Arthur 2nd. Grenadier Guards 20.9.14 (Mother lived Saffron Walden. Name on Debden & Radwinter memorials) - Guards Grave, Villers-Cotterets, France, Grave 23.

Sheffield Pte. Horace 5th. Northamptonshire Regt kia 17.3.16 (born Saffron Walden) - Vermelles British Cemetery, France, Plot 2 Row K Grave 10.

Sheriden Pte. Leslie 11th. Royal Warwickshire Regt. kia 16.7.16 (born Saffron Walden) - Pozieres British Cemetery, France, Plot 3 Row J Grave 16.

Simmonds 2nd. Lt. Percy Graham 9th. London Regt. (Queen Victorias' Rifles) kia 1.7.16 - Thiepval Memorial to the Missing, France, Panel 9C.

Smith Cpl. Samuel Frank 7th. Wiltshire Regt. kia 6.11.18 (born Saffron Walden. Name on Wimbish memorial) - Fontaine-au-Bois Communal Cemetery, France, Row E Grave 4.

Smith Pte. Walter Edward 2nd. East Surrey Regt. kia 9.5.15 (born Saffron Walden. Name on Ashdon memorial) - Menin Gate Memorial to the Missing, Belgium, Panel 34.

Speller Cpl. Fred 8th. Somerset Light Infantry kia 28.4.17 (born Saffron Walden) - Arras Memorial to the Missing, France, Panel 4.

Stacey Lce-Cpl. Frank 17th. London Regt. kia 8.12.17 (resided Saffron Walden) - Jerusalem Memorial, Palestine, Panels 47 to 53.

Stevenson Lce-Cpl. Edward 1st. North Staffordshire Regt kia 7.7.15 (born Saffron Walden. Name on Ickleton memorial) - Potijze Burial Ground, Ypres, Belgium, Row Z Grave 25.

Swann Pte. Harold William Essex Yeomanry dow 7.6.15 (born Saffron Walden) - Boulogne Eastern Cemetery, France, Plot 8 Row A Grave 72.

Tredgett Pte. Alfred 1st. Essex Regt. kia 12.10.16 (born & resided Saffron Walden) - Thiepval Memorial to the Missing, France, Panel 10D.

Turner Pte. Arthur William 1st. Essex Regt. kia 14.4.17 (resided Saffron Walden. Name on Hempstead memorial) - Arras Memorial to the Missing, France, Panel 7.

Watson Cpl. Frederick Henry No. 2 Base Hospital Canadian Army Medical Corps died 25.3.18 - Toronto (St.Johns Norway) Cemetery, Canada, Lot 16 Range 14 Section 3.

Weeden Pte. Alexander Sampson 7th. Suffolk Regt kia 9.4.17 (born Saffron Walden) - Duisans British Cemetery, Etrun, France, Plot 3 Row A Grave 19.

Wicks Pte. George 9th. Worcestershire Regt. kia 10.8.15 (born Saffron Walden) - Helles Memorial to the Missing, Gallipoli, Turkey, Panels 104 to 113.

Wilkinson Pte. Richard 72nd. Canadian Infantry (British Columbia) kia 9.4.17 - Vimy Memorial to the Missing, France.

Woodley Pte. Ernest 1st. Essex Regt kia 19.8.16 (born Saffron Walden. Name on

Littlebury memorial) - Potijze Burial Ground, Ypres, Belgium, Row A Grave 18.

Wright Pte. Ernest Lionel 11th. Royal Fusiliers kia 18.8.15 (born Saffron Walden. Name on Littlebury memorial) - Corbie Communal Cemetery, France, Plot 1 Row A Grave 17.

Wright Sgt. George 2nd. Essex Regt. kia 23.10.16 (born Saffron Walden. Name on Widdington memorial) - Thiepval Memorial to the Missing, France, Panel 10D.

(Total - 76 names)

A P P E N D I X 2

FRIENDS' SCHOOL MEMORIAL

Albright Pte. Joseph Pearson Northamptonshire Yeomanry kia 30th.October 1918 - Tezze British Cemetery, Italy, Plot 6 Row C Grave 4.

Arundel Lt. Philip Walter Rivers 43rd. Squadron Royal Air Force kia August 8th. 1918 - Arras Memorial to the Missing, France.

Cooper Pte. Cecil John 2nd. Bedfordshire Regt. kia December 12th. 1917 - Lijssenthoek Military Cemetery, Poperinghe, Belgium, Plot 27 Row DD Grave 7.

Deane Lt. Arthur Reginald 5th. Royal Sussex Regt. kia November 14th. 1917 - Dozinghem Military Cemetery, Westvleteren, Belgium, Plot 13 Row C Grave 7.

Duesbury Lce-Cpl. H Leslie Loyal North Lancashire Regt. died March 2nd. 1919 - Hertford (All Saints) Churchyard, Hertfordshire.

Elliott Pte. Joseph 1st. Middlesex Hussars died September 22nd. 1918 - Alexandria (Hadra) War Memorial Cemetery, Egypt, Row A Grave 2111.

Enock Chief Petty Officer Robert Royal Naval Air Service, H.M.S. President II died November 10th. 1916 - Southgate (Friends') Burial Ground, Middlesex. A/C by Special Memorial.

Gray Cpl. Gordon Cronin 9th. Norfolk Regt. kia September 26th. 1915 - Loos Memorial to the Missing, France, Panels 30 & 31.

Green Cpl. Donald R 5th. Dorsetshire Regt. kia September 26th. 1916 - Thiepval Memorial to the Missing, France, Panel 7B.

Harrison 2Lt. Percy Day 4th. Royal Sussex Regt. dow March 12th. 1917 - Bournemouth (Wimborne Road) Cemetery, Hampshire.

Hart Lt. Howard Victor 6th. London Regt. kia March 23rd. 1919 - Archangel Memorial, Russia and Brookwood (Russia) Memorial, Surrey.

Helliwell Pte. John William Noel 21st. Australian Imperial Forces kia February 26th. 1917 - Dernancourt Communal Cemetery Extension, France, Plot 6 Row A Grave 42.

Johnson Sapper. Charles Arthur 31st. Army Troop Company, Royal Engineers kia May 31st. 1916 - Vermelles British Cemetery, France, Plot 3 Row E Grave 23.

Newbery Pte. Frederic Walter 14th. Royal Warwickshire Regt. kia April 14th. 1918 - Ploegsteert Memorial to the Missing, Belgium, Panels 2 & 3.

Redding Pte. Lawrence H Australian Army Medical Corps died March 17th. 1919 - Cairo War Memorial Cemetery, Egypt, Row P Grave 47.

Roper Sgt. Richard S 4th. Australian Field Artillery kia May 26th. 1917 - Villers-Bretonneux Memorial to the Missing, France.

Roscher (Rosher) Pte. Max Leopold 1/5th. Northumberland Fusiliers kia October 26th. 1917 - Tyne Cot Memorial to the Missing, Belgium, Panels 19 to 23.

Sholl Gunner Arthur E 290th. Royal Field Artillery kia November 1st. 1917 - Buffs Road Cemetery, St. Jean-les-Ypres, Belgium, Row E Grave 17.

Skelton 2nd. Lt. Henry 11th. attached 16th. Lancashire Fusiliers (ex 28th. London Regt. Artists Rifles) kia October 2nd. 1918 - Joncourt East British Cemetery, France Row C Grave 15.

Skelton 2nd. Lt. Benjamin Dowell attached 10th. Essex Regt. dow November 7th. 1918 - St. Sever Cemetery Extension, Rouen, France, Block S Plot 5 Row G Grave 1.

Tawell Pte. Leslie R 18th. Battalion, Australian Imperial Forces August 27th. 1915 - Lone Pine Memorial, Gallipoli, Turkey, Panel 63.

Tilbrook Pte. Stanley James 6th. Connaught Rangers kia March 21st. 1918 - Pozieres Memorial to the Missing, France, Panel 77.

Tozer Cpl. Edward Gidley 9th. London Regt. (Queen Victoria's Rifles) kia July 1st. 1916 - Thiepval Memorial to the Missing, France, Panel 9C.

Walker 2nd. Lt. Stephen Cambridgeshire Regt. and Royal Air Force died May 14th. 1918 - Friends Burial Ground, Saffron Walden, Essex. (Name on Saffron Walden memorial).

(Total - 24 names)

IN ADDITION, BUT NOT ON THE SCHOOL MEMORIAL -

Lce-Cpl.Sidney Stuart Jenkins 1st. Honourable Artillery Company dow April 28th. 1917 - Etaples Military Cemetery, France, Plot 19 Row M Grave 10A. He was formerly a Classics master at the school.

A P P E N D I X 3

Some statistics.

Total Great War dead of Saffron Walden listed on town memorials - **159.**

Total of Great War dead not commemorated on our war memorial but who enlisted in the town - **247** (approx).

Totals killed by year -

1914 - 8.

1915 - 17.

1916 - 38.

1917 - 49.

1918 - 43.

1919 - 4. TOTAL - **159**

Day with highest number of deaths - **July 1st. 1916 - 4.**

Months with highest number of deaths - **July 1916 - 13.   April 1917 - 10. April 1918 - 8.**

Months with no deaths - **November, December 1914. January, April 1915. May 1916.   January, February, March and June 1918.**

Youngest to die - **Rifleman A.J. Brown and Pte. W.A. Crabb aged 18. Eleven others died aged 19.**

Oldest to die - **Pte. J. Pearson and Pte. A.S. Rushforth aged 42.**

Average age of death (estimated) - **28 years 3 months.**

Officer deaths - **8: Captain 1. Lieutenants 3. Second-Lieutenants 4.**

Non-Commissioned Officer (N.C.O.) deaths - **32: Sergeants 6. Corporals 9. Lance-Corporals 14. Stoker Petty Officer 1. Chief Steward 1. Leading Seaman 1.**

Other Ranks deaths - **119.**

Regiments

Essex: **43.**

London: **11.**

Middlesex: **11.**

Royal Fusiliers: **8.**

Dominion Forces: **Australian Imperial Forces 6.**
New Zealand Expeditionary Force 1.

Royal Navy: **6.**

APPENDIX 4

The war memorial was designed by the architect, T J Weatherall of Loughton in 1920. It was built by the firm of Whitehead and Day of Saffron Walden. Two of the late Mr. Osborne Whitehead's sons' names, Archibald and Osborne, are included on it. It was unveiled by General Lord Horne, G.C.G, K.C.M.G, G.O.C. Eastern Command. Standing thirty feet high it is octagonal in construction, erected upon a platform ten feet sixteen inches across. The platform is surmounted with three steps, upon which is a tapering pedestal upon which are eight sunk panels fitted with bronze tablets upon which are the names of the 159 fallen in raised lettering. (Interestingly, on its unveiling there were only 158 names. If you look at the bottom of one of the panels now you will see the addition of an extra name - George King. I believe he was originally omitted because of some confusion with Alfred George King).

There are carvings on four sides -

1. On the side facing down the High Street, a wreath of a wild rose, surrounding shield with St. George in relief.

2. On the side reverse to No.1, a wreath of English oak, surrounding shield with the arms of the County of Essex.

3. On the side towards London Road, a wreath of Saffron crocus, and a shield with embattled walls, enclosing three Saffron crocus flowers.

4. On the side towards Audley Road, a wreath of bay leaves, enclosing the old town seal of a lion rampant and fleur-de-lys in relief, in a sunk panel enclosed by a septfoil.

There are drip labels over the panels and carving. The base stone, on the top of the pedestal is carved with a large bay wreath. The shaft is tapering, with a moulded cap, mounted with a cross. The whole is worked in the finest brown whitened Portland stone.

The inscription says,

" For perpetual remembrance of the men of Saffron Walden who laid down their lives for their country in the Great War, 1914 - 1919. "

APPENDIX 5

LETTERS FROM A SOLDIER TO HIS MOTHER

2168 LANCE CORPORAL F. MARKING, 1ST BATTALION CAMBRIDGESHIRE REGIMENT (T.F).
Killed in Action, 26th June, 1915.

A DIARY OF FOUR MONTH 'S CAMPAIGNING IN FRANCE & BELGIUM, February-June, 1915.

(Postcard). 15/2/15.

> *Have arrived at Southampton (1) and been on board.*
> *Have just been allowed off for some tea.*

Much love, FRANK

[Undated].

My Dear Mother,

Have arrived safely after a rotten journey. It took us a fearful time to cross. We only arrived at quarter to four on Monday, and then they kept us hanging about till 4 or 5 hours later before we could land, and after that we had to wait and help unpack some limbers, etc., for the transport. To crown all, we had a 4 or 5 miles march after the journey up a terrific hill. (2) So you can imagine we were jolly glad to arrive last night and turn in. We are in bell tents, and 12 in a tent, so we keep fairly warm. Jack and I turn in together. (3)

Of course, we are not allowed to say where we are, and don't know how long we are to stop here. We came over with some of the -- ------

Much love, From FRANK.

19/2/15.

My Dear Mother,

This is my first opportunity of sending you a line to tell you a little of what we are doing.

We arrived at this place yesterday about dusk. (4) We had been travelling and hanging about the station, etc. since the morning of Wednesday, to-day being Friday. (5)

We are not a great way from the firing line, but suppose must not say any more than that. The hills are rotten for marching - both where we landed and here - and the roads seem to be all rough cobbles, which makes it extra tiring. We have been served out with fur coats, and I look rather like a tabby cat, having a sandy back, white front, and white and black sleeves. Where we are at present billeted in a barn, (6) which seemed very decent after trying to sleep in a troop train so crowded you couldn't lie down properly. We have had rather fun trying to talk to the people at the farm, and so far I have managed to make them understand what I want, even though we have to pay, and pay well, for everything we get from them.

The Germans have been here 4 or 5 times, and I understand shot some of the civilians here and made the rest dig trenches. This afternoon we are to have an inspection --- - - - left England -but we hope to get some proper rations soon. Am feeling very fit and enjoying myself.

Much love to all, from

FRANK

[Undated---Received 23/2/15].

My Dearest Mother,

I had hoped to be able to write you a decent letter to-day. But am afraid it will only be a short one after all, as we have been first on church parade, then about an 8-mile route march with full pack, and then had to dig trenches under the super-vision of some engineers with entrenching tools. So you will see they don't forget to keep us at work. Last night we could hear firing very distinctly all night, and we have had several aeroplanes flying overhead. There is always a certain amount of excitement over this, in case they should be German.

We were inspected yesterday by some Brigadier (7), who sent in a report to the effect that he had inspected 27 different Terrier Battalions in France (8), and we were the smartest and the only ones who were equal to "regulars" in what we did. To-morrow, General Smith-Dorrien is to inspect us, and at the end of the week, Sir John French, so they will be keeping us fairly busy.

Things seem very dear here -- bread is 6d. or 7d. a loaf, and sugar 1/3 a lb. I hope I shall get that 10/- soon, as Jack and I are both spent out, and as we have been going on bully and biscuits, we long for bread.

We are only to be paid once every 2 or 3 weeks, and then only small amounts. With our last coppers we bought two eggs, so we hope to enjoy our breakfast to-morrow. As a matter of fact, we are hoping to get better rations soon. The water is vile--- we are only allowed to drink what they serve out with, which tastes like medicine. The other water here is supposed to have been poisoned by the Germans.

Dad would he amused to see the pigs here. They are all ears and legs-more like racehorses. We feel certain the farmer we are with works his. They have the sauce to walk in our barn and eat biscuits out of our haversacks.

Do please send me weekly papers every week. We hear no news at all-only rumours. Is it right that the Dardenelles (sic) forts are smashed up and German submarines sunk in the Channel ?

I was very glad to get that card from you yesterday-it seems to take such a long time to hear from you.

I have had a vile cough and cold which I had before I started. In fact, sometimes I lost my voice entirely; am glad to say it is very much better and will soon be quite all right.

I wanted to wash out some hanks. to-day, but had no time.
They gave us some cigs. to-day - we were very glad to get them. Still, I haven't been able to smoke lately till to-day, so have plenty left. I believe they do give us plenty of cigs. to smoke. If you would like to send anything at any time, send me chocolate and one hank. occasionally, and a few shillings, please. A little money makes all the difference, as you can buy bread and cof-fee. The people here are not wonderfully generous, and make us pay for everything, such as boiling water for us.

I hope dad and you are quite alright now.

The scenery here is very picturesque, but all the land seems saturated with water. The farms are so filthy that an Englishman would think they were disgraceful. One man actually sleeps in with the cows in a shed that absolute-ly reeks.

Our journey over was a very trying experience, so much hanging about with so little sleep. Now, however, I am absolutely enjoying myself. Of course, we don't expect feather beds, though the last two nights I have had two splendid nights' rest.

Well, good-bye, and love to everyone. I will try to write to some of the others, but we get very little time.

Very much love,

From FRANK

My Dear Mother,

Thought I would send you a line to say I received your letter; evidently you hadn't got mine which I sent with the parcel. Still, I borrowed 5/- off Jack. (9) Will write as soon as I know my address. They got us up at 3 this morning.

Much love,

From FRANK.

P.S.-Expect money arrived after I left.

28/2/15.

My Dear Dad,

I was very pleased to hear from you, and to hear that you are feeling pretty fit again.

To-day we have had another move about a ten-mile route march and are now that much nearer to the firing line (10). From what we hear, we can expect to have a taste of trench work within the next fortnight. The place we are at now, will, I understand, be our base. We are billeted in a decent brick barn about I & a half miles from a village about the size of Chesterford. The country here is rather curious - one great advantage in being at a farm is that we can buy eggs. These are fine billets here we have all been in the house and had hot coffee and a warm. They charge us 1d. a cup for coffee.

Much love to all, from

FRANK

P.S.-I had a letter and P.P. from Lily.

I just stopped writing because a fellow lent me a Daily Mirror of 23rd date. The Germans didn't do much damage by their air raid on Braintree and Colchester, did they ? I expect they were trying to get at the troops.
I never mentioned, did I that the - - - -, on which we came out was tor-

pedoed on the return journey ? Lucky for us it wasn't coming over.

I haven't seen Eric and others lately, but might run across them any time.

Your letters to me are not censored at all as far as I know.

I should be glad to get some news of the War - we hear absolutely nothing.

I would like to write more than I do, but I get very little time and convenience for writing.

Did you send any money?

I didn't receive any. I should be glad of some, as I owe Jack 5/-, and we are able to buy food, etc., here - there is a Y.M.C.A. tent.

Love, FRANK

23/2/15.

My Dear Mother,

Many thanks for your letter, which I was very glad to get, and also to hear from Isie. I haven't heard anything about that money from the post office, and wonder how I shall get it when I do, as we are near no post office here. If I were you, I should enquire at the P.O. at home about it, as perhaps there are special arrangements for sending money to troops. In any case, don't send any more the same way, as there is so much delay even if I do get it.

The village we are in is about the size of Littlebury (11). We have only just left off work, and it is now too dark to see to write more.

Much love from

FRANK

I have been speaking to our officer who says there is some considerable delay in my getting the money that way.

I am on guard to-night, and am writing this at 2 a.m. in the guardroom. I was too late for the post to-day.

[By Censor. - He will receive this money to-morrow.]

26/2/l 5.

My Dear Mother,

I am very glad to say I have received the money order at last, and I have managed to get it changed. I got it yesterday, and meant to write to you then to let you know I had received it, but I did some washing, and then found I had no time to write, as we had to go on parade yesterday evening. We have to go on again this evening to man the trenches from about 6 to 1 we expect. We are not expecting to enjoy it very much, as they are beastly wet. They are some trenches we have been digging lately.

Lately, when they have been taking us out, they have got hold of the idea that we must be hardened, and no matter how it rains, they won't let us put on our overcoats. The other day we got absolutely wet through, and our officer was jolly decent and allowed us to go round to his billets to dry our things. Last night we got pretty wet, too, but I managed to get my things dry.

Did I say when I asked for chocolate that I would like plain chocolate~the sort of stuff you can get at grocers, I should imagine.

It is most extraordinary how everyone craves for chocolate - even fellows who never think of eating sweets in the ordinary way.

I was awfully pleased to hear from dad. I will write to him soon. I have also heard from Maggie and Cis.

General Smith-Dorrien inspected us yesterday, and paid us the compliment of saying that we were a "fine battalion" and "marched very well," so we really felt bucked with ourselves. (12)

Much love, From

FRANK

March 1, 1915.

My Dear Mother,

Just a line to say I have received your letter to-day and shall be glad to get the little parcel you mention.

We do nothing now but drink coffee all day at every opportunity. They charge us 1d. per cup - it is grand stuff.

Much love, From

FRANK

[Undated).

My Dear Mother,

I have just received the Weekly Dispatch, and am very glad to have it, as we hear so little war news except rumours. One of our companies left yesterday to go in the trenches, and our officer went with them to get experience. (13) I don't know when we are likely to go.

I started this yesterday, and have just received your letter saying you have sent of a small parcel which I haven't got yet. Expect it will turn up to-morrow. Did I tell you I received the P.O. for 3/- safely ? Thanks very much.

We heard to-day that our company I mentioned had bad luck to get under rifle fire while on fatigue work. One is killed and several wounded, I understand. The chap who was killed I knew fairly well. He was a very nice fellow. It seems to have been through sheer bad luck. (14) I had a parcel sent me by Nellie -- chocolates and cigarettes. Was very glad to have them, things are so expensive here.

Yes, a P.O. is the best way to send money - they change it for us at the orderly room through a Field Post Office.

Much love to all, From

FRANK

Jack wishes to he remembered to everyone at home. I have lost my spare shirt - had it pinched. Would you mind sending my old army shirt, perhaps they will leave me that.

March 6. 1915.

My Dear Mother,

Many thanks for parcel received yesterday. I was delighted with contents.

Would you mind sending me a pair of very stout leather gloves with tape stitched to them in such a way that it can run up my sleeves and across shoulders, joining gloves together, so as not to lose them?

I had a letter from Millie to-day and Punch from Cis.
Much love to all, From

FRANK.

March 8, 1915.

My Dear Mother,

I was very glad to hear from you again to-day, and to receive the Daily Mirror.

I should very much like some more of those beef tea things, and also some quinine lozenges would be useful, I think. Jack and I have both had very mild attacks of "flue," but have managed to cure them. Beef tea playing a large part in the cure.

I received a parcel from Cis to-day - very kind of her, I thought. Jack had two more arrive, so we shall live like lords for a little while.

I am getting very hot stuff at frying eggs in a mess tin.

Don't know for certain when we are likely to go in the trenches - perhaps about Thursday or Friday.

It seems to be fairly safe once you are in the trench-the difficulty is in getting there, and the Germans send up flares nearly all night trying to spot people going up to the trenches. We can see them distinctly every night here.

Much love from

FRANK

14/3/15.

My Dear Mother.

Many thanks for your letter. I am afraid you will wonder why you have not heard from me lately. As a matter of fact, we have had our first experience of the trenches, (15) and you must not worry or wonder if you don't hear from me for several days on occasion, as we get no chance of writing there, and in any case, there is delay in getting letters off. You'll hear soon enough if anything is wrong, so always remember no news is good news. I will write whenever I can.

The trenches are not so bad. We were in support trenches about 100 yards or so from the Germans. (16) The shell fire is the worst thing. Personally, I didn't mind the row as much as I thought I should. With regard to the shells themselves, a miss is as good as a mile, isn't it ? Some of the beggars drop unpleasantly near. The worst part really is the last mile walking up to the trenches at night to relieve. The road is full of holes caused by shells, and bullets whiz about in all directions. Whenever flares go up near you, as they do every few minutes, you have to keep perfectly still, and then they say they can't see you. If they are very near you have to flop down wherever you are even if you are nearly up to your neck in mud.

The mud is really rather terrible, but the worst thing, I think, is the fearful stenches everywhere.

If our first experience of the trenches is anything to go by, I must say it isn't really so very terrible. Of course, no one could be really fond of it, but I can honestly say I never felt a bit funky over it. I shouldn't want to do it as a hobby though.

I haven't received the parcel yet, but everything turns up in good time. Thanks for the P.O. shall be able to get it changed later on.

We shall, as a rule, go in the trenches for 48 hours, then have 48 hours off, and then 48 hours in again, and then have 8 days rest. While not in the trenches, we are in what is practically the 3rd line of defence, and are under shell fire. We have had one or two over just lately, as we are near one of our batteries billeted in stables belonging to a Chateau.

Our artillery is letting them have it just now. The Chateau which is about 20 yards off has been very much knocked about. We are not allowed out in the open or any lights, as if they knew troops were here, they would immediately shell us.

Must leave off now. We may be going in to-night. but don't know yet. We expect to start our eight days off on next Friday or Saturday.

Much love, from

FRANK

18/3/15.

Dearest Mother,

As you will see, I am writing this on my birthday, I received your parcels and letters last evening, so it was in nice time, you see (17).

I wonder if you got my letter written from the Chateau, after our first experience of the trenches. We had a night's rest, and the following evening were called out unexpectedly. Half of our section who had then relieved us were in the trenches and we were sent out with the other gun to be held in reserve in ease of need. We were kept hanging about 3/4 of a mile from the trenches, all night, as the situation was rather serious. The Germans had sapped and blown up a mound about 100 yards from the trench we had been in. They then must have attacked in thousands; they were the Prussian Guards, and new troops so I understand. They captured several trenches from our men, though their losses must have been tremendous. (18)

Our regiment, being in reserve trenches, was right in the thick of it, and some of them were compelled to evacuate their trenches. Our machine gun did splendid work-one officer and sergeant were in the half section in trenches at the time, and our fellows blazed away with their rifles as well. (19) They reckon they saved the trench and put no end of Germans out of action.

I wish I had been there - not one got a scratch, though several around were, killed and wounded.

That night, as I say, the rest of us were hanging about in a village 3/4 mile off firing line. About daybreak, we proceeded up the road leading to the trenches-it was pitiful to meet the streams of wounded coming down the road. It was just beginning to get light when we arrived in a field, and started digging a trench under rifle fire. This was abandoned after a bit, owing to the fact, I imagine, that our second counter-attack on the trenches (made by several different brigades) had succeeded. Troops simply streamed back along the road to the village-why on earth they didn't shell us is beyond my comprehension. We then received orders to return to the Chateau. Next night, they awoke us about 10, and we went to relieve the others in the trenches. It is awfully tedious work getting up to the trenches - the Germans sending up flares all the time.

We had a quiet time on the whole, and our trench wasn't shelled all day. In the afternoon, we dug earth and filled sandbags, while snipers tried to stop us-but it evidently takes something better than bullets to hit any of the gun section. We have been jolly lucky to sustain no casualties though our regiment has sustained several. We don't know quite how many, so I won't give figures or mention names, as nothing is certain. (20)

After leaving the trenches, we carried the gun, etc., back to the Chateau, and then found the battalion moving and we had to march here about 8 miles, I suppose, and we are now having a few days rest. (21) We arrived here at daylight yesterday. The roads are so bad, and it means halting all the way. I felt done up, and slept all yesterday, but am feeling quite fit again.

Thank Isie for letter; tell him that I quite expected to feel funky, but can honestly say I didn't a bit - you get beyond that. I was awfully glad to be with Jack in the trenches. I don't pretend I liked it - no one could - it is simply hell. But I didn't funk it, and it is certainly no good to do so. Shell fire is the most unpleasant thing.

Thanks for all your letters I received on my return. Much love to all. I will let you know when we are going up again.

I have several I must write to, so perhaps shall not send a line to-morrow.

Your affectionate son,

FRANK

March 22nd.

Just to let you know I am alright, and have received ginger-bread. Also parcel from Aunt Isobel. We move up again to-morrow.

Love from FRANK

March 24, 1915.

My Dear Mother,
    I was very glad to hear from you again to-day -- expect by now you will have received some of my letters.
    We have not moved up to the trenches yet; expect we shall go on Friday now. I understand we are moving to a fresh part of the line. Have heard nothing of the Staffs. I have had my writing pad pinched, and don't like to use all Jack's up for him. Will you send another -- can't buy notepaper here.
    Love, from FRANK

March 25th.

My Dear Mother,

I have just received letter and postcard, thanks very much. I did not receive shirt or gloves, though the papers in which latter had been wrapped up arrived. Do not send any more of either, as some leather gloves have been given me, and I will try to get shirt off the regiment.
    We are still having a rest, and are not certain when we move -- perhaps to-morrow. Don't forget to send writing pad.

    Much love, from

FRANK

March 27th, 1915.

My Dear Mother,

Just a line to let you know I am all right. We are still on our rest cure -- don't know how much longer it will last.
    I had a letter from Cis to~day - very pleased to receive it.
Have absolutely no news.

Love to all,

FRANK.

March 29, 1915.

My Dear Mother,

Just a line to let you know I am quite all right. We hear we may be moving off to-morrow, but don't know for certain.

Love to all, From FRANK

March 30th.

[Postcard].

Am quite alright. No news at all. Lovely weather here, but cold north wind.

Love to all, from

FRANK

2/4/15.

No hot cross buns to-day.

We have marched about 8 miles and have arrived at a well-known town near the firing line. (22) We are going into the trenches to-night. (23) Expect to have a fairly slack time. Love to all, and kind regards from Jack, with thanks to you for Easter Egg.

11/4/15.

My Dear Mother,

I am not quite sure of the date, but imagine it to be the eleventh. I would have liked to have written you before to let you know I am alright, but that was impossible.

The morning we left the place where we had been resting, we turned out at 2 a.m. and fell in and marched here with the battalion. This is the place of which I have spoken before not much larger than Stortford, I should imagine, but possessing several beautiful buildings and churches. The place has suffered terribly from bombardment; photographs convey no idea of the effect of shell fire. The houses are riddled with small holes from shrapnel, as well as having lumps knocked off them by high explosives.

What strikes one most forcibly is the heroism of the civil population, who continue to live in the remains of what was once their home, and carry on their ordinary occupation as though nothing had happened, though this place is shelled daily.

On our way from here to the trenches, we pass several farmhouses -- perhaps half the house will be gone, even then, in many cases, the people still continue to live there, and their dogs still hang about the farm yard. It brings home the misery of war more clearly than anything. Poor little Belgium. Suppose it was my home I always think ! - or poor little Billy, and still clinging to what had been his favourite haunts. -

On arriving here, there was nowhere for the gun section to go, the place being packed. Fortunately it was fine, and we lay down all day in the shade of a church. That evening, half the gun section was detailed for the trenches, among whom were Jack and I. We left at eight, and after a fearfully tedious march, arrived at the dumping ground, which is as far as the limbers are allowed to go. After this, all our guns, tripods, etc., had to be carried. (24)

It was cold and wet, and perfectly miserable. We arrived at the trenches after a struggle - the last man getting in about 4-30.

We were supposed to stop in this trench for 48 hours - it was our first experience of the actual fire trench, the Germans, in some parts, being only about 10 yards away. (25) The first day -- Saturday - passed very quietly, the next was Easter Sunday and the Germans then put up a notice wishing us a Happy Easter, and said they wouldn't fire unless we did. However, about 2 hours afterwards, they shelled us rather heavily, the earth thrown up by the explosion falling in our trench in quite large lumps.

Being under shell fire is beastly. We were not relieved on Sunday, as arrangements were altered, and we were to put in four days straight off. On the Tuesday night, however, we expected an attack, and had the order for every man to "stand to" practically all night. It was pitch dark, you couldn't see your hand in front of your face; very few flares were sent up. You can imagine it being rather uncanny peering out and listening, trying to see if the Germans are creeping up to your parapets. Of course, that meant having to stop in another 2 days, by which time we got almost in difficulties as to whether we were relieved or not. About five of "A" Company fellows went off their heads, owing to the strain, and they were only in four days.

I was put in charge of one of the guns, and what, with extra duties and the beastly weather (rain all the time), I got very little sleep; still I feel wonderfully fit. On Thursday evening we were actually relieved at last. We had to carry all our stuff back to some dug-outs in a wood, where we were to spend the night. We were all feeling so tired, that owing to the awful mud, shell holes, stumps of trees, etc., the journey took us over 4 hours. The next day we were moved to some dug-outs about 150 yards in rear of our fire trench at a different part of the line -a part of our section being in the trenches. That evening I was put in charge of a fatigue party going to the dumping ground to draw rations. We had a guide from the communicating section. He took us there after a fashion, but gave us the slip there. However, our fellow decided to trust to my tender mercies and risk it, and we managed to find our way back. We lost the road once in a wood, and I made them halt, and pushed ahead myself to try to discover the way, and succeeded in finding a very hot corner, bullets all round me. You can imagine how relieved I was I had left them behind.

A sergeant of another regiment put us on the right road, and we returned safely, wet and tired, but quite cheerful. The next day (yesterday) we were sent here (the town of which I have spoken) for a much-needed rest. On Thursday next we return to the trenches.

Tell Cis her cookery is magnificent - her parcel and the one from Lolly's girl came at the best possible times - one in the trenches and the other when I arrived at the dug-outs on Friday.

I heard from Maggie to-day; she sent me several snaps.

Would you mind sending me a parcel soon after you get this, as I shall then get it after my next four days in the trenches. I should love more meat patties and potted meat.

Much love to all - you don't know how much I was thinking of you all at Easter, and wishing I could have been with you. Not that I am not quite content with what I am doing.

Your affectionate son,

FRANK

Tell dad I did get his letter some while ago, and was delighted with it.

Jack wants to be remembered to you. We are sitting up in "bed" after our first good night's rest.

13/4/15

My Dearest Mother,

Just a line to let you know that we are off to the trenches again for four days, I believe.

I have been fitted out with a new uniform, so am feeling quite smart for the occasion.

Have just been out with Jack and had a good feed-actually managed to get a bath of sorts this morning. Have no news but plenty to do.
Much love, From FRANK.

My Dearest Mother,

Thanks so much for your ripping letter and parcel, which arrived to-day. The greater part of the grub I intend saving up to take with us to the trenches, as we expect to return in four days time, which will be on Wednesday next.

We came out of the trenches, last night, having been in for four days. We had our first casualties in the gun section on this occasion-one of our fellows was shot through the head and killed; (26) another had a narrow escape, being slightly wounded in the head, but he is practically alright again now. We feel awfully sorry about the poor chap who was killed, although he only came on the gun section recently; he was a general favourite, as he was always cheerful and full of jokes - never out of temper, which is a great thing in this life.

Jack wishes to be remembered to all at home. We are both feeling in the pink. Last night there was a pretty big scrap near us. Our fellows were advancing on our right and making a demonstration with rapid fire and artillery on our left to mislead the enemy. According to what we hear, the attack was thoroughly successful and accomplished with surprisingly small losses.

We are all looking forward to the expected big attack -- of course, we know there will be big losses, but we are getting anxious to get the beggars on the run, and feel confident of being able to do so. The Germans are past masters in the art of trench warfare, and all its tricks, but in a good stand up fight, our fellows have the advantage.

I should very much like that wrist watch sent out if it is in good going order, as when I am in charge of the gun, I have to arrange about reliefs for look-outs, etc., and time the chaps to see they go on at the appointed time, etc. It will be frightfully useful to me.

Last night, while I was on look-out from 1/4 to 12 till 1/4 to 2, it was a lovely night, the sky was studded with stars, our trench was in a wood, and you could see the tall trees all round us clearly silhouetted against the sky. The attack on the German lines had been made (27), and we imagined our fellows digging them-selves in at their new positions against the counter-attack, which would be certain to take place about dawn. Occasional flares lit up the sky, and over the fitful rifle fire sounded the booming of the German artillery (or what was left of it), shelling our fellows in their new position, and searching for our big guns. We keep a sharp look-out all the while, in case they make a counter-attack at this point, and take an occasional shot at the parapet of their trench. It may sound a rather eerie experience, but it has its charms.

Shortly after we were relieved by the other half of our section. We had about a 5 or 6 mile march back to our billets. Part of the journey some shells fell fairly near us-the nearest one, fortunately, failed to explode. We imagined they were trying to hit the batteries concealed near the road along which we were marching.

We were rather startled at the loud report of one of the batteries which fired several shells while we were passing behind it.

I had a parcel from Aunt Isabel, containing some knitted things, which we don't really need, and some sweets and condensed milk, which were highly acceptable.

Please don't send any more tobacco (pipe) for some while. I should like a packet of cocoa when you send next, please.

You ought to see us frying steak and onions in the trenches in our mess tins. That always seemed to annoy Fritz (the sniper over the way), as about dinner time he always potted our sandbags, sending the earth flying all over our dinner. He must have had a rare nose for onions.

Jack and I took a loaf and 8 hard boiled eggs with us to the trenches, and on the whole fared sumptuously.

I had a letter from Cis to-day. I will try to write to some of the many people I owe letters to, but as you know, we are only allowed one letter a day.

Oh ! please send me some tooth powder; true, I only clean my teeth occasionally, but still it is very enjoyable to do so when I get the chance.

Thank Isie for his letter and P.C.'s.

Fortunately, the weather was very good during our last pic-nic in the trenches. After the war, I intend looking round all the little ditches we have lived in, I'm sure It will be highly entertaining.

No more paper here or time to write more.

Very much love to all,

From FRANK.

[Postcard]. 19/4/15.

Thanks very much for P.O. and parcel. Delighted with both. The Germans have been shelling us pretty heavily to-day; the dirty dogs.

Love to all,

From FRANK

April 20.

My Dearest Mother,

Just to let you know I am quite alright, in spite of everything. Poor Jack has had the toothache badly lately, so perhaps will not accompany us on our next trip, that is, if they will pull a tooth out and alter his false tooth plate for him. He wouldn't see about it till I made him.

Have received writing pad, as you will doubtless notice. Tell Mary that at present I am full of meat patty and sausage roll, and that the feeling is a beautiful one.

I could not write to Mrs. Waturley, as she gave me no address.

Will you send it to me, and also let her know that I received and much appreciated the parcel on Easter Monday ?

Love to all, FRANK

27/4/15.

My Dear Mother,

Many thanks for parcel I received last night. On Sunday we completed another four days in the trenches, and are now spending 4 days in dug-outs about 200 yards to rear of trenches. I wrote you yesterday, but failed to get the letter sent.

We had a fellow in the gun section killed yesterday (28), and Lieut. Ollard has gone home ill. Our last four days "rest" we were subjected to a terrific bombardment at the town where we were. One day, 180 ordinary high explosive shells fell in the place. (29) It is a wretched experience, and one of our chaps had his nerves completely shattered. However, it didn't stop me eating or sleeping, so you will see that it didn't worry me very badly. Two big shells together put 127 men out of action. It is fearful to see the women and kiddies and dead civilians. **[Paragraph deleted by Censor].**
I suppose, and last night about a mile or so, from the firing line, a day after a German attack, the fumes hung about and made your eyes water. (30)

While in the trenches we had several thrilling moments of rapid fire, etc., and bullets started coming through our parapet. We repaired it at the first opportunity. We had very little rest all the time, and we were quite expecting an attack, which never came off. We were quite ready for them.

Love to all,

FRANK

P.S.-Will you please send in next parcel some Colgate Shaving Soap. The Cocoa you sent was very acceptable, but came loose all over parcel. I rescued the greater part of it.

Watch not yet arrived, expect it to-night. When you send more chocolate, would you mind sending Cadbury's Mexican, as I prefer that.

Would you please send another shirt, as I have found a few undesirables (31). We all have them. I am afraid you worry an awful lot with all my requests, but it does make a difference. If they only feed us well, we feel we can put up with anything else.

Much love,

FRANK.

29/4/15.

My Dearest Mother,

Many thanks for the parcel I received last night. I haven't got the watch yet, but if you registered it, that would, of course, account for the delay.

We return to the trenches to-night for another four days. unless the batt. is relieved on Saturday, of which there is some talk.

With regard to the news you have been reading in the papers at home, things, from what we hear, are hardly as bad as one would suppose. While we were in the trenches last time, things were critical at one period, and we were practically cut off, but they seem to have the situation well in hand, and from what we hear, to have more than made amends for any ground lost.

We are having lovely weather here now; if it were not for the war and other small enemies, things would be very enjoyable. As it is, however, we make the best of things, and have many a good laugh in spite of everything.

Thanks particularly for the condensed milk and cocoa -- if I may mention it, I would really prefer Van Houten's or some cocoa that goes farther. We always get plenty of sugar near these dug-outs.

We get a plentiful supply of water by a little stream that runs into a Jack Johnson hole (32) -- in fact, in and out of the trenches we get most of our water from these miniature ponds kindly supplied by the Germans. Of course, we always have to boil the water before drinking it. It makes, me feel glad that I have been inoculated.

I didn't tell you that, apart from Mitchell being killed since we left the trenches last, Wakefield (a Sawston chap, who was slightly wounded before) was shot through the ear, and is now in hospital.

No end of our battalion have gone sick, and what with casualties, we only have about 600 of our men left.

We hear that our Colonel has gone back to England "sick" or "something," chiefly "something," I imagine. There seems to be a great dearth of officers heaven alone knows where they have all got to.

We can only congratulate ourselves on having the best sergeant in the regiment, and a section that feels pretty confident of its capacity to look after itself.

Am afraid I have nothing to write about, as though only about 200 yards from the trenches, we hear and see and do practically nothing.

Yesterday was enlivened by some shells, but no damage was done.

Love to all. From FRANK.

11/5/15.

My Dearest Mother,

I am afraid you must be feeling rather anxious at having so little news from me lately. Well, I am quite alright, I am glad to say, though naturally we are none of us feeling particularly fit, as we have had rather a rough and tiring time. We have not been relieved yet, though, I think, It cannot be very long before we are. Our other half section relieved us in the trenches last night, and we are now back in dug-outs. I suppose you will have heard the news of the Allies' advances, just lately (33). It puts fresh heart into all of us, as the Germans are so much better than us at trench warfare, but no match for our men at a real fight.

One day soon I will try to give you a proper account of what we have been doing lately, but just now I feel too lazy, and besides,, must not say too much, as I am sending this letter uncensored.

Two days we went without rations, and the third had only bully and biscuits, so you can tell things have been rather upset. In spite of everything, we still keep our pecker up, although, of course, we are feeling the strain a bit. Your parcel (for which many thanks), and one from Miss Suddaby, came on the day we got decent rations, together with several letters that had been hung up.

The weather here is simply gorgeous. The life would be delightful if there were no war.

One of our companies lost heavily the other day, while in support under shell fire -- about 40 casualties in all. (34)

I believe we have the Germans whacked at last. We all feel that we would much rather attack and take risks that way than sit still and wait for it.

I have had a washing day to-day, and am wearing a clean shirt -- the first change since I left Bury. Fancy the Zepp. over Bury (35). Thank Isaac for his letter. I will write to him to-morrow, all being well.

Much love to everyone, FRANK.

12/5/15.

Dear Isie,

I was very glad to have your letter, and at last have found time to reply to it.

I see in the paper from home that the retirement to a line of trenches some distance back has been reported (36). Well, we took part in that affair. We knew it was coming off some while before it happened, as we were making preparations to evacuate our trench. That is to say, emptying all available sandbags, removing everything possible in the way of planks and corrugated iron, etc. Just before we left, we slit all the remaining sandbags, and cleared out of the trench to a position already prepared. It was rather amusing to us, as we wondered how long the Germans would solemnly sit in front of the trenches before they discovered we had left them. One of our "B Company chaps got left behind in a dug out, and was awakened at daybreak by the Germans opening rapid fire, evidently smelling a rat. He cleared out just in time (37), as shortly afterwards the Germans discovered we had gone, and advanced down the road in fours, a chap leading them on horseback, and some with bicycles; and soon as our fellows saw them, they opened machine gun fire, and caught them beautifully. Needless to say, any idea of a march through to Calais was immediately knocked on the head.

As they, of course, had no trenches within several hundred yards of ours, they of course shelled our trenches unmercifully. Still, I have known them send hundreds of shells at our trenches, and do practically no damage at all. One thing is certain, and that is that they suffer from no shortage of ammunition-an artillery officer reckoned that they sent seven shells to our one, and then didn't do anything like the same damage.

Last time we were in the trenches, they shelled us pretty considerably and also sent some " lobdobs " from trench mortars (38). These are fearfully unpleasant -- quite the nastiest things I've stuck bar 17 inch shells. They make a fearful report, and explode with terrific force. One fellow near us had his head blown off and every stitch of clothing. You can see the wretched things coming, and there is quite a rush up the trench, trying to dodge them. The only difficulty is they wobble on their course, and when quite near, it is hard to gauge where they are coming. From our other fellows who relieved us I heard that our artillery shelled them yesterday, and made them shift their mortar farther down the line.

Our Brigade still seems as far as ever from being relieved, so I expect we shall return to the trenches, in two days time for another four days. We continue to hear good news of advances from all quarters. I wonder if Italy will come in-have just heard of her ultimatum to Germany. The United States should be upset over the "Lusitania" too I should imagine (39).

Love to all,

From FRANK.

The Lilacs, Maple Copse,(40)

"Somewhere in Flanders,"

Friday, May 21, 1915.

My Dear Mother,

Very many thanks for your letters, etc., which I have been unable to acknowledge before. I heard yesterday that various letters, etc., I wrote while here in the " dug-outs " last time were not despatched till then, so perhaps you will understand why there has been all that delay before you heard from me.

Our Brigade has not yet been relieved, but should be to-morrow, unless arrangements are altered again.

I did receive that first parcel from Maggie and Cis, but really things have been so very muddled with us lately that I cannot say for certain if I acknowledged it or not. I also got another one from you, which was sent later. I got two P.O.'s from you fairly lately, and hope to be able to spend them soon when we go back for our well-earned rest.

It is a strain, of course, and the conditions are pretty hard. yet Jack and I keep wonderfully fit really.

You would be surprised at what an expert cook I am becoming, while here in dug-outs, about a mile at the back of the trenches. We get plenty of time on our hands, and if we are not shelled, and it only keeps fine, life is really very bearable.

Yesterday I ransacked several farms in the neighbourhood, and got some potatoes, leeks, and kind of sorrel, and some lilac and stocks. With the latter I made a garden in front of our dug-out -- hence its name. With the potatoes and meat I made some "shepherd's pie." Very good it was, too, with two or three cubes to help the gravy. For pudding we crushed some biscuits of the Army order to a kind of flour, and mixed it with some cocoa and milk stuff and water into a batter, added some butter we were lucky enough to have served out, and made so much we could hardly eat it all, and had to give some away - greedy brutes I can hear you say.

To-day's programme will also be very varied.

For breakfast, coffee (Miss Suddaby sent me some coffee and milk), ham cooked, issued in rations, and potted meat sent by Cis. For dinner, "shepherd's pie," as yesterday (only, of course, much better !), for pudding, biscuits soaked all night in water and Nestle's Milk, and cooked up this morning at 3 a.m. with some damson jam (served out in tins), followed, perhaps, by cheese and a cigarette. For tea, we have some salmon and vinegar Jack had sent him, toast, perhaps, and then a bar of chocolate. If we can eat any more, we may have some Welsh rabbit for supper.

We appreciate these meals because in the trenches we have no convenience for cooking, and are very often very short of grub. It is difficult and dangerous to bring rations up to this point, and consequently we have very often had to go short, especially when there has been any attack round about.

Love to all,

From FRANK

Since finishing your letter, Jack and I have been out again, and found some flowers and few leeks and some rhubarb. Am sending a forget-me-not and another flower.

Our dug-out is decorated now with a scheme of lilac and pink stocks, with some pretty green I picked in the wood-it looks great ! (41)

24/5/15.

My Dear Mother,

Just a line or two to let you know I am quite well and we are now back on rest (42), but don't know how long -- expect to return too. To-day we are "standing to," and may have to move off at any moment as there is something happening near here. Must leave off now to catch post, bot hope to write a proper letter to-morrow.

Much love

From FRANK

My Dearest Mother,

At last I am going to try to write you a really decent letter, and give you some account of my doings. I only hope the Censor will be fairly indulgent and leave enough of my letter for it to be recognised.

We are sleeping here in a ripping field, under bivouacs made out of waterproof sheets. The weather is ideal-May weather at its best. I got up at four this morning and made some cocoa, and I am now sitting on a gun limber writing this, having written to Mr. Ollard to thank him for a parcel he was kind enough to send me. A sweet little dog who slept in our bivouac all last night is sitting beside me while I am writing. It is now nearly seven, but everyone else still sleeps on. All one can hear at present are the fowls and cows, and a skylark singing over-head-a very welcome change from the continuous roar of rifle fire and artillery. All that reminds us there is a war on is the occasional hum of an aeroplane overhead and the distant rumbling of guns.

I am glad to say I got my watch all right yesterday, and it now goes beautifully. Thanks also for last parcel containing cakes, etc.

I have just heard this morning that we have had a very important victory round this way. All yesterday we were "standing to," and I believe are still doing so. I was told we have made a big advance and taken large numbers of prisoners, and I only hope it is true. I don't particularly want to be called out again just yet, but if to chase the beggars, I shouldn't grumble. I think we all regard them as personal enemies now after what we have seen and been through. There seems to be no trick too dirty or contemptible for them.

I think the last time I gave you an account of any doings was while we were "resting" at Ypres during the bombardment. That was "some" bombardment, I can tell you. However, it is much worse now, and is quite in ruin, with not a living soul in the place. It seems terribly sad.

We returned from there back to our old trench, and had a very warm time (43). When the Germans broke through, we were cut off, and I don't know what would have happened if the line hadn't been re-established. I saw - -------- blown up, but I believe I told you something about that. In this trench the Germans continually used to open rapid fire, and we always expected an attack, which never came off, though at one time the bullets came through our parapet till I had it built up from the inside. We were in a bit of trench this shape--

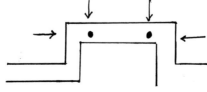

the dots representing gun positions, and we used to get fire from all directions, even from the back. Every time we have been in the trenches we have been in a very advanced position, and could see the flares being sent up nearly all round. As you stand in the trenches at night, you would see these flares all round you like this--

This, of course, means that getting into the trench is risky work, as you are quite liable to get enfiladed.

The next thing we had to do was, when, as I see has been stated in the papers, we shortened our line. This was a rather ticklish job, but accomplished very successfully. The new trenches we retired into were good trenches, much narrower, and with no dug-outs, which means that any sleep you get you have to get sitting up, and under no cover at all. I have seen men so tired in the trenches that at night on getting up to look over the parapet, they have fallen back as though shot -- asleep.

From there we went to dug-outs in" Maple Copse," and expected to go back on rest, but after 3 days, we went up to the trenches in a rather different part of the line, but only a short distance off. In this trench the most serious things we had to contend with were shells of the "whizz bang" variety (44) and trench mortars -- these latter are particularly horrible. The explosion from them is simply terrific. We had 3 doses of 4 days in that trench, and had pretty well enough of it -- it is impossible to describe things to you as they are. One has to experience it to realise what it is like. As long as it keeps fine, and they can get the rations up, it is fairly bearable, but other-wise!

Anyway, we are jolly glad of a rest, however short, and hope to return to the fray fit and well to do our little bit towards the "advance" we all hope for and look forward to, to try and end the war as soon as possible.

Much love to all,

FRANK.

May 30, 1915.

My Dear Mother,

Many thanks for your letter received yesterday. We have had 3 days marching during which time we received no letters, nor were able to dispatch any (45). We arrived the night before last in these trenches in a different part of the line, and near another and bigger town (46). I intended writing to you yesterday, but learnt too late that the post had to be in by 12 o'clock. You can tell Millie that on the way here we passed through the place where Howard used to be billeted, but I had no time to enquire if he was still there. Anyway, I expect he

157

has a commission by now.

These trenches are simply great. I had no idea that trenches could be so good. There is a communicating trench reaching to a suburb of the town at the back. There is a plentiful supply of magnificent dug-outs. The Germans are 400 or 500 yards away, and never seem to do much shelling or firing. The result is the place is an absolute rest cure after the rough time we have been used to.

Poor Jack Brand is in hospital with a burnt, and, I am afraid, poisoned arm, and also a temperature of 100-6. Expect to hear from him shortly where he is and how he is. I learn that Penketh's lot have been round this quarter for a short space, but have shifted. I was very glad to. hear from Miss Osborn, and I hope Bob is alright. Poor old Gillespie. I often wondered about him. Was sorry to hear about Mary's sister, and hope she is much better now.

It is awfully good being so near the town, as we can get grub sent up in the shape of eggs, beer, and tinned stuffs. The beer is, of course, very thin stuff, but highly acceptable in these days.

We are all as happy as lords here. I only wish Jack was here to enjoy it as well.

Yesterday we had omelette made of eggs, one onion, and tomatoes. It was grand!

Just at the back of our trenches is a farmhouse with a moat. Yesterday we repaired ---------, which had been faked up as a punt, and two of our fellows got on it. About midstream they started to sink, and finally the thing capsized. Another fellow and I, who were looking on, simply yelled. In fact, my only regret is that I laughed so much I couldn't see it all.

It was just too funny to see them striking out for the shore !

Much love, from FRANK

June 2, 1915.

My Dear Mother,

Thanks for your letter and postal order received to-day. I have already had it changed and shall he able to spend the proceeds on grub in the village. Things have been quiet here since I wrote last, - in fact, life in these trenches, unless things alter considerably, is a very enjoyable thing.

I heard from Jack yesterday; he said he was better, but that his arm is still bad. Nevertheless, he hopes to see us all again very shortly.

I had a thrilling and unpleasant experience last night. Day - one of our gunners - and I volunteered and obtained permission to reconnoitre in front of our gun position. (47)

Just as we were on the point of going out, we received orders to go with two officers who were also going out. We were all armed with revolvers and some wire cutters.

By walking at first and then crawling, we managed to get over two lots of barbed wire, and when about 100 yards of their trenches, they seemed to have had some suspicion that we were crawling towards them.

They sent up a flare and fired a shot or two in our direction.

By resting whenever they sent up flares, we crawled up to their "knife rests" (barbed wire entanglements), which were not more than 25 yards off their trench. For some while we could hear them talking and also the click as of loading rifles, and we heard the murmuring as of an order being passed down the line, and a suppressed cough.

We reached there at 10 minutes to 12, having taken 1 1/2 hours to get there. At 12, they suddenly fired a shot which hit one of the officers, who called out, and they at once peppered us at short range (48). The other officer who was next to him examined him, and the first one who had been groaning suddenly left off. In a minute or so they ceased fire, and Day and I started to crawl to try and render assistance, but at once the officer who had examined got up and ran like a hare to our lines (49). Under these circumstances, we assumed the officer first hit was dead, and after a hurried consultation, followed suit.

On reaching our lines, we found the officer being bandaged up, and enquired if the other was dead. He said' "I don't know, but he was shot through the chest." We at once volunteered to try and get him in (while realizing, as the officer said when we had gone, that it was practically a forlorn hope). By this time the moon was well up, and we knew it would be impossible to get cover, so we ran and got over their first lot of barbed wire, when they spotted us, and sent up a flare and a shot or two. We agreed to try to get farther, and ran another 50 or 70 yards to within about 30 yards of the first position; they then sent up another flare and opened fire in such a way it was impossible to get any further.

We reluctantly returned and reported to Major Saint (50), who, on examination, said it was impossible to do anything further. I feel cut up about the officer. Doubtless he was dead, as they peppered that spot so freely, and the other officer was hit four times though not dangerously, I believe. We had no idea he was hit till we returned to the trench.

I have just looked at the position through glasses, and find we were even nearer the German lines (51) -15 yards is quite the farthest we can have been from their parapet.

Day and I had a marvellous escape.

As I have previously mentioned, I have received watch some little while back, and also have my cigarette case with me.

Was surprised to hear about Mr. Evans - what did you think of him?
I wonder if Gillespie is in Walden.

Much love to all, from

Your affectionate son,

FRANK.

3/6/15.

My Dear Mother,

I am fit and well, and feeling as right as rain.

Love to all,

From FRANK

Sunday, June 6, 1915.

My Dear Mother,

Thanks for your letter. I cannot understand how it was that you have not received any of my letters, but suppose they will turn up eventually. There are so many possible causes of delay.

That officer I told you about, who we thought was dead was found to be wounded (52). This was ascertained two days afterwards by getting in communication with the Germans, who had taken him into their trench (53). They wouldn't say how had he was, but from what the other officer said, he must be pretty bad, I'm afraid. I feel awfully pleased about it. We said at the time that was his only chance.

I haven't heard from Jack again yet, but hope to see him shortly. Thanks so much for parcel-have just remembered that I have not acknowledged it,

It is still frightfully hot. We have been using our machine gun the last two nights, and seem to he tickling them up a bit. We are going to use her again to-night.

Love to all,

From FRANK

My Dearest Mother,

I expect you will be surprised to hear that I am no longer in the trenches. Another fellow and I are back in the town with our Transport looking after the Gun Section rations. We are to have a week of this, and then go back and another two will take our places. We only came out yesterday, and are thoroughly enjoying our first holiday since we came out to France.

This morning I got up at five and went on horseback with the rest of the transport to exercise the horses. I am feeling rather stiff and sore in consequence. There is a decent canal about 100 yards from here, where one can have a swim.

Did I tell you that we found out two days afterwards that that officer had been taken in by the Germans, wounded, of course, how badly, they wouldn't say. I need not tell you how pleased we were. I had said to Major Saint that night that I thought it was his only chance.

I have heard that Jack is practically well and expects, to rejoin us in a day or two. I shall be awfully glad to see him back.

The last 3 nights I was in the trenches we used our machine gun, and succeeded in doing a certain amount of damage, according to current slang, "fairly put the wind up the Germans."

There are one or two funny tales I have never told you. While at Ypres, some of our fellows went into a shop one day and got talking to a Belgian civilian. He said to them, -" English good, Allemand no good -- no ammunition; English, plenty ammunition." The next day they started the bombardment of Ypres, and when our fellows went by his house, they found the top knocked off and the poor old chap pushing all his goods and chattels along in a push-cart. Evidently there was no dearth of ammunition on the German side there.

On another occasion, some of our fellows were going up to the trenches and passed along Tillebecke (sic) Lake. As I daresay, you know, on meeting a party of soldiers, each party challenges the other. One of our fellows thought he was being challenged, and said -" Cambridgeshires, Cambridgeshires ------- ------ you I keep telling you Cambridgeshires;" he then tumbled to the fact that he was answering the challenge of some bull frogs in the Lake. Everyone in the battalion knows the joke now.

We are having two new machine guns, so shall now have four in all, and a bigger section again.

There is a rumour that we may be sent back to "Blighty" (as England is called by the Tommies), as several Terrier regiments have returned for a rest, so we understand. Of course, no one really takes the rumour seriously.

By the way, if ever you see the 82nd Brigade or 27th Division mentioned in the papers, you will know that it is our Brigade or Division. Perhaps you saw General French's message in the paper about the conduct of the 27th and 28th Divisions before Ypres.

Our Brigade is hot stuff, and has already had more casualties in these trenches than the chaps they relieved had in two months. We are not content to stand still and do nothing.

Much love to all,

From FRANK

June 12, 1915.

My Dear Mother,

Very many thanks for your letter and P.O. I expect by this time you will know that I have received those two parcels. Bill Lane says I am to tell you I got up this morning at 5-30, and his horse took me out for a ride.

No news.

Love to all,

From FRANK

June 15, 1915.

My Dear Mother,

Just to let you know I am quite alright. We came in the trenches on Sunday, and go out for six days rest next Thursday.

Jack has not rejoined us yet. Have absolutely no news.

Love to all,

From FRANK

My Dear Mother,

Very many thanks for your letter and parcel. I think the snap of you is quite the best you have had taken-I was awfully pleased to get it.

Jack has returned from the hospital, and has rejoined us. I was awfully pleased to see him again. We were relieved in the trenches last night. Jack Day (54) and I have returned to where the transport are billeted, and are looking after the Gun Section rations again. I expect we shall be out again for six days.

I received a parcel from Millie yesterday containing another shirt and some sweets.

I was very glad to receive all the contents of the parcel. Tea we usually have enough and to spare, but it will most likely come in useful. I should be glad to have some lemonade stuff that will mix in cold water some time or other.

Have no other news.

Much love to all,

From FRANK

24/6/15.

My Dear Mother,

Many thanks for your letter.

I had two letters from Maggie to-day and a parcel from Miss Suddaby - very kind of her, I thought.

I should be glad if you would send me some cigarettes and some stuff for making lemonade to be mixed with cold water.

We go back to the trenches to-morrow for twelve days, I believe.

Have absolutely no news.

Love to all,

FRANK

Gunner J. Brand,

2145 1st Cambs. Regt
B. E. F.
Dear Mr. Marking,

To my great sorrow I have to tell you that Frank was killed yesterday morning about 10 o'clock by a piece of shell. The Germans started shelling about eight o'clock (55), and we had just been debating whether we should move. Frank said, - "Well, boys, we have been lucky up to the present, no reason why we shouldn't he now." Myself and two others just moved away - what made us do it, I couldn't say - got about six yards when we heard another shell coming - stood still - turned round, saw that the shell had exploded in the trench; rush up, saw Frank's hand sticking out of the top of some rubbish, as the shell had struck a dug-out then - then I think I went mad, worked like mad, got Frank out. A piece of shell had struck him on side of the head. Death must have been instantaneous. I was demented with grief, as we were inseparable chums. The same shell wounded three others, including a captain who was walking by at the time. Frank had only been made full corporal the day before, five of us were under him. There is a lot more I should like to say, but I am too full of grief to write it now. We are going to bury him this afternoon, 4-30, as near as I can tell you. Frank had asked me to write to you a long time ago should anything happen. I little thought that I should he called upon to do it.

In deepest sympathy for yourself and Mr. and Mrs. Marking, Senr.,

His sorrowful chum,

JACK.

P.S. The Sergeant is writing to let you know full particulars, also, anything I could let you know I should only be too pleased to write.

1591 Sergeant G Bowyer
Machine Gun Section,
1st Batt. Cambs. Regt.,
Expeditionary Force,

27/6/15.

Dear Mr. Marking,

A letter from the front in a strange hand-writing may have prepared you more or less, for the sad news which it is my painful duty to have to acquaint you with - that your brother Frank was killed early yesterday morning while on duty in the trenches in charge of one of our guns. A high explosive shell struck the dug-out in which he was, killing him instantly and wounding 2 more of our section one of them, I am afraid, fatally (56) - and also severely wounding a Company Officer who was passing at the time (57). I can hardly tell you how cut up we all were when we heard of it, as by his cheery disposition and his willingness to do anything that required doing he had endeared himself to us all. A better soldier or a truer comrade one could not wish for, and I can only express, on behalf of myself and his comrades of the gun section, how much we sympathise with you all in your loss, and hope that you will try and bear up as well as possible, in the knowledge that he died fighting for the honour of his King and Country, and the safety of those dear to him at home. He will he buried this Sunday afternoon with full military honours, and by a Church of England Clergyman in a soldier's grave in a soldiers' cemetery just outside the town which lies behind our trenches (58). His bosom chum, Jack Brand, will no doubt write to you in a few days, but at present he is too much cut up. His private effects will he sent on to you in due course.

Again expressing my sincere sympathy,

I remain,

Yours sincerely,

G. BOWYER, Sergt.
1st Cambridgeshire Regt
B. E. F.

30/6/15.

165

Dear Mrs. Marking,

It is with feelings of the deepest sympathy that I write to you to inform you that your son 2168 L/Cpl. Marking, was killed on Saturday. I am thankful to state that death was instantaneous. He was a most conscientious and valuable N.C.O., and only an hour previous to his death I told him that I had recommended him for promotion. He was a hard worker, always ready to do anything. and was one of the party that accompanied Lieut. Hopkinson of this regt. on an expedition which resulted in all being recommended for their gallant conduct. (59)

I feel that I have lost the best of a good section, and shall miss him greatly. He was buried some distance behind the firing line with full military honours by a clergyman of the Church of England, and his grave will be honoured by us as long as our Regt. is in this district. All his comrades, of the Gun Section join with me in expressing their deep sympathy to you in your sad loss. Please believe me to be.

Yours very sincerely,

F. A. MANN,
2nd Lieut. Machine Gun
Officer, 1st Cambs Regt.

THE END

1. *The battalion arrived at Bury from Southampton.*

2. *The battalion arrived at Le Havre on February 15th. 1915.*

3. *No. 6 Camp.*

4. *Terdeghem.*

5. *The train was taken to Cassel and then a march to Terdeghem.*

6. *Billets were made in local farms.*

7. *Probably Plumer.*

8. *Territorial or Special Reservist Battalions.*

9. *Frank's closest friend Jack Brand who survived the war.*

10. *Marched to Dickebusch.*

11. *Bosechepe.*

12. *The Regimental History desribes Smith-Dorrien as, "..a real human General, who did the men no end of good."*

13. *The company was digging in the rear of the front line.*

14. *The first casualty was Corporal Noble Dewey, 1st. Cambridgeshire Regiment, died of wounds on March 4th. 1915. Buried in Dickebusch New Military Cemetery, Row A Grave 1.*

15. *On March 15th. the battalion went into front-line trenches with a new Brigade.*

16. *Support trenches at St. Eloi with Lieutenant Ollard.*

17. *Behind Voormezeele.*

18. *Six trenches were evacuated. The mound was blown on March 14th. at 5.30 p.m.*

19. *Lieutenant Ollard and Sergeant G Bowyer in Trench S.9. Both men survived the war.*

20. *Casualties were at least one officer and seven other ranks.*

21. *The battalion moved to Westoutre leaving at 10.30 p.m. and arriving at 5.30 a.m.*

22. *Arrived in Ypres at 8 a.m. Billetted in the Ramparts.*

23. *Trenches in Sanctuary Wood.*

24. B Company with machine-guns to Sanctuary Wood.

25. Spells of four days in and four days out of the trenches with C Company. The close proximity of the German trenches precluded enemy shelling, at least.

26. The battalion was much troubled by German snipers.

27. The 5th. Division attacled Hill 60 on the Cambridgeshire's right.

28. Private John Mitchell, 1st. Cambridgeshire Regiment killed in action April 26th. 1915. Commemorated on the Menin Gate Memorial to the Missing, Panels 50 and 52.

29. According to the Regimental History, "..the greatest bombardment we had yet experienced....the Cloth Hall and soon the whole of the sky behind us was reddened by the glare of big conflagrations."

30. The Cambridgeshire's first dose of lachrymatory gas shells.

31. Lice !

32. A 15 centimetre high-explosive German shell emitting black smoke. Named after the negro heavy-weight boxer and also known as marmites and coal-boxes.

33. The attack on Aubers Ridge.

34. C Company securing Fosse Wood.

35. Bombing raids on English cities began on January 19th. 1916.

36. On the night of May 3rd. at 10.30 p.m. they were withdrawn to shorten the line.

37. The Regimental History states, "..that individual came panting in half-an-hour late; situated in a lonely travers he had not heard, or had misunderstood, the order to withdraw. He kept firing his rifle at intervals and then suddenly became aware that the trenches were deserted and that he alone was facing the German army ! "

38. Stokes mortars were much feared

39. The " Lusitania " was torpedoed on May 7th. 1915 with the loss of 1198 passengers; of these 128 were Americans and this did much to encourage the U.S.A's entry into the war.

40. Zillebeke. Later Maple Copse Cemetery.

41. The period between May 15th. and May 22nd. is summed up as, "..digging, wiring, whizzbangs and hoping for rest. "

42. Relieved on May 22nd. to Busseboom.

43. Into Sanctuary Wood again.

44. A 77 millimetre field-gun shell.

45. Marched to Dranoutre on May 26th.

46. The line at Armentieres, "..a little light shelling absolutely peaceful. "

47. In the area of Ploegsteert (Plugstreet) Wood.

48. Lieutenant Eric H Hopkinson MC MID killed June 2nd. 1915. Commemorated on the Ploegsteert Memorial to the Missing, Panel 10.

49. Captain Kenneth C Gill, MC, 1st. Cambridgeshire Regiment and 22 Squadron, Royal Air Force, killed October 22nd. 1918. Buried in Fillievres British Cemetery, Row A Grave 32.

50. Later Lieutenant-Colonel Edward T Saint DSO 1st. Cambridgeshire Regiment, killed August 29th. 1918. Buried in Daours Communal Cemetery Extension, Plot 7 Row A Grave 43.

51. These were Saxon troops.

52. A Scholar of Trinity College and a cross-country blue, who spoke German, Hopkinson was never heard of again.

53. The Germans communicated with a board and a megaphone.

54. This is possibly Private John William Day, from Cambridge, who died of wounds on May 28th. 1915 and is buried in Lijssenthoek Military Cemetery, Poperinghe, Belgium, Plot 12 Row B Grave 26A.

55. The Regimental History states, " The enemy was beginning to liven up...tormenting them with rifle grenades of a superior type to the British. Casualties were getting more frequent. "

56. Private Francis Willmott died of wounds June 28th. 1915. Buried in Houpline Communal Cemetery Extension, Plot 3, Row A, Grave 12, next to Frank Marking.

57. Captain Richard E Sindall, 1/1st. Cambridgeshire Regiment, died of wounds July 1st. 1915. He came from Great Shelford and is buried in Bailleul Communal Cemetery Extension, Plot 1 Row D, Grave 30.

58. Frank now rests in Houplines Communal Cemetery Extension, Plot 3 Row A Grave 13, one of 506 soldiers from the United Kingdom, 3 from Canada, 3 from New Zealand, 1 Australian and 1 Special Memorial.

59. No award was ever forthcoming.

Selective Index